SATPREM

A sailor and Breton, althou͟   ͟ ͟ ͟ ͟ ͟ ͟ in
1923, Satprem took part in the French Resistance and was
arrested by the Gestapo when he was twenty years old.
Devastated after one and a half years in concentration
camps, he traveled to Upper Egypt, then to India, where
he served in the French government of Pondicherry. There
he discovered Sri Aurobindo and the Mother. Deeply struck
by their Message—"Man is a transitional being"—he re-
signed his post in the French Colonies and left for French
Guiana, where he spent a year in the middle of the jungle,
then on to Brazil and Africa.

In 1953, at thirty, he returned to India to be near Mother,
who sought the secret of the passage to the "next species,"
becoming her confidant and the witness of her experiences
for almost twenty years. His first nonfiction work was
dedicated to *Sri Aurobindo or The Adventure of Consciousness.* At the age of fifty, he brought out the fabulous logbook
of Mother's own journey, *The Agenda,* in 13 volumes, then
wrote a trilogy on Mother—*The Divine Materialism, The
New Species, The Mutation of Death.*

At fifty-nine, he withdrew completely from public life to
attempt the last Adventure: the search for the "great passage" leading to man's evolutionary future. In a last inter-
view in 1984, *Life Without Death,* he described the beginning of his experience in the body.

In 1989, after seven years spent "digging in the body," he
wrote a short autobiographical essay, *The Revolt of the
Earth,* in which he took stock of the human situation.

In 1992, as the process of transformation in his own body
became increasingly "pounding" and "burning," he wrote
Evolution II to outline HOW, despite Darwinian laws, a
completely different human species is emerging on this
very earth.

Sri Aurobindo
or
The Adventure of Consciousness

ALSO BY SATPREM

The Mind of the Cells (1980)
By the Body of the Earth (1990)
Mother :
I. *The Divine Materialism* (1980)
II. *The New Species* (1983)
III. *The Mutation of Death* (1987)
On the Way to Supermanhood (1986)
Life without Death (1988)
My Burning Heart (1989)
The Revolt of the Earth (1990)
Evolution II (1992)

Mother's Agenda
1951-1973
13 Volumes

Recorded by Satprem in the course of numerous personal conversations with Mother, the complete logbook of her fabulous exploration in the cellular consciousness of the human body. Twenty-three years of experiences which parallel some of the most recent theories of modern physics. Perhaps the key to man's passage to the next species. (Vols. 1, 2, 3, 4, 5, 6, 7, 8, 12 & 13 published in English)

Satprem

Sri Aurobindo
or
The Adventure
of Consciousness

Translated from the French by
Luc Venet

INSTITUTE FOR EVOLUTIONARY RESEARCH
1621 FREEWAY DRIVE, MT VERNON, WA 98273

For information address:
  U.S.A:
    Institute for Evolutionary Research
    1621 Freeway Drive, Suite 220
    Mount Vernon, WA 98273

  India & Asia:
    Mira Aditi Centre
    62 Sriranga, 1st Cross
    4th stage, Kuvempunagar
    Mysore 570023, India

Library of Congress Cataloging-in-Publication Data
Satprem, 1923-
  Sri Aurobindo, or, The adventure of consciousness
  Translated from French.
  Includes bibliographies.
  1. Ghose, Aurobindo, 1872-1950 2. Hindus–India–
Biography. I. Title. II. Title: Sri Aurobindo.
BL1273.892.G56S2713 1984   294.5'5[B]   83-22725
ISBN 0-938710-04-4

Manufactured in the United States of America
Second Edition. Third printing 1993

CONTENTS

to
The Mother

PREFACE

The age of adventures is over. Even if we reach the seventh galaxy, we will go there helmeted and mechanized, and it will not change a thing for us; we will find ourselves exactly as we are now: helpless children in the face of death, living beings who are not too sure how they live, why they are alive, or where they are going. On the earth, as we know, the times of Cortez and Pizarro are over; one and the same pervasive Mechanism stifles us: the trap is closing inexorably. But, as always, it turns out that our bleakest adversities are also our most promising opportunities, and that the dark passage is only a passage leading to a greater light. Hence, with our backs against the wall, we are facing the last territory left for us to explore, the ultimate adventure: ourselves.

Indeed, there are plenty of simple and obvious signs. This decade's [the 60's] most important phenomenon is not the trip to the moon, but the "trips" on drugs, the student restlessness throughout the world, and the great hippie migration. But where could they possibly go? There is no more room on the teeming beaches, no more room on the crowded roads, no more room in the ever-expanding anthills of our cities. We have to find a way out *elsewhere.*

But there are many kinds of "elsewheres." Those of drugs are uncertain and fraught with danger, and above all they *depend* upon an outer agent; an experience ought to be possible at will, any-where, at the grocery store as well as in the solitude of one's room—otherwise it is not an experience but an anomaly or an enslavement. Those of psychoanalysis are limited, for the mo-ment, to the dimly lit caves of the "unconscious," and, most importantly, they lack the agency of consciousness, through which a person can be in full control, instead of being an impotent witness or a sickly patient. Those of religion may be more enlightened, but they too depend upon a god or a dogma; for the most part they confine us in *one* type of experience, for it is just as possible to be a prisoner of other worlds as it is of this one—in fact, even more so. Finally, the value of an experience is measured by its capacity to transform life; otherwise, it is simply an empty dream or an hallucination.

Sri Aurobindo leads us to a twofold discovery, which we so urgently need if we want to find an intelligible meaning to the suffocating chaos we live in, as well as a key for transforming our world. By following him step by step in his prodigious exploration, we are led to the most important discovery of all times, to the threshold of the Great Secret that is to change the face of this world, namely, that *consciousness is power.* Hypnotized as we are by the "inescapable" scientific conditions of the present world, we have come to believe that our only hope lies in an ever greater proliferation of machines, which will see better than we do, hear better than we do, calculate better than we do, heal better than we do—and finally, perhaps, live better than we do. Indeed, we must first realize that we can do better than our machines, and that the enormous Mechanism that is suffocating us is liable to collapse as quickly as it came into being, provided we are willing to seize on the true power and go down into our own hearts, as methodical, rigorous, and clearheaded explorers.

Then we may discover that our splendid twentieth century is still the Stone Age of psychology, that, in spite of all our science, we have not yet entered the true science of living, the real mastery of the world and of ourselves, and that there lie before us horizons of perfection, harmony and beauty, compared to which our most superb scientific discoveries are like the roughcasts of an apprentice.

Satprem
Pondicherry, January 27, 1970

I become what I see in myself. All that thought suggests to me, I can do; all that thought reveals in me, I can become. This should be man's unshakable faith in himself, because God dwells in him.[1]

INTRODUCTION

There once was a wicked Maharaja who could not bear to think that anyone was superior to him. So he summoned all the pandits of the realm, as was the practice on momentous occasions, and put to them this question: "Which of us two is greater, I or God?" The pandits began to tremble with fear. Being wise by profession, they asked for time; they were also concerned for their positions and their lives. Yet, they were worthy men who did not want to displease God. As they were lamenting their predicament, the oldest pandit reassured them: "Leave it to me. Tomorrow I shall speak to the Prince." The next day, the whole court was gathered in a solemn *durbar* when the old pandit quietly arrived, his hands humbly joined together, his forehead smeared with white ashes. He bowed low and spoke these words: "O Lord, undoubtedly thou art the greater." The Prince twirled his long mustache thrice and tossed his head high. "Thou art the greater, King, for thou canst banish us from thy kingdom, whilst God cannot; for verily, all is His kingdom and there is nowhere to go outside Him."

This Indian tale, which comes from Bengal, where Sri Aurobindo was born, was not unknown to him who said that all is He—gods, devils, men, the earth, not just heaven—and whose entire experience leads to a divine rehabilitation of matter. For the last half century, psychology has done nothing but reinstate the demons in man; it is possible, as André Malraux believed, that the task of the next half century will be "to reinstate the gods in man," or, rather, as Sri Aurobindo put it, to reinstate the Spirit in man and in matter, and to create "the life divine on earth": *The heavens beyond are great and wonderful, but greater yet and more wonderful are the heavens within you. It is these Edens that await the divine worker.*[2]

There are many ways to set out to work; each of us has, in fact, his or her own particular approach: for one it may be a well-crafted object or a job well done; for another a beautiful idea, an encompassing philosophical system; for still another a piece of music, the flowing of a river, a burst of sunlight on the sea; all are ways of breathing in the Infinite. But these are brief moments, and we seek permanence. These are moments subject to many uncontrollable conditions, and we seek something inalienable, independent of conditions and circumstances—a window within us that will never close again.

And since those conditions are difficult to meet here on earth, we speak of "God," of "spirituality," of Christ, of Buddha, and the whole lineage of great religious founders; all are ways of finding permanence. But it may be that we are not religious or spiritual men, but just men, tired of dogmas, who believe in the earth and who are suspicious of big words. We also may be somewhat weary of too much intelligent thinking; all we want is our own little river flowing into the Infinite. There was a great saint in India who, for many years before he found peace, used to ask whomever he met: "Have you seen God? Have you seen God?" He would always go away frustrated and angry because people told him stories. He wanted to *see*. He wasn't wrong, considering all the deception men have heaped onto this word, as onto many others. Once we have seen, we can talk about it; or, most probably, we will remain silent. Indeed, we do not want to deceive ourselves with words; we want to start from what we have, right where we are, with our cloddy shoes and the little ray of sunshine on the good days; such is our simplehearted faith. We see that the world around us is not so great, and we aspire for it to change, but we have become wary of universal panaceas, of movements, parties, and theories. So we will begin at square one, with ourselves such as we are; it isn't much, but it's all we have. We will try to change this little bit of world before setting out to save the other. And perhaps this isn't such a foolish idea after all; for who knows whether changing the one is not the most effective way of changing the other?

What can Sri Aurobindo do for us at this low altitude?

There is Sri Aurobindo the philosopher, and Sri Aurobindo the poet, which he was essentially, a visionary of evolution; but not everyone is a philosopher or a poet, much less a seer. But would we not be content if he gave us a way to believe in our own possibilities, not only our human but our superhuman and divine possibilities, and not only to believe in them but to discover them ourselves, step by step, to *see* for ourselves and to become vast, as vast as the earth we love and all the lands and all the seas we hold within us? For there is Sri Aurobindo the explorer, who was also a yogi; did he not say that *Yoga is the art of conscious self-finding?* ³ It is this exploration of consciousness that we would like to undertake with him. If we proceed calmly, patiently, and with sincerity, bravely facing the difficulties of the road—and God knows it is rugged enough—there is no reason that the window should not open at some point and let the sun shine on us forever. Actually, it is not one but several windows that open one after another, each time on a wider perspective, a new dimension of our own kingdom; and each time it means a *change of consciousness* as radical as going from sleep to the waking state. We are going to outline the main stages of these changes of consciousness, as Sri Aurobindo experienced them and described them to his disciples in his *integral yoga*, until they take us to the threshold of a new, still unknown experience that may have the power to change life itself.

For Sri Aurobindo is not only the explorer of consciousness, he is the builder of a new world. Indeed, what is the point of changing our consciousness if the world around us remains as it is? We would be like Hans Christian Andersen's emperor walking naked through the streets of his capital. Thus, after exploring the outermost frontiers of worlds that were not unknown to ancient wisdom, Sri Aurobindo discovered yet another world, not found on any map, which he called the *Supermind* or *Supramental,* and which he sought to draw down upon Earth. He invites us to draw it down a little with him and to take part in the beautiful story, if we like beautiful stories. For the Supermind, Sri Aurobindo tells us, brings a dramatic change to the evolution of consciousness on earth; it is *the* change of consciousness that will have the power to transform our physical world, and it will do so—for the better, we hope—as thoroughly and lastingly as the Mind did when it first appeared in living matter. We will see, therefore, how the integral yoga leads to a *supramental yoga,* or yoga of terrestrial transformation, which we will try to outline only, because the story is still in the making; it is quite new and difficult, and we do not quite know yet where it will take us, or even whether it will succeed.

That, in fact, depends a little upon us all.

CHAPTER 1

An Accomplished Westerner

Humanly speaking, Sri Aurobindo is close to us, because once we have respectfully bowed before the "wisdom of the East" and the odd ascetics who seem to make light of all our fine laws, we find that our curiosity has been aroused but not our life; we need a practical truth that will survive our rugged winters. Sri Aurobindo knew our winters well; he experienced them as a student, from the age of seven until twenty. He lived from one lodging house to another at the whim of more or less benevolent landladies, with one meal a day, and not even an overcoat to put on his back, but always laden with books: the French symbolists, Mallarmé, Rimbaud, whom he read in the original French long before reading the Bhagavad Gita in translation. To us Sri Aurobindo personifies a unique synthesis.

He was born in Calcutta on August 15, 1872, the year of Rimbaud's *Illuminations*, just a few years before Einstein; modern physics had already seen the light of day with Max Planck, and Jules Verne was busy probing the future. Yet, Queen Victoria was about to become Empress of India, and the conquest of Africa was not even completed; it was the turning point from one world to another. Historically, it appears that the birth of a new world is often preceded by periods of trial and destruction, but perhaps this is simply a misreading: it may be because the new seeds are *already* alive that the forces of subversion (or clearing away) are raging. In any event, Europe was at the peak of its glory; the game seemed to be played in the West. This is how it appeared to Dr. Krishnadhan Ghose, Sri Aurobindo's father, who had studied medicine in England, and had returned to India completely anglicized. He did not want his three sons, of whom Sri Aurobindo was the youngest, to be in the least contaminated by the "steamy and retrograde" mysticism in which his country seemed to be running to ruin. He did not even want them to know anything of the traditions and languages of India. Sri Aurobindo was therefore provided not only with an English first name, Akroyd, but also with an English governess, Miss Pagett, and then sent off at the age of five to an Irish convent school in Darjeeling among the sons of British administrators. Two years later, the three Ghose boys would leave for England. Sri Aurobindo was seven. Not until the age of twenty would he learn his mother tongue, Bengali. He would never see his father again, who died just before his return to India, and barely his mother, who was ill and did not recognize him on his return. Hence, this is a child who grew up outside every influence of family, country, and tradition—a free spirit. The first lesson Sri Aurobindo gives us is perhaps, precisely, a lesson of freedom.

Sri Aurobindo and his two brothers were entrusted to an Anglican clergyman of Manchester, *with strict instructions that they should not be allowed to make the acquaintance of any Indian or undergo any Indian influence.*[1] Dr. Ghose was indeed a peculiar man. He also ordered Pastor Drewett not to give his sons any religious instruction, so they could choose a religion themselves, if they so wished, when they came of age. He then left them to their fate for thirteen years. He believed his children should become men of character. Dr. Ghose may appear to have been a hardhearted man, but he was nothing of the kind; not only did he donate his services as a doctor but also gave his money to poor Bengali villagers (while his sons had hardly anything to eat or wear in London), and he died of shock when he was mistakenly informed that his favorite son, Aurobindo, had died in a shipwreck.

The first few years in Manchester were of some importance to Sri Aurobindo because this is where he learned French (English was his "mother tongue") and discovered a spontaneous affinity for France: *There was an attachment to English and European thought and literature, but not to England as a country; I had no ties there. . . . If there was attachment to a European land as a second country, it was intellectually and emotionally to one not seen or lived in in this life, not England, but France.*[2] The poet had begun to awaken in him; he was already listening to *the footsteps of invisible things,* as he put it in one of his early poems; his inner window had already opened, although he was quite unimpressed with religion, as is evident from the account he gives of his "conversion." Predictably, Clergyman Drewett's mother had undertaken the task of saving the souls of the three heretic children, or at least that of the youngest one, whom she took one day to a meeting of "nonconformist" ministers. *After the prayers were over,* wrote Sri Aurobindo, *nearly all dispersed, but devout people remained a little longer, and it was at that time that conversions were made. I was feeling completely bored. Then a minister approached me and asked me some questions. (I was about ten at that time.) I did not give any reply. Then they all shouted, "He is saved, he is saved," and began to pray for me and offer thanks to God.*[3] Sri Aurobindo, the seer, was never to become a religious man, not even in India, and he often emphasized that religion and spirituality are not necessarily synonymous: *True theocracy,* he would write later, *is the kingdom of God in man and not the kingdom of a Pope, a priesthood or a sacerdotal class.*[4]

When he began his life in London, at the age of twelve, Sri Aurobindo knew Latin and French thoroughly. The headmaster of St. Paul's School, where he had enrolled, was so surprised at the aptitude of his young student that he personally coached him in Greek. Three years later, Sri Aurobindo could skip half his classes and spend most of his time engrossed in his favorite occupation:

reading. Nothing seemed to escape this voracious adolescent (except cricket, which held as little interest for him as Sunday school). Shelley and "Prometheus Unbound," the French poets, Homer, Aristophanes, and soon all of European thought—for he quickly came to master enough German and Italian to read Dante and Goethe in the original—peopled a solitude of which he has said nothing. He never sought to form relationships, while Manmohan, the second brother, roamed through London in the company of his friend Oscar Wilde and would make a name for himself in English poetry. Each of the three brothers led his separate life. However, there was nothing austere about Sri Aurobindo, and certainly nothing of the puritan (*the prurient*,[5] as he called it); it was just that he was "elsewhere," and his world was replete. He even had a way of jesting with a straight face, which never left him: *Sense of humour? It is the salt of existence. Without it the world would have got utterly out of balance—it is unbalanced enough already—and rushed to blazes long ago.*[6] For there is also Sri Aurobindo the humorist, and that Sri Aurobindo is perhaps more important than the philosopher whom Western universities speak of so solemnly. Philosophy, for Sri Aurobindo, was only a way of reaching those who could not understand anything without explanations; it was only a language, just as poetry was another, clearer and truer language. But the essence of his being was humor, not the sarcastic humor of the so-called spiritual man, but a kind of joy that cannot help dancing wherever it passes. Now and then, in a flash that leaves us somewhat mystified, we sense behind the most tragic, the most distressing human situations an almost facetious laughter, as if a child were playing a tragedy and suddenly made a face at himself because it is his nature to laugh, and ultimately because nothing in the world and no one can affect that place inside ourselves where we are ever a king. Indeed, perhaps this is the true meaning of Sri Aurobindo's humor: a refusal to see things tragically, and, even more so, a sense of inalienable royalty.

Whether St. Paul's School appreciated his sense of humor we do not know, but it certainly appreciated his astonishing culture;

he was awarded a scholarship to attend Cambridge (just in time; the family remittances had practically stopped), which was not enough, however, to relieve him from cold and hunger since his older brothers also partook heartily of the windfall. He was just eighteen. What was he going to that nursery-of-gentlemen for? For one reason, he was fulfilling his father's wishes—though not for long. In his first year at King's College, he won all the prizes in Greek and Latin verse, but his heart was no longer in it. It was Joan of Arc, Mazzini, the American Revolution that haunted him—in other words, the liberation of his country, India's independence, of which he would become one of the pioneers. This unforeseen political calling was to hold him for almost twenty years, even though at the time he did not exactly know what an Indian was, let alone a Hindu! But he learned fast. As with Western culture, he managed to learn and assimilate Hinduism by leaps and bounds; in fact, he would be truly "Sri Aurobindo" only after assimilating both cultures and finding the point where the two worlds met in something that was neither one, nor even a synthesis of both, but what we might call with Mother, who would later continue Sri Aurobindo's work, a *third position*, a "something else" we desperately need, we who are neither narrow-minded materialists nor exclusive spiritualists.

Thus, he became secretary of the "Indian Majlis," an association of Indian students at Cambridge, delivered revolutionary speeches, cast off his English first name, and joined a secret society called "Lotus and Dagger"(!) (Though, in this case, romanticism could lead one straight to the gallows.) Ultimately, he attracted the attention of the authorities, and his name was put on Whitehall's blacklist. Nonetheless, he earned his Bachelor of Arts degree, only to fail to attend the graduation ceremony, as if that were enough of that. In the same casual way, he took the celebrated Indian Civil Service examination, which would have opened the doors of the government of India to him among the ranks of the British administrators; he passed brilliantly, but neglected to appear for the horsemanship test, going for a walk that day instead of trotting at Woolwich, and was consequently disqualified. This time the Senior Tutor of Cambridge was moved to write to the authorities: "That a man of this calibre should be lost to the Indian government merely because he failed to sit on a horse or did not keep an appointment appears to me, I confess, a piece of official short-sightedness which it would be hard to surpass. . . . He has had a very hard and anxious time of it for the last two years. Supplies from home have almost entirely failed, and he has had to keep his two brothers as well as himself. . . . I have several times written to his father on his behalf, but for the most part unsuccessfully. It is only lately that I managed to extract from him enough to pay some tradesmen who would otherwise have put his son into the County Court."[7] The tutor's pleading would be in vain; the Colonial Office was convinced that Sri Aurobindo was dangerous. They were not wrong.

When he sailed back to India, Sri Aurobindo was twenty. He had no position, no titles. His father had just died. What remained of his fourteen years in the West? We are tempted to recall Edouard Herriot's perfect definition, for if it is true that education is what remains when everything is forgotten, then what remains of the West after one has left it is not its books, its museums, and theaters, but an urge to translate into living acts what has been theorized. There, perhaps, lies the true strength of the West. Unfortunately, we in the West have too much "intelligence" to have anything truly substantial to translate outwardly, while India, too inwardly replete, does not possess the necessary urge to match what she lives with what she sees. This lesson would not be lost on Sri Aurobindo.

CHAPTER 2

The Eternal Law

The proletariat among us is sunk in ignorance and overwhelmed with distress![1] exclaimed Sri Aurobindo soon after disembarking in India. It was not metaphysical questions that preoccupied him, but questions of *action*. To act: we are in the world to act. But what action? And above all, what *method* of action would be the most effective? This very practical concern would remain with Sri Aurobindo from his very first days in India right up to his highest yogic realizations. I personally recall (if you will excuse the digression) traveling to the Himalayas and enjoying a few wonderful days there in the company of a holy man, lost among the pines and the red laurels, with snow sparkling all around us between sky and valley. It was very beautiful, and I remember saying to myself how easy it is to have divine thoughts, or perhaps even visions, at that altitude, but what about in the valley below? I was not entirely wrong, although I later learned that one can act and work for the world in the silence and stillness of one's own body. (A clinging illusion makes us confuse agitation with action.) Still, what remains of our divine moments once we are removed from our solitude and brought down to the plains? This is a mirage that Western enthusiasts of Hinduism should consider, for if we merely want to escape the world, a retreat in the Alps or the Yosemite Valley, or even a small whitewashed cell, would do just as well; the

Pilgrimage to the Source* has little, if nothing, to do with the
Ganges or the Brahmaputra. What was India going to bring to Sri
Aurobindo, then? Did she hold some secret relevant to action in
life?

Reading books on Hinduism, it would appear that it is a kind
of spiritual paleontology interspersed with polysyllabic Sanskrit
words, as if Indians were a mixture of arcane philosophers and
unrepentant idolaters. But if we look at India simply, from within,
without trying to divide her into paragraphs of Hinduism (which
are necessarily false, like the conclusions of the traveler who went
to Delhi in May and found India torrid and hot, whereas if he had
gone to the south or the east in November or March, he would
have found India at once cold, boiling, sodden, desert-like, Medi-
terranean, and gentle; she is a world as indefinable as her "Hinduism," which does not exist, moreover, because Hinduism is not
a belief or a spiritual longitude; one does not take bearings there,
for all possible bearings are contained in it), we find that India is
first and foremost a country of exceptional spiritual freedom. The
so-called Hinduism is a creation of the West; Indians speak only
of "the eternal law,"; *sanatana dharma*, which they know is not an
Indian monopoly but belongs also to the Moslems, the Africans,
the Christians, and even to the Anabaptists. What seems to a
Westerner to be the most important part of a religion (namely, the
structure that *distinguishes* it from all other religions, insisting that
a person is not a Catholic or a Protestant unless he or she thinks
this way or that way and subscribes to this or that articles of faith)
is in fact the least important aspect for an Indian, who instinctively
seeks to remove external differences in order to find everyone at
the central point where all communicates.

This open-mindedness is not "tolerance," which is only the
reverse of intolerance; it is a positive understanding that every
human being has an inner need, which we may call "God" or by
any other name, and that he needs to love what he himself

---

*   A French book on Hinduism by Lanza del Vasto.

understands of God at his own level and particular stage of inner development, and Peter's way is not John's. That everyone should love a crucified god, for instance, seems unnatural to the average Indian, who will bow respectfully before Christ (with as much spontaneous reverence as before his own image of God), but who will see also the face of God in the laughter of Krishna, the terror of Kali, the sweetness of Saraswati, and in the thousands upon thousands of other gods who dance, multicolored and musta-chioed, mirthful or terrifying, illuminated or compassionate, on the deliriously carved towers of Indian temples. *A God who cannot smile could not have created this humorous universe,*[2] said Sri Aurobindo. All is His face, all is His play, terrible or beautiful, as many-faceted as our world itself. For this country so teeming with gods is also, at the same time, the country of a monolithic faith in Oneness: "One, He presides over all wombs and natures; Himself the womb of all." (*Swetaswatara Upanishad* V.5) But not everyone can at once merge with the Absolute; there are many degrees in the Ascent, and one who is ready to understand a little Lalita's childlike face and to bring her his incense and flowers may not be able to address the Eternal Mother in the silence of his heart; still another may prefer to deny all forms and plunge into the contemplation of That which is formless. "Even as men come to Me, so I accept them. It is my path that men follow from all sides," says the Bhagavad Gita (IV,11).* As we see, there are so many ways of conceiving of God, in three or three million persons, that we should not dogmatize, lest we eliminate everything, finally leaving nothing but a Cartesian God, one and universal by virtue only of his narrowness. Perhaps we still confuse unity with uniformity. It was in the spirit of that tradition that Sri Aurobindo was soon to write: *The perfection of the integral Yoga will come when each man is able to follow his own path of Yoga, pursuing the development of his own nature in its upsurging towards that which transcends the nature. For freedom is the final law and the last consummation.*[3]

---

* All quotations from the Upanishads, the Veda, and the Bhagavad Gita in this book are taken from Sri Aurobindo's translations.

Nor does an Indian ever ask: "Do you believe in God?" The question would seem to him as childish as: "Do you believe in CO_2?" He simply says: "Have the experience yourself; if you do this, you'll get that result; if you do that, you'll get another result." All the ingenuity, the skill and precision we have expended for the last century or two in the study of physical phenomena, the Indian has brought, with equal exactness for the last four or five millennia, to the observation of inner phenomena. For a people of "dreamers," they have some surprises in store for us. And if we are a little honest, we will soon admit that our own "inner" studies, i.e., our psychology and psychoanalysis, or our knowledge of man, is still at an embryonic stage, simply because self-knowledge demands an ascesis as methodical and patient, and sometimes as tedious, as the long studies required to master nuclear physics. If we want to take up this path, it is not enough to read books or to collect clinical studies on all the neuroses of an unbalanced society: we *must implicate ourselves.* Indeed, if we brought as much sincerity, meticulousness, and perseverance to the study of the inner world as we do to the study of our books, we would go fast and far—the West also has surprises in store for us—but it must first get rid of its preconceptions (Columbus did not draw the map of America before leaving Palos). These simple truths may be worth repeating, for the West seems to be caught between two falsehoods: the overly serious falsehood of the spiritualists, who have already settled the question of God in a few infallible paragraphs, and the not-serious-enough falsehood of the rudimentary occultists and psychics, who have reduced the invisible to a sort of freak-show of the imagination. India, wisely, refers us to our own direct experience and to experimental methods. Sri Aurobindo would soon put this fundamental lesson of experimental spirituality into practice.

But what kind of men, what human substance, was he going to find in that India he did not know? Once we have set aside the exotic facade and the bizarre (to us) customs that amuse and intrigue tourists, there nevertheless remains something strange;

and saying that Indians are a gentle, dreamy, fatalistic people, detached from the world, only describes the effect, not the cause. "Strange" is indeed the word, because spontaneously, in their very physical substance, without the least "thought" or even "faith," Indians sink their roots very deeply into other worlds; they do not altogether belong here. In them, these other worlds rise constantly to the surface; *at the least touch the veil is rent,* remarks Sri Aurobindo. This physical world, which for us is so real and absolute and unique, seems to them but one way of living among many others, one modality of the total existence among many others; in other words, a small, chaotic, agitated, and rather painful frontier on *the margin of immense continents which lie behind, unexplored.*[4] This substantial difference between Indians and other peoples appears most strikingly in their art, as it does also in Egyptian art (and, we assume without knowing it, in the art of Central America). If we leave behind our light and open cathedrals that soar high like a triumph of the divine thought in man suddenly to find ourselves before Sekmeth in the silence of Abydos on the Nile, or face to face with Kali behind the peristyle of Dakshineshwar, we do feel something; we suddenly gape before an unknown dimension, a "something" that leaves us a little stunned and speechless, which is not at all there in our Western art. There are no secrets in our cathedrals! Everything is there for every outer eye to see, all neat and tidy, open to the four winds; yet, there are many secrets. The intent here is not to weigh one form of art against the other—that would be rather absurd—but simply to say we have *forgotten* something. If so many civilizations, which were once as glorious and refined as ours, and whose elites were no less "intelligent" than those of our universities, have seen and experienced invisible (to us) hierarchies and great psychic rhythms that exceed the brief pulsation of a human life, how has it not dawned on us that this may have had nothing to do with a silly superstition or a mental aberration—a strange aberration indeed, found thousands of miles apart in civilizations totally unknown to one another? True, the Age of the Mysteries is behind us; everything is wonderfully Cartesian and pragmatic, but still, something is missing. The first sign announcing a new being, probably, is the dawning sense of a terrible lack of something, which neither his science nor his churches nor his garish pleasures can ever fulfill. Man cannot be dispossessed of his secrets with impunity. This, too, was a living testimonial India imparted to Sri Aurobindo, unless he knew it already in his own flesh.

However, if we expect India, the land where ancient Mysteries survive, to give us the practical solution we are seeking, we may be disappointed. Sri Aurobindo, who soon learned to appreciate the freedom, spiritual breadth, and immense experimental knowledge India offers a seeker, did not subscribe to everything there, far from it; not that there was anything to reject; there is nothing to reject anywhere, not in so-called Hinduism any more than in Christianity or in any other aspiration of man; but there is everything to widen, to widen endlessly. What we take for a final truth is most often only a partial experience of the Truth, and certainly the total Experience exists nowhere in time and space, in no place and no being however luminous he may be; for Truth is infinite, forever marching onward. *But man always takes upon himself an endless burden,* said the Mother in a talk about Buddhism. *He refuses to let go of anything from his past, and so he stoops more and more beneath the weight of a useless accumulation. Have a guide for part of the way, but once you have travelled that part, leave it and the guide behind, and move on. This is something men do very reluctantly; once they get hold of something that helps them, they cling to it; they won't let go of it. Those who have made some progress with Christianity do not want to give it up, and carry it on their backs; those who have made some progress with Buddhism do not want to leave it, and carry it on their backs. This weighs you down and slows you terribly. Once you have passed through a stage, drop it; let it go! And move on!* Yes, there is an eternal law, but it is eternally young and eternally progressive. Although India was also able to appreciate that God is the Eternal Iconoclast in his cosmic march, she did not always have the strength to withstand her own wisdom. The *vast invisible* that pervades this country was to extract from it a double ransom, both human and spiritual; human, because these people, saturated with the Beyond, conscious of the Great Cosmic Game and the inner dimensions in which our little surface lives are just points, periodically flowering and soon re-engulfed, came to neglect the material world—inertia, indifference to progress, and resignation often wore the face of wisdom; a spiritual ransom also (this one far more serious), because in that immensity too great for our *present* little consciousness, the destiny of the earth, our earth, became lost somewhere in the deep confines of the galaxy, or nowhere, reabsorbed in Brahman, whence perhaps it had never emerged after all, except in our dreams—illusionism, trance, the closed eyes of the yogi were also often mistaken for God. It is therefore essential to define clearly the goal that religious India has in view, then we will better understand what she can or cannot do for we who seek an integral truth.

To begin with, we must admit that we are faced with a surprising contradiction. India is a country that brought forth a great revelation: "All is Brahman," she said, all is the Spirit; this world also is the Spirit, as is this earth, this life, these men; nothing is outside Him. "All this is Brahman immortal, naught else; Brahman is in front of us, Brahman behind us, and to the south of us and to the north of us and below us and above us; It stretches everywhere. All this is Brahman alone, all this magnificent universe." (*Mundaka Upanishad* II,12) At long last, the dichotomy that is tearing this poor world apart between God and the Devil— as if one always had to choose between heaven and earth, and could never be saved except when mutilated—was healed for good. Yet, *in practice*, for the last three thousand years, the entire religious history of India has taken the view that there is a true Brahman, as it were, transcendent, immobile, forever beyond this bedlam, and a false Brahman, or rather a minor one (there are several schools), for an intermediate and more or less questionable reality (i.e., life, the earth, our poor mess of an earth). "Abandon this world of illusion," exclaimed the great Shankara.* "Brahman is real, the world is a lie," says the Nirlamba Upanishad: *brahma satyam jaganmithya.* Try as we might, we just don't understand through what distortion or oversight "All is Brahman" ever became "All, except the world, is Brahman."

If we leave aside the Scriptures—for the human mind is so skillful that it can easily dream up sheep grazing on the Empire State building—and if we look at the practical disciplines of India, the contradiction becomes even more striking. Indian psychology is based on the very intelligent observation that all things in the universe, from mineral to man, are made up of three elements or qualities (*gunas*), which may be called by different names depending on the order of reality one considers: *tamas*, inertia, obscurity, unconsciousness; *rajas*, movement, struggle, effort, passion, action; *sattva*, light, harmony, joy. Nowhere does any of these three elements exist in a pure state; we are always a mixture of inertia, passion, and light; we may be sattvo-tamasic, good but a bit dull, well-meaning but a little unconscious; or sattvo-rajasic, impassioned upwardly; or tamaso-rajasic, impassioned downwardly; most often we are an excellent mixture of the three. In the darkest *tamas* the light also shines, but unfortunately the opposite is equally true. In other words, we are always in a state of unstable equilibrium; the warrior, the ascetic, and the brute happily share our dwelling-place in varying proportions. The various Indian disciplines seek therefore to restore the equilibrium, to help us emerge from the play of the three *gunas*, which rock us endlessly from light to dark, enthusiasm to exhaustion, gray apathy to fugitive pleasures and recurring sufferings, and to find a poise above—in other words, to recover the divine consciousness (*yoga*), the state of perfect equilibrium. In order to achieve this goal, they try to take us out of the state of dispersion and waste in which we live daily, and to create in us a concentration powerful enough to break our ordinary limits and, in time, to propel us into another

---

* Shankara (788-820 A.D.), mystic and poet, theorist of *Mayavada* or the doctrine of illusionism, which supplanted Buddhism in India.

state. This work of concentration can be done at any level of our being—physical, vital, or mental. Depending on the level we choose, we undertake one kind of yoga or another: *hatha yoga, raja yoga, mantra yoga,* and many others, countless others, like so many stages of our effort. We won't discuss here the great value of these methods, or the remarkable intermediate results they can lead to; we will examine only their goal, their final destination. The truth is, this "poise above" seems to have no relation with real life whatsoever; first, because all these disciplines are extremely demanding, requiring hours and hours of work every day, if not complete solitude; secondly, because their ultimate result is a state of trance or yogic ecstasy, *samadhi,* perfect equilibrium, ineffable bliss, in which one's awareness of the world is dissolved, annihilated. Brahman, the Spirit, appears therefore to have absolutely nothing to do with our regular waking consciousness; He is outside all that we know; He is not of this world. Others who were not Indians have said the same.

In fact, all the religions of the world have said it. And whether we speak of "salvation" in the West, of "liberation," or *mukti,* in the East, whether we speak of paradise or ending the cycle of rebirths, makes little difference, since ultimately the common goal is to "get out." Yet, things were not always this way. Between the end of the Age of the Mysteries and the advent of the great religions, both in the West and in the East, a chasm appeared, a Knowledge that did not make such a formidable distinction between God and the world was obscured; all the traditions, all the legends testify to this. The conflict between Matter and Spirit is a modern creation; the so-called materialists are really the offspring, legitimate or not, of the spiritualists, much as prodigal sons are begotten by miserly fathers. Between the first Upanishads of about three or four thousand years ago—themselves heirs to the Veda, which saw God everywhere in this "marvelous universe"—and the last Upanishads, a Secret was lost; it was lost not only in India but in Mesopotamia, in Egypt, in Greece, and in Central America. It is this Secret that Sri Aurobindo was to rediscover, perhaps because his being combined the finest Western tradition and the profound spiritual yearning of the East. *East and West,* he said, *have two ways of looking at life which are opposite sides of one reality. Between the pragmatic truth on which the vital thought of modern Europe enamoured of the vigour of life, all the dance of God in Nature, puts so vehement and exclusive a stress and the eternal immutable Truth to which the Indian mind enamoured of calm and poise loves to turn with an equal passion for an exclusive finding, there is no such divorce and quarrel as is now declared by the partisan mind, the separating reason, the absorbing passion of an exclusive will of realisation. The one eternal immutable Truth is the Spirit and without the Spirit the pragmatic truth of a self-creating universe would have no origin or foundation; it would be barren of significance, empty of inner guidance, lost in its end, a fire-work display shooting up into the void only to fall away and perish in mid-air. But neither is the pragmatic truth a dream of the non-existent, an illusion or a long lapse into some futile delirium of creative imagination; that would be to make the eternal Spirit a drunkard or a dreamer, the fool of his own gigantic self-hallucinations. The truths of universal existence are of two kinds, truths of the spirit which are themselves eternal and immutable, and these are the great things that cast themselves out into becoming and there constantly realize their powers and significances, and the play of the consciousness with them, the discords, the musical variations, soundings of possibility, progressive notations, reversions, perversions, mounting conversions into a greater figure of harmony; and of all these things the Spirit has made, makes always his universe. But it is himself that he makes in it, himself that is the creator and the energy of creation and the cause and the method and the result of the working, the mechanist and the machine, the music and the musician, the poet and the poem, supermind, mind, and life and matter, the soul and Nature.*[5]

But for Sri Aurobindo it was not enough to reconcile Spirit and Matter on paper. That the Spirit is or is not of this world does not make much difference, after all, if knowledge of the Spirit in life is not associated with a power over life:

For truth and knowledge are an idle gleam,
If Knowledge brings not power to change the world.[6]

The lost Secret was not a theoretical truth, it was an actual power of Spirit over Matter. It is this pragmatic Secret that Sri Aurobindo was to find again, step by step, experientially, by daring to go beyond his Western background as well as the Hindu religious tradition; it is indeed true that the real essence emerges when all else is forgotten.

CHAPTER 3

The End of the Intellect

Sri Aurobindo had spent fourteen years traveling the Western path; it would take him almost as much time to travel India's path and to reach the "peak" of traditional yogic realizations, the starting-point of his own work. What is most interesting for us, however, is that Sri Aurobindo traveled this traditional path, which we may therefore consider as a preparation, outside all customary rules, as a freelancer, as it were, or rather as an explorer who does not care about precautions and maps, and hence avoids many unnecessary detours simply because he has the courage to forge straight ahead. Thus, it was not in seclusion or in the lotus position or under the guidance of an enlightened Master that Sri Aurobindo undertook the journey, but just as we might do it ourselves, without any special knowledge, right in the midst of everyday life—a life as busy and hectic as ours can be—and all alone. Sri Aurobindo's first secret is probably a persistent refusal to cut life in two—action vs. meditation, inner vs. outer, and the whole range of our false divisions; from the day he thought of yoga, he put everything into it, high and low, inside and outside, and he set out without ever looking back. Sri Aurobindo does not come to demonstrate exceptional qualities in an exceptional environment; he comes to show us what is possible for man, and to prove that the exceptional is only a normal possibility not yet mastered, just as *the supernatural,* as he said, *is that the nature of which we have not attained or do not yet know, or the means of which we have not yet conquered.*[1] Ultimately, everything in this world is a matter of proper concentration; there is nothing that will not finally yield to a well-applied concentration.

When he went ashore on the Apollo Bunder in Bombay, he was overtaken by a spontaneous spiritual experience, *a vast calm;* but he had more immediate concerns of food and survival. Sri Aurobindo was twenty. He found a position with the Maharaja of Baroda, as professor of French, then taught English at the state college, where he soon became vice-principal. He worked also as private secretary to the Prince. Between the court and the college he was busy enough, but in truth, it was the destiny of India that preoccupied him. He traveled many times to Calcutta, familiarizing himself with the political situation and writing several articles that created a scandal, for he didn't just refer to the Queen-Empress of India as *an old lady so called by way of courtesy,*[2] but he urged his countrymen to shake off the British yoke, and attacked the *mendicant policy* of the Indian Congress party: *no reforms, no collaboration.* His aim was to gather and organize all the energies of the nation toward revolutionary action. This must have required some courage, considering the year was 1893, when the British ruled over three-fourths of the world. But Sri Aurobindo had a very special way of dealing with the problem; he did not lay any blame on the English, but on the Indians themselves: *Our actual enemy is not any force exterior to ourselves, but our own crying weaknesses, our cowardice, our purblind sentimentalism.*[3] Already, we see a dominant theme of Sri Aurobindo, who, in the political as in the spiritual struggle and in all circumstances, urges us to look within ourselves for the cause both of our misfortunes and of the world's troubles—not outside or elsewhere. *Outer circumstances are merely the unfolding of what we are,* the Mother, who shared his work, would later emphasize. Sri Aurobindo soon realized that newspaper articles were not enough to awaken a country; he began an underground activity, which would lead him to the foot of the gallows. For thirteen years Sri Aurobindo would play with fire.

However, this young man was neither restless nor fanatical: "His smile was simple like that of a child, as limpid and as sweet," wrote his Bengali teacher who lived with him for two years (Sri Aurobindo had naturally begun to study his mother tongue). With touching ingenuousness, his teacher adds: "Before meeting Aurobindo, I had imagined him as a stalwart figure dressed like a European from head to foot, immaculate, with a stern look behind his spectacles, a horrible accent (from Cambridge, of course!) and a very difficult disposition. Who could have thought that this tanned young man with gentle, dreamy eyes, long wavy hair parted in the middle and falling to the neck, clad in a common coarse Ahmedabad *dhoti*, a close-fitting Indian jacket, and old-fashioned slippers with upturned toes, and whose face was slightly marked with smallpox, was no other than *Mister* Aurobindo Ghose, a living treasure of French, Latin and Greek?"

Actually, Sri Aurobindo was not yet through with books; the Western momentum was still there; he devoured books ordered from Bombay and Calcutta by the case. "Aurobindo would sit at his desk," his Bengali teacher continues, "and read by the light of an oil lamp till one in the morning, oblivious of the intolerable mosquito bites. I would see him seated there in the same posture for hours on end, his eyes fixed on his book, like a yogi lost in the contemplation of the Divine, unaware of all that went on around him. Even if the house had caught fire, it would not have broken this concentration." He read English, Russian, German, and French novels, but also, in ever larger numbers, the sacred books of India, the Upanishads, the Bhagavad Gita, the Ramayana, although he had never been in a temple except as an observer. "Once, having returned from the College," one of his friends recalls, "Sri Aurobindo sat down, picked up a book at random and started to read, while Z and some friends began a noisy game of chess. After half an hour, he put the book down and took a cup of tea. We had already seen him do this many times and were waiting eagerly for a chance to verify whether he read the books from cover to cover or only scanned a few pages here and there. Soon the test began. Z opened the book, read a line aloud and asked Sri Aurobindo to recite what followed. Sri Aurobindo concentrated for a moment, and then repeated the entire page without a single mistake. If he could read a hundred pages in half an hour, no wonder he could go through a case of books in such an incredibly short time." But Sri Aurobindo did not stop at the translations of the sacred texts; he began to study Sanskrit, which, typically, he learned by himself. When a subject was known to be difficult or impossible, he would refuse to take anyone's word for it, whether he were a grammarian, pandit, or clergyman, and would insist upon trying it himself. The method seemed to have some merit, for not only did he learn Sanskrit, but a few years later he discovered the lost meaning of the Veda.*

The day came, however, when Sri Aurobindo had had enough of these intellectual exercises. He probably realized that one can go on amassing knowledge indefinitely, reading and learning languages, even learning all the languages in the world and reading all the books in the world, and yet not progress at all. For the mind does not seek truly to know, even though it may appear to—it seeks to grind. Its need of knowledge is primarily a need for something to grind. If by chance the machine were to come to a stop because knowledge had been obtained, it would soon rise up in revolt and find something new to grind, just for the sake of grinding and grinding; such is its function. That within us which seeks to know and to progress is not the mind, but something behind it which uses it: *The capital period of my intellectual development,* Sri Aurobindo confided to a disciple, *was when I could see clearly that what the intellect said might be correct and not correct, that what the intellect justified was true and its opposite also was true. I never admitted a truth in the mind without simultaneously keeping*

---

* The Vedic Age, prior to that of the Upanishads, which was its heir, dates back before 4000 B.C.

it open to the contrary of it. . . . And the first result was that the prestige of the intellect was gone![4]

Sri Aurobindo had come to a turning point; temples did not interest him and books were empty. A friend advised him to practice yoga, but Sri Aurobindo refused: *A yoga which requires me to give up the world is not for me,*[5] he moreover added: *a solitary salvation leaving the world to its fate was felt as almost distasteful.*[6] Then one day Sri Aurobindo witnessed a curious scene, though one not uncommon in India (to be sure, banality is often the best trigger of inner movements), when his brother Barin was ill with a severe fever. (Barin, born while Sri Aurobindo was in England, was Sri Aurobindo's secret emissary in the organization of Indian resistance in Bengal.) One of those half-naked wandering monks known as *naga-sannyasins*, whose bodies are smeared with ashes, appeared. He was probably begging for food from door to door as is their custom, when he saw Barin rolled up in blankets, shivering with fever. Without a word, he asked for a glass of water, drew a sign, chanted a *mantra*, and had Barin drink the water. Five minutes later Barin was cured, and the monk had disappeared. Sri Aurobindo had heard about the strange powers of these ascetics, but now he had seen it with his own eyes. He suddenly realized that yoga could serve other purposes than escape from the world. And he needed *power* to liberate India: *The agnostic was in me, the atheist was in me, the skeptic was in me and I was not absolutely sure that there was a God at all. . . . I felt there must be a mighty truth somewhere in this yoga. . . . So when I turned to the yoga and resolved to practise it and find out if my idea was right, I did it in this spirit and with this prayer to Him, "If Thou art, then Thou knowest my heart. Thou knowest that I do not ask for Mukti [liberation], I do not ask for anything which others ask for. I ask only for strength to uplift this nation, I ask only to be allowed to live and work for this people whom I love."*[7] That is how Sri Aurobindo set out on the road.

CHAPTER 4

The Silent Mind

Mental Constructions

The first stage in Sri Aurobindo's yoga, and the major task that opens the door to many realizations, is mental silence. Why mental silence, one may ask? Clearly, if we wish to discover a new country within us, we must first leave the old one behind; everything depends upon our determination in taking this first step. Sometimes it can happen in a flash. Something in us cries out: "Enough of this grinding!" We at once are on our way, walking forth without ever looking back. Others say *yes* then *no*; they vacillate endlessly between two worlds. Let us emphasize here that the aim is not to amputate from ourselves any painfully acquired possession in the name of Wisdom-Peace-Serenity (we will also avoid using big and empty words); we are not seeking holiness but youth—the eternal youth of an ever-progressing being; we are not seeking a lesser being but a better being and above all a vaster one: *Has it not occurred to you that if they really sought for something cold, dark and gloomy as the supreme good, they would not be sages but asses?* [1] Sri Aurobindo once humorously remarked.

Actually, one makes all kinds of discoveries when the mental machine stops, and first of all one realizes that if the power to think is a remarkable gift, *the power not to think* [2] is a far greater one yet;

let the seeker try it for just a few minutes, and he will soon see
what this means! He will realize that he lives in a surreptitious
racket, an exhausting and ceaseless whirlwind exclusively filled with
his thoughts, his feelings, his impulses, his reactions—him, always
him, an oversized gnome intruding into everything, obscuring
everything, hearing and seeing only himself, knowing only himself
(if even that!), whose unchanging themes manage to give the
illusion of novelty only through their alternation. *In a certain sense
we are nothing but a complex mass of mental, nervous and physical
habits held together by a few ruling ideas, desires and associations—an
amalgam of many small self-repeating forces with a few major vibrations.*[3] By the age of eighteen we are set, one might say, with our
major vibrations established. Then the deposits of the same perpetual thing with a thousand different faces we call culture or
"our" self will ceaselessly settle around this primary structure in
ever thicker layers, increasingly refined and polished. We are in
fact shut in a *construction*, which may be like lead, without even a
small opening, or as graceful as a minaret; but whether in a granite
skin or a glass statue, we are nonetheless confined, forever buzzing
and repetitive. The first task of yoga is to breathe freely, to shatter
that *mental screen*, which allows only one type of vibration to get
through, in order to discover the multicolored infinity of vibrations; that is, the world and people as they really are, and another
"self" within ourselves, whose worth is beyond any mental appreciation.

Active Meditation

When we sit with our eyes closed to silence the mind, we are at
first submerged by a torrent of thoughts; they crop up from every
side, like frightened or even aggressive rats. There is only one way
to stop this racket: to try and try again, patiently and persistently;
above all, we must shift our concentration elsewhere, and not
make the mistake of struggling mentally with the mind. All of us

have, above the mind or deep inside ourselves, an *aspiration*, the very thing that has put us on the path in the first place, a yearning of our being, a password that has a special meaning for us; if we cling to that, the work becomes easier, positively rather than negatively oriented, and the more we repeat our password, the more powerful it becomes. We can also use an image, for instance that of a vast ocean without a ripple upon which we float, becoming that tranquil vastness. We thus learn not only silence but expansion of consciousness. Each person must find his own method, and the less tension he brings to it, the more quickly he will succeed: *One may start a process of one kind or another for the purpose which would normally mean a long labour and be seized, even at the outset, by a rapid intervention or manifestation of Silence with an effect out of all proportion to the means used at the beginning. One commences with a method, but the work is taken up by a Grace from above, from That to which one aspires or an irruption of the infinitudes of the Spirit. It was in this last way that I myself came by the mind's absolute silence, unimaginable to me before I had its actual experience.*[4] This is a most important point indeed. For we might think that these yogic experiences are all very nice and interesting, but that they are far beyond our ordinary human grasp; how could we, such as we are, ever get there? Our mistake is in judging with our present self possibilities that belong to another self. By the simple fact of setting out on the path, the yoga automatically awakens a whole range of latent faculties and invisible forces that far exceed the possibilities of our outer being and can do for us things that we are normally incapable of doing: *One has to have the passage clear between the outer mind and something in the inner being . . . for they (the Yogic consciousness and its powers) are already there within you,*[5] and the best way of "clearing" the passage is to silence the mind. We do not know who we are, and still less what we are capable of.

But exercises of meditation are not the true solution to the problem (though they may be necessary at the beginning to provide an initial momentum), because even if we achieve a relative silence, the moment we set foot outside our room or retreat, we fall right back into the usual turmoil as well as into the familiar separation between inner and outer self, inner life and worldly life. What we need is a total life; we need to live the truth of our being every day, at every moment, not only on holidays or in solitude, and blissful meditations in pastoral settings simply will not achieve this. *We may get incrusted in our spiritual seclusion and find it difficult later on to pour ourselves triumphantly outwards and apply to life our gains in the higher Nature. When we turn to add this external kingdom also to our inner conquests, we shall find ourselves too much accustomed to an activity purely subjective and ineffective on the material plane. There will be an immense difficulty in transforming the outer life and the body. Or we shall find that our action does not correspond with the inner light: it still follows the old accustomed mistaken paths, still obeys the old normal imperfect influences; the Truth within us continues to be separated by a painful gulf from the ignorant mechanism of our external nature. . . . It is as if we were living in another, a larger and subtler world and had no divine hold, perhaps little hold of any kind, upon the material and terrestrial existence.*[6] The only solution is therefore to practice silencing the mind just where it is *seemingly* the most difficult: on the street, in the subway, at work, everywhere. Instead of going through Grand Central Station four times a day like someone hounded and forever in a rush, we can walk there consciously, as a seeker. Instead of living haphazardly, dispersed in a multitude of thoughts, which not only lack any excitement but are also as exhausting as a broken record, we can gather the scattered threads of our consciousness and work on ourselves at every moment. Then life begins to become surprisingly exciting, because the least little circumstance becomes an opportunity for victory; we are *focused*; we are going somewhere instead of going nowhere.

For yoga is not a way of doing but of being.

The Transition

We are thus in search of another country; but, we must admit, between the one we leave behind and the one we have not yet reached, there is a rather uncomfortable no-man's-land. It is a period of trial, whose length depends upon our own determination; but, as we know, from time immemorial, from the Eastern, Egyptian, or Orphic initiations to the quest for the Holy Grail, the story of man's ascent has always been attended by trials. In the past they were mainly romantic. What was so earthshaking, after all, about getting oneself sealed in a sarcophagus while the fifes were playing, or celebrating one's own funeral rites around a pyre? Today the sarcophagi have become public, and some human lives are a kind of burial. It is therefore worthwhile to make some effort to get out. When we take a good look around, we see we haven't much to lose by making that effort.

The main difficulty of this transition is the inner void. After living in a condition of mental effervescence, we suddenly feel like a convalescent, rather lost, with strange echoes in our head, as if this world were horribly noisy and tiring. We become extremely sensitive, with an impression of bumping into everything, into gray or aggressive people, heavy objects, brutal events; the world appears enormously absurd. This is a sure sign of the beginning of interiorization. Yet if we try to go consciously inside ourselves in meditation, we find a similar void, a sort of dark well or amorphous neutrality. If we persist inward, we might even drop off to sleep for a few seconds or minutes, or sometimes even longer. Yet this is no ordinary sleep: we have passed into another consciousness, but there is still no *link* between the two, and we come out of this state apparently no more enlightened than when we entered it. This transitory condition might easily lead to a sort of absurd nihilism: nothing outside or inside. Here is where we must be very careful, once we have demolished our outer mental constructions, not to become confined in another construction of false profundity, an absurd, illusionist or skeptical, perhaps even rebellious, construction. We must go farther. Once we have begun yoga, we must go *to the end*, no matter what, because if we let go of the thread, we may never find it again. There, indeed, is the trial. The seeker must understand that he is being born to another life, and his new eyes, his new senses are not yet formed; he is like a newborn child just coming into the world. There is not a lessening of consciousness but, in reality, a passage to a new consciousness: *The cup [has to be] left clean and empty for the divine liquor to be poured into it.*[7] The only resource in these circumstances is to cling to our aspiration and, precisely because everything is so terribly lacking, allow it to grow like a fire into which we throw all our old clothes, our old life, our old ideas and old feelings; we have to have an unshakable faith that behind this transition, a door will open. And our faith is not foolish; it is not a credulous stupidity but a *foreknowledge*, something within us that knows before we do, sees before we do, and which sends its vision and knowledge to the surface in the form of a yearning, a seeking, an inexplicable faith. *Faith*, says Sri Aurobindo, *is an intuition not only waiting for experience to justify it, but leading towards experience.*[8]

The Descent of the Force

Little by little the void is filled. We then make a series of observations and experiences of considerable importance, which cannot be listed in a logical sequence, because from the moment we leave the old world we find that everything is possible, and, above all, that no two cases are alike—hence, the falsehood of all spiritual dogmas. We can only mention a few broad lines of experience.

First, when calm, if not absolute silence, is relatively well established in the mind, when our aspiration, our need, has grown and become constant, throbbing, as if we carried a hole within ourselves, we start noticing a phenomenon that will have enormous consequences over the entire course of our yoga. We feel around the head, and particularly in the nape of the neck, a kind of unusual pressure, which may give the sensation of a false headache. At the beginning we cannot bear it for very long, and we try to shake it off, distract ourselves or "think of something else." Gradually, this pressure takes on a more definite form, and we actually begin to feel a *descending* current, a current of force that does not resemble an unpleasant electric current but rather a flowing mass. We then begin to realize that the "pressure" or false headache was caused simply by our own resistance to the descent of this Force, and that the obvious thing to be done is not to obstruct the passage by blocking the current in the head, but to allow it to flow through all the levels of our being, from head to toe. This current is at first rather spasmodic, irregular; a slight, conscious effort is required of us to reconnect with it when it vanishes; then it becomes continuous, natural and automatic, giving the very pleasant sensation of a fresh energy, like another breathing, fuller than that of our lungs, enveloping us, bathing us, making us lighter, while also filling us with strength. The physical feeling is very similar to that of a brisk walk in the wind. We do not realize its true effect (it settles in very gradually, in small doses) until, for one reason or another—distraction, error, or excess—we cut ourselves off from the current. Then we feel empty, shrunken, as if lacking oxygen, with a very unpleasant impression of a physical shriveling, not unlike an old apple whose sunshine and juice have been squeezed out. At this point, we really wonder how we were ever able to live without that current before. This is a first transmutation of our energies. Instead of drawing from the common source, below and around us, in universal life, we draw from above. And that energy is far clearer, far more sustained, uninterrupted, and especially far more dynamic. In daily life, in the midst of our work and our myriad other occupations, the current of force is at first rather diluted, but the moment we stop and concentrate, there is a massive inrush. Everything comes to a standstill. We are like a jar filled to the brim; the sensation of "current" disappears, as if the whole body from head to foot were charged with a mass of energy at once compact and crystalline (*a solid cool block of peace*,[9] says Sri Aurobindo). And if our inner vision has begun to open, we may notice that everything has become bluish; we are like an aquamarine, and vast, vast, tranquil, without a ripple— such indescribable freshness, truly the feeling of bathing in *the* Source. Indeed, this "descending force" is the very Force of the Spirit—*Shakti*. Spiritual Force is not just a word. Ultimately, it will no longer be necessary to close our eyes and withdraw from the surface to feel it; it will be there every second of our life, no matter what we are doing, whether we are eating, reading, or speaking; we will see it take on a greater and greater intensity as our being becomes accustomed to it. It is actually a formidable mass of energy, limited only by the smallness of our receptivity and capacity.

When the disciples speak of their experience with this descending Force, they call it "Sri Aurobindo's and the Mother's Force." But they do not mean that this *Shakti* is the personal property of Sri Aurobindo and Mother; they merely express, unwittingly, the fact that it has no equivalent in any other known yoga. Here, experientially, we touch upon the fundamental difference between Sri Aurobindo's integral yoga (*purna yoga*) and the other yogas. If one has practiced other methods of yoga before Sri Aurobindo's, one does notice a basic practical difference: after some time, one experiences an *ascending* Force (called *kundalini* in India), which awakens rather brutally at the base of the spine and rises from level to level until it reaches the top of the head, where it blossoms into a sort of luminous and radiating pulsation, bringing a sensation of immensity (and often a loss of consciousness called ecstasy), as if one had forever emerged Elsewhere. All yogic methods, which might be called thermogenetic—the *asanas* of hatha yoga, the concentrations of raja yoga, the breathing exercises or *pranayama*, etc.—aim at arousing that ascending Force; they can be dangerous and cause profound perturbations, which make the presence and protection of an enlightened Master indispensable. We will return to this later. The difference in the direction of the current, ascending vs. descending, has to do with a difference in goals which cannot be overemphasized. Traditional yogas and, we suppose, Western religious disciplines aim essentially at a liberation of consciousness: the yearning of the whole being is directed upward, in an ascending aspiration; the seeker strives to break through the appearances and to found his station above, in peace or ecstasy. Hence the arousing of the ascending Force. As we have seen, however, Sri Aurobindo's goal is not only to ascend but also to descend, not only to find eternal peace but to transform life and matter, beginning with the little bit of life and matter that we are, hence the arousing, or rather the response, of the descending Force. To experience the descending current is to experience the transforming Force. It is this Force that will do the yoga for us, automatically (if we let it), this Force that will rejuvenate our soon-exhausted energy and awkward efforts, this Force that will begin where other yogas end, illuminating first the top of our being, then going down from level to level, gently, peacefully, irresistibly (it is never violent; its power is amazingly measured, as if it were directly guided by the wisdom of the Spirit), and it is this Force that will universalize our entire being, right down to the lowest layers. This is the fundamental experience of the integral yoga. *When the Peace is established, this higher or Divine Force from above can descend and work in us. It descends usually first into the head and liberates the inner mind centres, then into the heart centre . . . then into the navel and other vital centres . . . then into the sacral region and below. . . . It works at the same time for perfection as well as liberation; it takes up the whole nature part by part and deals with it, rejecting what has to be rejected, sublimating what has to be sublimated, creating what has to be created. It integrates, harmonizes, establishes a new rhythm in the nature.*[10]

Emergence of a New Mode of Knowledge

With the silence of the mind comes another change, one that is

very significant but more difficult to recognize because it sometimes extends over several years, and its signs are at first imperceptible. It could be called the emergence of a new mode of knowledge,
and thus of a new mode of action.

It is conceivable to maintain a silent mind when walking in a
crowd, eating, dressing or resting, but how is it possible at work,
at the office, for example, or while having a discussion with
friends? We need to think, to call upon our memory, to look for
ideas, to bring in a whole mental process. Experience shows,
however, that this is not inevitable, that it is only the product of
a long habit in which we have grown accustomed to depending
on the mind for knowledge and action; but it is only a *habit*, and
it can be changed. In essence, yoga is not so much a way of learning
as a way of unlearning a mass of supposedly imperative habits we
have inherited from our animal evolution.

If the seeker undertakes to silence his mind while working, for
instance, he will go through several stages. At first, he will barely
manage to remember his aspiration from time to time, and to stop
his work a few minutes to recapture the right wavelength, only to
see everything swallowed up again in the routine. But as he
develops the habit of making an effort in other places—on the
street, at home, anywhere—the dynamism of his effort will tend
to keep alive and to draw his attention unexpectedly in the midst
of his other activities: he will recall more and more often. Then
the *character* of that recall will gradually change: instead of a
voluntary interruption to recapture the true rhythm, the seeker
will feel something *living* deep within him, in the background of
his being, like a little muffled vibration; at any time, all it will take
is a slight inner movement of stepping back to regain the vibration
of silence, in a second. He will realize it is always there, like a bluish
depth in the background; he will discover he can refresh himself
in it whenever he chooses, relax in it in the very midst of turmoil
and problems, and that he carries within himself an inviolable
haven of peace.

Soon this vibration behind will become more and more perceptible and continuous, and the seeker will feel a *separation* take place in his being: a silent depth vibrating in the background, and the rather thin surface being where activities, thoughts, gestures, words occur. He will have brought to light the *Witness* in him, and will allow himself less and less to be taken in by the outside play, which, octopus-like, constantly tries to devour us alive. This discovery is as old as the Rig Veda: "Two birds beautiful of wing, friends and comrades, cling to a common tree, and one eats the sweet fruit, the other regards him and eats not." (I.164.20) At this point, it will become easier for him to substitute, voluntarily at first, a habit of referring silently to this vibrating depth for the old superficial habit of mental reflection, memory, planning, and calculation. In practice, this is a long period of transition, with setbacks and breakthroughs (the feeling is not so much one of setbacks and breakthroughs as of something being veiled and unveiled in turn) as well as a confrontation of the two processes, the old mental mechanism tending constantly to interfere and to recapture its rights, namely, to convince us that we can't do without it; it may also find some support in a sort of laziness whereby we find it easier "to do as usual." On the other hand, this work of disentanglement is powerfully aided, first by the experience of the descending Force, which automatically and tirelessly puts our house in order and exerts a quiet pressure on the rebellious mechanism, as if each wave of thought were seized and frozen in place; secondly, by the accumulation of thousands of increasingly perceptible little experiences, which makes us realize that we can do amazingly well without the mind, and are actually better off without it.

In fact, gradually we discover that there is no necessity to think. Something behind, or above, does all the work, with a precision and infallibility that grow as we get into the habit of referring to it. There is no necessity to remember, since the exact information comes forth when needed; there is no necessity to plan any action, since a secret spring sets it in motion without our willing it or thinking about it, and makes us do exactly what is needed with a wisdom and foresight of which our mind, forever shortsighted, is quite incapable. We notice also that the more we trust and obey these unexpected intimations or flash-suggestions, the more frequent, clear, compelling, and natural they become, somewhat like an intuitive functioning, but with the important difference that our intuitions are almost always blurred and distorted by the mind, which delights at imitating them and making us mistake its vagaries for revelations, while here the transmission is clear, silent, and accurate, because the mind is quiet. We have all experienced certain problems which are "mysteriously" solved during sleep, precisely when the thinking machine is hushed. There will no doubt be errors and stumblings before the new functioning is securely established; the seeker must be ready to be often mistaken; in fact, he will notice that mistakes are always the result of a mental intrusion; each time the mind intervenes, it blurs, splinters, and delays everything. Eventually, after many trials and errors, we will understand once and for all and see with our own eyes that *the mind is not an instrument of knowledge but only an organizer of knowledge*, as Mother put it, and that knowledge comes from elsewhere.* When the mind is silent, words come, speech comes, action comes, everything comes, automatically, with striking exactness and speed. It is indeed another, much lighter way of living. For *there is nothing the mind can do that cannot be better done in the mind's immobility and thought-free stillness.*[11]

The Universal Mind

So far, we have discussed the progress of the seeker in inner terms, but this progress manifests outwardly also. Actually, the wall between inner and outer grows increasingly thin; it seems more and more like an artificial convention set up by an adolescent mind, self-absorbed and self-centered. The seeker will feel this wall

---

*   This "elsewhere" will be discussed later, in the study of the Superconscient.

slowly losing its consistency; he will experience a kind of change in the texture of his being, as if he were becoming lighter, more transparent, more porous, as it were. This change of texture will be felt at first through unpleasant symptoms, for while the ordinary person is generally protected by a thick hide, the seeker no longer has this protection: he receives people's thoughts, intentions, and desires in their true forms and in all their starkness, exactly as they are—assaults. And here we must emphasize that "bad thoughts" or "ill will" are not the only forms to share a virulent character; nothing is more aggressive than good intentions, kindly sentiments, or altruism; either way, it is the ego fostering itself, through sweetness or through violence. We are civilized only on the surface; underneath the cannibal in us lives on. It is therefore very necessary for the seeker to be in possession of the Force we have described; with It he can go anywhere. Actually, the cosmic wisdom is such that this transparency would not come without adequate protection. Armed with "his" Force and a silent mind, then, the seeker will gradually find he is open to all outside impacts; he receives everything; distances are unreal barriers—no one is far away, no one is gone, everything is together, and everything is simultaneous; he can perceive a friend's thought ten thousand miles away, a person's anger, or a brother's suffering. The seeker will need only to tune in to that place or person, in the silence, to have a more or less exact perception of the situation, depending upon his own capacity for silence; for in this case, too, the mind jams everything, because it has desires, fears, prejudices, and anything it perceives is instantly distorted by this desire, that fear, or that prejudice (there are other causes of jamming, which we will discuss later). Therefore, it would seem that silencing the mind brings an expansion of consciousness, which becomes capable of projecting itself at will onto any point of the universal reality and learning there what it needs to know.

In this silent transparency, we will soon make another discovery, of capital importance in its implications. We will notice that not only do other people's thoughts come to us from the outside, but our own thoughts, too, *come from outside*. Once we are sufficiently transparent we will be able to feel, in the motionless silence of the mind, little swirling eddies coming into contact with our atmosphere, like faint little vibrations drawing our attention; if we pay closer attention in order to "see" what they are, that is, if we let one of these little swirls enter us, we suddenly find ourselves "thinking" of something. What we had felt at the periphery of our being was a thought in its pure form, or rather *a mental vibration* before it enters us and comes to the surface of our being clad in a personal form, enabling us to claim: "This is *my* thought." This is how a good mind-reader can read what goes on in a person whose language he does not even know, because it is not the "thoughts" that he catches but the vibrations, to which he then attributes his own corresponding mental form. But we should not really be too surprised, because if we were capable of creating a single thing ourselves, even a tiny little thought, we would be the creators of the world! *Where is the I in you that can create all that?* Mother used to ask. It is just that the process is not perceptible to the ordinary man, firstly, because he lives in constant tumult, and secondly because the process through which vibrations are appropriated is almost instantaneous and automatic. Through his education and environment, a person becomes accustomed to selecting from the universal Mind a given, narrow range of vibrations with which he has a particular affinity. For the rest of his life he will pick up the same wavelength, repeating the same vibratory mode in more or less high-sounding words and with more or less innovative turns of phrase; he will spin around in a cage, the illusion of progress being given only by a greater or lesser extent and sparkling range of vocabulary used. True, we do change our ideas, but changing ideas is not progressing. It is not rising to a higher or faster vibratory mode; it is merely a new set of acrobatics within the same environment. This is why Sri Aurobindo spoke of a *change of consciousness*.

Once the seeker has seen that his thoughts come from outside, and after he has repeated this experience hundreds of times, he will hold the key to the true mastery of the mind. For while it is difficult to get rid of a thought we believe to be ours, once it has become entrenched in us, it is easy to reject the same thought when we see it coming from the outside. Once we master silence, we necessarily master the mental world, because instead of perpetually picking up the same wavelength, we can run through the whole range of wavelengths and choose or reject as we please. But let us listen to Sri Aurobindo himself describe the experience as he first had it with another yogi, Bhaskar Lele, who spent three days with him: *All developed mental men, those who get beyond the average, have in one way or other, or at least at certain times and for certain purposes to separate the two parts of the mind, the active part, which is a factory of thoughts and the quiet masterful part which is at once a Witness and a Will, observing them, judging, rejecting, eliminating, accepting, ordering corrections and changes, the Master in the House of Mind, capable of self-empire, samrajya. The Yogi goes still further,—he is not only a master there but even while in mind in a way, he gets out of it as it were, and stands above or quite back from it and free. For him the image of the factory of thoughts is no longer quite valid; for he sees that thoughts come from outside, from the universal Mind, or universal Nature, sometimes formed and distinct, sometimes unformed and then they are given shape somewhere in us. The principal business of our mind is either a response of acceptance or a refusal to these thought waves (as also vital waves, subtle physical energy waves) or this giving a personal-mental form to thought-stuff (or vital movements) from the environing Nature-Force. It was my great debt to Lele that he showed me this. "Sit in meditation," he said, "but do not think, look only at your mind; you will see thoughts coming into it; before they can enter throw these away from your mind till your mind is capable of entire silence." I had never heard before of thoughts coming visibly into the mind from outside, but I did not think either of questioning the truth or the possibility, I simply sat down and did it. In a moment my mind became silent as a windless air on a high mountain summit and then I saw one thought and then another coming in a concrete way from outside; I flung them away before they could enter and take hold of the brain and in three days I was free. From that moment, in principle, the mental being in me became a free Intelligence, a universal Mind, not limited to the narrow circle of personal thoughts as a labourer in a thought factory, but a receiver of knowledge from all the hundred realms of being and free to choose what it willed in this vast sight-empire and thought-empire.*[12]

Having started from a small mental construction in which he felt quite at ease and highly enlightened, the seeker looks back and wonders how he ever managed to live in such a prison. He is particularly struck to see how for years and years he lived surrounded by impossibilities, and how humans in general live behind bars: "You can't do this; you can't do that; it's against this law, against that law; it's illogical; it's not natural; it's impossible." He discovers that everything is possible; the true difficulty is in the belief that it is difficult. After living for twenty or thirty years in his mental shell, like a sort of thinking periwinkle, he begins to breathe freely.

He finds, too, that the eternal opposition of inner versus outer is resolved—that this also was part of the mental sclerosis. In reality, "outside" is everywhere inside! We are everywhere! It is wrong to believe that if we could only realize perfect conditions of peace, beauty, or bucolic serenity things would be so much easier, because there would *always be something* to disturb us, everywhere. So we might as well decide to break our constructions and embrace all the "outside" in ourselves; we will then be at home everywhere. The same holds for the opposition between action and meditation; the seeker has established inner silence, and his action *is* meditation (he will even glimpse the fact that meditation can be action); whether he is taking a shower or going about his business, the Force flows and flows in him. He is forever tuned in elsewhere. Finally, he will see his actions becoming more clear-sighted, effective and powerful, without in the least encroaching upon his peace: *The substance of the mental being . . . is still, so still that nothing disturbs it. If thoughts or activities come, they . . . cross the mind as a flight of birds crosses the sky in a windless air. It passes, disturbs nothing, leaving no trace. Even if a thousand images or the most violent events pass across it, the calm stillness remains as if the very texture of the mind were a substance of eternal and indestructible peace. A mind that has achieved this calmness can begin to act, even intensely and powerfully, but it will keep its fundamental stillness— originating nothing from itself but receiving from Above and giving it a mental form without adding anything of its own, calmly, dispassionately, though with the joy of the Truth and the happy power and light of its passage.*[13]

Need we recall that Sri Aurobindo was then leading a revolutionary movement and preparing guerrilla warfare in India?

CHAPTER 5

Consciousness

A disciple once had to make a critical decision. He wrote to Sri Aurobindo for advice and was quite puzzled when he was told to make his decision from the "summit of his consciousness." He was a Westerner and wondered what on earth this could mean. Was this "summit of consciousness" a special way of thinking very intensely, a sort of enthusiasm produced when the brain warms up? For this is the only kind of "consciousness" we know in the West. For us, consciousness is always a mental process: "I think, therefore I am." Such is our own particular bias; we place ourselves at the center of the world and bestow the gift of consciousness upon all those who share our way of being and perceiving things. Not so long ago, we marveled that one could be Persian. However, if we want to understand and discover what consciousness truly is, and utilize it, we must indeed go beyond this narrow perspective. After having attained a certain degree of mental silence, Sri Aurobindo was able to make the following observations: *Mental consciousness is only the human range which no more exhausts all the possible ranges of consciousness than human sight exhausts all the gradations of color or human hearing all the gradations of sound—for there is much above or below that is to man invisible and inaudible. So there are ranges of consciousness above and below the human range, with which the normal human has no contact and they seem to it*

unconscious,—supramental or overmental and submental ranges.[1]
. . . What we call unconsciousness is simply other-consciousness. . . .
We are really no more unconscious when we are asleep or stunned or
drugged or "dead" or in any other state, than when we are plunged in
inner thought oblivious of our physical selves and our surroundings.
For anyone who has advanced even a little way in Yoga, this is a most
elementary proposition. And Sri Aurobindo adds: *As we progress and*
awaken to the soul in us and things, we shall realize that there is a
consciousness also in the plant, in the metal, in the atom, in electricity,
in everything that belongs to physical nature; we shall find even that
it is not really in all respects a lower or more limited mode than the
mental; on the contrary, it is in many "inanimate" forms more intense,
rapid, poignant, though less evolved towards the surface.[2] The task of
the beginning yogi is therefore to become conscious in every way,
at all the levels of his being and all the degrees of universal
existence, not just mentally; to become conscious in himself and
in others and in all things, while awake and in sleep; and finally,
to learn to become conscious in what people call "death," because,
to the extent that we have been conscious in our life, we shall be
conscious in our death.

But we do not have to take Sri Aurobindo's word for it. On the
contrary, he strongly urges us to see for ourselves. We must
therefore strive to unravel that in us which connects all our modes
of being—sleep, waking and "death"—and enables us to come
into contact with other forms of consciousness.

The Centers of Consciousness

Pursuing our experimental method based on mental silence, we
are led to several discoveries that will gradually put us on the track.
First, we see the general confusion in which we live slowly settle;
more and more clearly, strata will appear in our being as if we were
made up of separate fragments, each with its own individual
personality and specific center, and, what is more, with its own

life independent of the others. This polyphony (or, rather, cacophony) is generally masked from us by the voice of the mind, which drowns out and appropriates everything. There is not a single movement of our being, at any level, not a single emotion, not a single desire, not the batting of an eyelash, that is not instantly snatched up by the mind and covered over with a layer of thought; in other words, we *mentalize* everything. This is the great purpose of the mind in evolution: it helps bring to our conscious surface all the movements of our being that would otherwise remain as a formless subconscious or superconscious magma. It also helps us establish some semblance of order in this anarchy by organizing all these tiny feudal states under its sovereignty. But, in so doing, it veils from us their voices and true workings; there is only one step from sovereignty to tyranny. The supermental mechanisms are totally obstructed; or if something of the superconscious voices manages to get through, it is immediately distorted, diluted, and obscured. Similarly, the submental mechanisms become atrophied, depriving us of spontaneous senses that were very useful at an earlier stage of our evolution and could still be. Other minorities of our being line up in rebellion, while still others secretly accumulate their little power, waiting for the first opportunity to fly in our faces. But the seeker who has silenced his mind will begin to discern all these states in their bare reality, without their mental veneer; he will feel, at various levels of his being, certain centers of concentration, or nodes of force, each with its own particular vibratory quality or frequency. We have all experienced, at least once in our lives, vibrations radiating at different levels of our being and with different densities; a great revelatory vibration, for example, when a veil seems to be suddenly rent and we are shown a whole vision of truth, without words, without our even knowing exactly what the revelation consists of; something simply vibrates, which makes the world inexplicably wider, lighter, and clearer; or heavier vibrations of anger or fear, vibrations of desire, vibrations of sympathy. Thus, there is in us an entire gamut of vibratory nodules or *centers of consciousness,*

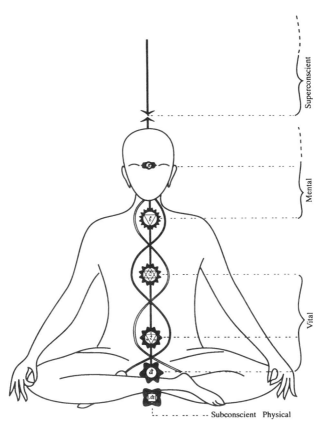

The Centers of Consciousness
According to the Indian Tantric Tradition

The central channel and the two interlacing side channels correspond to the medullary canal and, probably, to the sympathetic nervous system. They are the paths through which the ascending Force (Kundalini) travels, after awakening in the lower center, and rises from center to center "like a serpent" to blossom at the top of the head in the Superconscient. (This seems to be also the significance of the uraeus, the Egyptian naja that adorned the Pharaohs' headdress; the Mexican quetzalcoatl, or plumed serpent; and perhaps the naga snakes overhanging Buddha's head.) The detailed features of these centers are of interest only to professional clairvoyants; we will discuss later some details of general interest. A complete study on the question can be found in the remarkable work of Sir John Woodroffe (Arthur Avalon), *The Serpent Power* (Madras: Ganesh & Co., 1913).

each specialized in a specific type of vibration, which can be distinguished and perceived directly according to the degree of our silence and the acuity of our perceptions. The mind is only *one* of these centers, *one* type of vibration, *one* of the forms of consciousness, though it seeks to take first place.

We will not dwell here on the description of these centers as tradition refers to them, for it is better to experience things oneself rather than to talk about them, nor will we discuss their positions in the body; the seeker will feel them himself without any difficulty as soon as he becomes a little clear. Suffice it to say that these centers (called *Chakras* in India) are not located in our physical body but in another dimension, though their concentration may at times become so intense that we have an acute, localized physical sensation. Some of them, though not all, are in fact quite close to the body's nervous plexuses. Roughly speaking, there are seven centers distributed in four zones: (1) *The Superconscient,* with one center slightly above the top of the head,* which controls our thinking mind and communicates with higher mental realms: illumined mind, intuitive mind, overmind, etc. (2) *The Mind,* with two centers: one between the eyebrows, which controls the will and dynamism of our mental activity (it is also the center of subtle vision, the "third eye" certain traditions speak of); the other, at throat level, controls all the forms of mental expression. (3) *The Vital,* with three centers: one at heart level, which controls our emotional being (love, hatred, etc.); the second at the level of the navel, which controls our impulses for domination, possession and conquest, as well as our ambitions, etc.; and a third, the lower vital, between the navel and the sex center, at the level of the mesenteric plexus, which controls the lowest vibrations: jealousy,

---

* According to Indian tradition, this center, called "the thousand-petaled lotus" to express the luminous fullness one perceives when it opens up, is located at the top of the head. According to Sri Aurobindo and the experience of many others, what is felt at the top of the head is not the center itself, but the luminous reflection of a solar source located *above* the head.

envy, desire, greed, anger. (4) *The Physical and the Subconscient,** with a center at the base of the spine, which controls our physical being and sexual impulses; this center also opens up to the subconscious regions farther below.

Generally, in a "normal" man, these centers are asleep or closed, or they only let through whatever small current is necessary for his limited existence; he is truly confined in himself and communicates only indirectly with the outside world, in a very narrow range; in fact, he does not see other people or things but himself in others, himself in things, himself in everything, interminably. With yoga, the centers open. They can open in two ways: from bottom to top or from top to bottom, depending on whether we practice traditional yogic and spiritual methods, or Sri Aurobindo's yoga. As mentioned earlier, through concentration and exercises, we can eventually feel a Force awakening at the bottom of the spine and ascending from level to level up to the top of the head, with an undulating movement, just like a snake. At each level this Force *pierces* (rather violently) through the corresponding center, which opens up, thereby putting us in contact with all the universal vibrations or energies associated with the frequency of that particular center. With Sri Aurobindo's yoga, the descending Force opens the same centers, slowly and gently, from top to bottom. Often, the lower centers do not even fully open until much later. This process has a distinct advantage if we appreciate that each center corresponds to a *universal* mode of consciousness or energy. To open the lower vital or subconscious centers at the beginning is to run the risk of being flooded not only by our own small personal problems, but by torrents of universal mud; we are automatically in contact with the confusion and mud of the world. This is why traditional yogas require the protective presence of a

---

* Throughout this book we have kept Sri Aurobindo's terminology—Subconscient, Inconscient—to emphasize the etymological sense in which he used these words, i.e., that which is historically sub-conscious, not below the level of our waking consciousness but below the conscious stage in the evolutionary sense.

Master. With the descending Force this danger is avoided; we confront the lower centers only after our being is firmly established in the higher, superconscious light. Once the seeker controls his centers, he begins to know things and beings, the world and himself, as they really are, for he is no longer receiving external signs, dubious words or gestures—the charade of the confined man or the closed face of things—but the pure vibration at each level, in each thing and each being, which nothing can disguise.

But our foremost discovery concerns ourselves. If we follow a discipline similar to that described for mental silence, and remain perfectly transparent, we will soon notice that not only mental vibrations come from outside before entering our centers, but *everything* comes from outside: the vibrations of desire, of joy, of will, etc. From top to bottom, our being is a receiving station: *Truly, we do not think, will or act but thought occurs in us, will occurs in us, impulse and act occur in us.*[3] If we say: "I think, therefore I am," or "I feel, therefore I am," or "I want, therefore I am," we are like a child who believes that the disc jockey or the orchestra is hidden in the radio set and that TV is a thinking medium. Indeed, none of these I's is ourselves, nor do they belong to us, for their music is universal.

The Frontal Being

Nonetheless, we might be tempted to protest that these are *our* feelings, *our* pains, *our* desires; this is our *own* sensitive nature, not some kind of telegraphic machinery! True, it is our nature, in the sense that we have grown accustomed to responding to certain vibrations rather than to others, to being moved or pained by certain things rather than by others; and this set of habits has, apparently, crystallized into a personality we call our "self." Yet, if we look more closely, we can hardly say that it is "we" who have acquired all these habits. Our environment, our education, our atavism, our traditions have made the choice for us. At every instant they choose what we want or desire, what we like or dislike. It is as if life took place without us. When does a real "I" burst forth in all this? *Universal Nature*, Sri Aurobindo wrote, *deposits certain habits of movement, personality, character, faculties, disposi- tions, tendencies in us, and that is what we usually call ourselves.*[4] Nor can we say that this "self" has any true fixity: *The appearance of stability is given by constant repetition and recurrence of the same vibrations and formations,*[4] because it is always the same wave- lengths that we pick up or, rather, that pick us up, consistent with the laws of our environment or education; it is always the same mental, vital or other vibrations that return through our centers, and that we appropriate automatically, unconsciously, and end- lessly. In reality, everything is in a state of *constant flux*, and everything comes to us from a mind vaster than ours (a universal mind), a vital vaster than ours (a universal vital), from lower subconscious regions, or from higher superconscious ones. Thus this small *frontal being*[5] is surrounded, overhung, supported, pervaded by and set in motion by a whole hierarchy of "worlds," as ancient wisdom well knew: "Without effort one world moves in the other," says the Rig Veda (II.24-5), or, as Sri Aurobindo says, by a gradation of *planes of consciousness*, which range without break from pure Spirit to Matter, and are directly connected to each of our centers. Yet we are *conscious only of some bubbling on the surface.*[6]

What remains of ourselves in all this? Not much, to tell the truth, or everything, depending on which level we focus our consciousness.

The Individualization of Consciousness

We are beginning to have an idea of what consciousness is and to sense that it is everywhere in the universe, at every level, with corresponding centers in ourselves, but we have not yet found "our" consciousness—perhaps because consciousness is not something to be found ready-made, but something to kindle like a fire. At certain privileged moments in our existence, we have felt something like a warmth in our being, a kind of inner *impetus* or vivid energy that no words can describe, no reason can explain, because it arises from nowhere, without cause, naked like a need or a flame. Our childhood often bears witness to this pure enthusiasm, this inexplicable nostalgia; but soon we grow out of adolescence. The mind seizes upon this force as it does with everything else and covers it with pretentious, idealistic words; it channels it into a physical undertaking, a job, or a church. Or else the vital captures it and daubs it with more or less lofty sentiments—unless it uses it for some personal adventure, or for domination, conquest or possession. In some cases, this force gets bogged down even lower. And sometimes everything is swallowed up, such that only a diminutive shadow remains beneath an onerous burden. But the seeker who has silenced his mind and no longer falls prey to ideas, who has quieted his vital being and is no longer overcome and scattered at every instant by the great confusion of feelings and desires, discovers in the newly acquired clarity of his nature something like a new youth, a new and unrestrained *impetus*. As his concentration grows stronger through his "active meditations," through his aspiration and need, he will feel this impetus begin to acquire a *life* of its own within him: "It widens, bringing out that which lives," says the Rig Veda (I.113-8), "awakening someone who was dead." He will feel it assume an increasingly distinct consistency, an ever denser strength and, above all, an *independence*, as if there were both a force and a being within his own being. He will notice, first in his passive meditations (when he is quiet, at home, his eyes closed), that this force in him has mass, varying intensity, and movement, that it moves up and down inside him as if it were fluid—much like the shifting of a living substance. These movements inside him can even be powerful enough to bend his body as the force descends, or to straighten it and draw it backward as it rises. In our active meditations, in daily external life, this force inside is more diluted and feels like a tiny muffled vibration in the background, as we have said earlier; further, we feel it not only as an impersonal force but as a presence, a *being* in our depths, as if we had a support, something giving us solidity and strength, almost like an armor, as well as a serene outlook on the world. With this imperceptible vibration inside, we are invulnerable, and we are no longer alone. It is there in all circumstances, all the time. It is warm, intimate, strong. Strangely enough, once we have found it, we find *the same thing* everywhere, in all beings and in all things; we can communicate directly, as if everything were the same, without separation. We have touched something within us that is not the mere puppet of universal forces, not the narrow and dry "I think, therefore I am," but the fundamental reality of our being, our true self, true center, warmth and being, consciousness and force.*

As this inner urge or force takes on a distinct individuality, as it grows as indeed a child grows, the seeker will become aware that it does not move at random, as he had thought at first, but converges at certain points of his being, depending upon his current activity, and is in fact behind each of the centers of consciousness: behind the mental centers when we think, assert a will or express something; behind the vital centers when we feel, suffer or desire; or farther down or farther up. That force actually becomes aware of things; all the centers, including the mind, are only its openings on the different levels of universal reality, its instruments of transcription and expression. It is *the traveller of the worlds*,[7] the explorer of the planes of consciousness; it connects our various modes of being together, from waking to sleep to death, when the small outer mind is no longer there to inform or guide us; it pervades the entire range of universal existence and communicates everywhere.

In other words, we have discovered *consciousness*. We have isolated what in ordinary man is constantly mixed with other things, dispersed, entangled in his endless mental or sensory

---

* We will return to this center, which Sri Aurobindo calls the *psychic center* or *psychic being*, and others call the soul.

activities. Instead of being forever positioned somewhere between the abdomen and the forehead, we are now able to shift our consciousness to deeper or higher regions, inaccessible to the mind and our sense organs; for consciousness is not a way of thinking or feeling (or at least not just that), but a power to come in contact with the multitude of gradations of existence, either visible or invisible. The more our consciousness develops, the greater its range of action and the number of gradations it can reach. We will also find that this consciousness is independent of the thoughts, feelings, and desires of our small frontal being; it is independent of the mind, of the vital being, and even of the physical body; in certain particular conditions, which we will discuss later, it can even go outside the body to have its own experiences. Our body, our thoughts, our desires are only a thin layer of our total existence.

Consciousness-Force, Consciousness-Joy

When we discover consciousness, we find it is a force. Remarkably, we even start noticing it as a current or inner force before realizing it is a consciousness. Consciousness is force, *consciousness-force*, as Sri Aurobindo calls it, for the two terms are truly inseparable and interchangeable. The ancient wisdom of India knew this well, and never spoke of consciousness, *Chit*, without adjoining to it the term *Agni*, heat, flame, energy: *Chit-Agni* (sometimes also called *Tapas*, a synonym of *Agni: Chit-Tapas*). The Sanskrit word for spiritual or yogic discipline is *tapasya*, that which produces heat or energy, or, more correctly, consciousness-heat or conscious-ness-energy. *Agni*, or *Chit-Agni*, is the same everywhere. We speak of descending or ascending Force, of inner force, of mental, vital, or material force, but there are not a hundred different kinds of forces; there is only *one* Force in the world, a single current that circulates through us as it circulates through all things, and takes on one attribute or another, depending upon the particular level of its action. Our electric current can light up a tabernacle or a bar, a schoolroom or a restaurant; it is still the same current, though it illuminates different objects. So too, this Force, this Warmth, *Agni,* is still the same whether it animates or illuminates our inner recesses, our mental factory, our vital theater, or our material lair; depending on the level, it takes on a more or less intense light, heavier or lighter vibrations: superconscious, mental, vital, physical, but it does link everything together, animates everything. It is the fundamental substance of the universe: *Consciousness-Force, Chit-Agni.*

While consciousness is a force, the reverse is also true: force is consciousness; *all the forces are conscious.*[8] Universal Force is universal Consciousness. This is what the seeker discovers. After coming in contact with the current of consciousness-force in himself, he can attune himself to any plane of universal reality, at any point, and perceive or understand the consciousness there, and even act upon it, since the same current of consciousness is everywhere with only different modes of vibration, whether in a plant or in the thoughts of a human mind, whether in the luminous superconscient or the instinct of an animal, whether in metal or in our deepest meditations. If a piece of wood were not conscious, no yogi could displace it through concentration, because there would be no possibility of contact with it. If a single point of the universe were totally unconscious, the whole universe would be totally unconscious, because there cannot be *two* things. With Einstein we have learned—a great discovery indeed—that Matter and Energy are interchangeable: $E=mc^2$; Matter is condensed Energy. We must now discover experientially that this Energy, or Force, is Consciousness, that Matter too is a form of consciousness, just as the Mind is a form of consciousness, and the Vital and Superconscient are other forms of consciousness. Once we find this Secret—consciousness in force—we will have the true, and direct, mastery of material energy. But we are merely rediscovering very ancient truths; four thousand years ago the Upanishads knew that Matter is condensed Energy, or rather condensed Consciousness-Energy: "By energism of Consciousness* Brahman is massed; from that Matter is born and from Matter Life and Mind and the worlds." (*Mundaka Upanishad* I.1.8)

All here is Consciousness, because all is Being or Spirit. All is *Chit*, because all is *Sat—Sat-Chit*—at every level of Its own manifestation. The history of our earthly evolution is nothing but a slow conversion of Force into Consciousness or, more exactly, a slow remembering of Itself by the Consciousness buried in its own Force. During the primary stages of evolution, the consciousness of the atom, for example, is absorbed in its whirling, as the consciousness of a potter is absorbed in the pot he is making, oblivious to everything else, as the plant is absorbed in its photosynthesis, as our own consciousness can be absorbed in a book or a desire, oblivious to all the other levels of its own reality. All evolutionary progress is ultimately measured by the capacity to extricate and free the element of consciousness from its element of force—this is what is meant by "individualization of consciousness." At the spiritual or yogic stage of evolution, consciousness is completely freed, released from its mental, vital, and physical turmoil; it is its own master and can move through the entire range of vibrations of consciousness, from the atom to the Spirit; the Force has totally become Consciousness, totally remembered Itself. Finally, to remember oneself is to remember everything, because it is the Spirit in us remembering the Spirit in everything.

Simultaneously, as the Force regains its Consciousness, it regains the mastery of its force and of all forces; because to be conscious is to have power. Neither the whirling atom nor the man treading the biological rut and laboring in his mental factory has any control over the mental, vital, or atomic forces: they merely go round and round. At the conscious stage, by contrast, we are free and in control of our actions, verifying tangibly that consciousness is a force, a *substance*, which can be handled as one handles hydroxides or electric fields: *If one becomes aware of the*

---

* *Tapas.*

inner consciousness, wrote Sri Aurobindo, *one can do all sorts of things with it, send it out as a stream of force, erect a circle or wall of consciousness around oneself, direct an idea so that it shall enter somebody's head in America, etc. etc.*[9] He further explains: *The Invisible Force producing tangible results both inward and outward is the whole meaning of the Yogic consciousness. . . . If we had not had thousands of experiences showing that the Power within could alter the mind, develop its powers, add new ones, bring in new ranges of knowledge, master the vital movements, change the character, influence men and things, control the conditions and functionings of the body, work as a concrete dynamic Force on other forces, modify events . . . we would not speak of it as we do. Moreover, it is not only in its results but in its movements that the Force is tangible and concrete. When I speak of feeling Force or Power, I do not mean simply having a vague sense of it, but feeling it concretely and consequently being able to direct it, manipulate it, watch its movements, be conscious of its mass and intensity and in the same way as of other opposing forces.*[10] Later we will see that Consciousness can act upon Matter and transform it. This ultimate conversion of Matter into Consciousness, and perhaps one day even of Consciousness into Matter, is the aim of the *supramental yoga,* which we will discuss later. There are many degrees of development of the consciousness-force, from the seeker or aspirant just awakening to his inner need, to the yogi; even among yogis there are many degrees—that is where the true hierarchy begins.

There remains a final equivalence. Not only is consciousness force, not only is consciousness being, but consciousness is also joy, *Ananda*—Consciousness-Joy, *Chit-Ananda.* To be conscious is joy. When consciousness is released from the thousands of mental, vital or physical vibrations in which it was buried, we awaken to joy. The whole being is in effect filled with a mass of vibrant, crystalline, motionless, aimless force ("like a well-shaped pillar," as the Rig Veda says, V.45)—pure consciousness, pure force, pure joy, for it is all the same thing—a *concrete* joy, a vast and peaceful substance of joy, which seems to have neither beginning nor end nor reason, and seems to be everywhere, in all things and beings, as their secret foundation and secret need to grow. No one wants to give up life because this joy is there—everywhere. It needs nothing to exist; it *is*, irrefutably, like a bedrock throughout time and space, like a smile behind everything. There lies the entire Riddle of the universe. That's all there is. An imperceptible smile—a mere nothing that is everything. All is Joy because all is the Spirit which is Joy, *Sat-Chit-Ananda*, Existence-Consciousness-Joy—the eternal trinity that is the universe, and which we are, the secret we must discover and live through the long evolutionary journey. "From Delight all these beings are born, by Delight they exist and grow, to Delight they return." (*Taittiriya Upanishad*, III.6)

CHAPTER 6

Quieting the Vital

The Limitations of Morality

There is an area of our being which is a source of both great difficulty and great power. A source of difficulty, because it blurs all the communications from outside or above by frantically opposing our efforts to silence the mind and bogging down the consciousness at its own level of petty occupations and interests, thus hindering its free movement toward other regions. A source of power, because it is the outcropping of the great force of life in us. This is the region located between the heart and the sex center, which Sri Aurobindo calls *the vital*.

It is a place full of every possible mixture: pleasure is inextricably mixed with suffering, pain with joy, evil with good, and make-believe with truth. The world's various spiritual traditions have found it so troublesome that they have preferred to reject this dangerous zone altogether, allowing only the expression of so-called religious emotions and strongly advising the neophyte to reject everything else. Everyone seems to agree: human nature is unchangeable. But this kind of *moral surgery*,[1] as Sri Aurobindo calls it, has two drawbacks: first, it does not bring about any real purification, because the higher emotions, however refined they may appear to be, are as mixed as the lower ones, since they are sentimental in essence and hence partial; secondly, it does not really prevent anything—it merely represses. The vital is a force of its own, entirely independent of our rational or moral arguments. If we try to overpower it or ill-treat it by radical asceticism or discipline, the slightest letup can bring on an open rebellion—and it knows how to take revenge with interest. Or, if we have enough willpower to impose our mental or moral rules upon it, we may prevail, but at the cost of drying up the life-force in ourselves, because the frustrated vital will go on strike and we will find ourselves purified not only of the evil but also of the good in life: we will have become colorless and odorless. What is more, morality works only within the bounds of the mental process; it does not have access to the subconscious or superconscious regions, or to death, or to sleep (which happens to take up one day out of every three in our existence, so that a sixty-year life span would entitle us to forty years of waking moral life and twenty years of immorality—a strange arithmetic). In other words, morality does not go beyond the limits of our small frontal personality. Therefore, it is not a rigid moral or fanatic discipline that we want to impose on our being, but a spiritual and comprehensive one that respects each part of our nature while freeing it from its particular mixture; for in truth, there is no absolute evil anywhere—only mixtures.

Furthermore, the seeker no longer thinks in terms of good and evil (assuming he still "thinks" at all), but in terms of exact and inexact. When a sailor needs to take his ship's bearing, he does not use his love of the sea to do so, but a sextant, and he makes quite sure that the mirror is clean. If our mirror is not clean, we can never see the reality of things or people, because everywhere we will meet only the reflection of our own desires or fears, the echo of our own turmoil, not only in this world but in all the other worlds, in waking, in sleep, and in death. In order to *see*, we need to stop being in the center of the picture. The seeker will therefore need to discriminate between those elements that blur his vision and those that clarify it; such will be the essence of his "morality."

The Habit of Response

The first thing the seeker will detect in his vital exploration is a part of the mind whose only role seems to be to give form, and justification, to his impulses, feelings or desires; this is what Sri Aurobindo terms *the vital mind.* Since we already know the necessity for mental silence, we will now strive to extend our discipline of silence to this lower mental layer, too. Once this has been achieved, we will see things far more clearly—without all their mental embellishments; the various vibrations of our being will appear in their true light and at their true level. Most importantly, however, we will be able to see these vibrations coming. In this zone of silence we have now become, the slightest movement of substance—mental, vital or other—will be like a signal for us; we will immediately know that something has touched our atmosphere. We will thus become aware, spontaneously, of the many vibrations people constantly emanate without realizing it; we will know exactly what is going on and whom we are facing (a person's external veneer having usually nothing to do with that unostentatious vibrating reality). Our relationships with the outer world will become clear: we will understand why we instinctively like or dislike someone, why we feel afraid or ill at ease—then we will be able to correct our reactions, accept the helpful vibrations, deflect the darker vibrations, and neutralize the harmful ones. Indeed, we will notice quite an interesting phenomenon: our inner silence has power. If, instead of responding to the incoming vibration, we maintain an absolute inner stillness, we will notice that this stillness *dissolves* the vibration; it's as if we were surrounded by a field of snow in which all impacts are absorbed and neutralized. Let us take the simple example of anger: if, instead of vibrating inwardly in unison with the person facing us, we can remain absolutely still within, we will see that person's anger gradually dissolving. Mother observed that this inner stillness, this power not to respond, can even stop an assassin's hand or a snake's bite. But wearing an impassive mask while we are still boiling on the inside will not do; we cannot cheat with vibrations (as animals know full well). This has nothing to do with so-called self-control, which is only a mastery of appearances, but with true inner mastery. Moreover, this silence can neutralize any vibration at all, for the simple reason that all vibrations are *contagious,* from the highest vibrations to the lowest (this is how a master can pass on spiritual experiences or a power to a disciple), and it is up to us to accept the contagion or not; if we become afraid, it means we have already accepted the contagion, and hence have already accepted the angry man's blow or the snake's bite. (One can also accept a blow out of love, like Sri Ramakrishna, who at the sight of a cart driver beating an ox, suddenly cried out in pain and found himself lacerated and bleeding, his back covered with lash marks.) The same holds for physical pain; we can allow the contagion of a painful vibration to overcome us, or, instead, circumscribe the area of pain and eventually, depending on the degree of our mastery, neutralize the pain by disconnecting the consciousness from that area. The key to mastery is always *silence*, at every level, because silence enables us to discern the vibrations, and to discern them is to be able to act upon them. This has countless practical applications, and hence countless opportunities for progress. Ordinary everyday life (which is ordinary only for those who live it ordinarily) becomes an extraordinary field of experience and handling of vibrations, which is why Sri Aurobindo always wanted his yoga to encompass it. It is very easy to live isolated in a flawless illusion of self-mastery.

This power of silence or inner immobility has even more significant applications, for our own psychological life. The vital is not only a place of many troubles and perturbations, it is also the source of a great energy; we must therefore try to separate the life energy from its complications, without separating ourselves from life. The real complications are not in life but in ourselves, and all external circumstances are the exact reflection of what we are. The main problem with the vital is that it mistakenly identifies with just about everything that comes out of itself. It says: "This is 'my' pain, 'my' depression, 'my' personality, 'my' desire," and thinks of itself as all sorts of little me's it is not. If we are convinced that all these occurrences are ours, then there is obviously nothing we can do about them, except put up with the trivial family until the attack is over. But if we can remain silent within, we soon realize that none of this has anything to do with us: everything comes from outside. We keep picking up the same wavelengths, and becoming overwhelmed by every contagion. For example, we are with some people, completely silent and still within (which doesn't prevent us from talking and acting normally), when suddenly, in this transparency, we feel something trying to draw us or to enter us, a kind of pressure or vibration in the atmosphere (which may cause a vague sense of unease). If we take in the vibration, we are soon struggling against a depression, having a particular desire, or feeling restless; we have caught the contagion. Sometimes it is not just a vibration but a whole wave that falls upon us. Another's physical presence is unnecessary; we can be alone in the Himalayas and still receive the world's vibrations. So where is "my" restlessness, "my" desire in all this, except in a habit of perpetually picking up the same vibrations? But the seeker who has cultivated silence will no longer let himself become caught in this *false identification*[2]; he will have become aware of what Sri Aurobindo calls *the circumconscient, the environmental consciousness*,[3] that field of snow around him, which can be extremely luminous, strong and solid, or become dark, corrupted, and sometimes even completely disintegrated, depending upon his own inner state. It is an individual atmosphere, as it were, a *protective envelope* (sensitive enough to enable us to feel somebody approaching, or avoid an accident just before it happens) where we can feel and stop the psychological vibrations *before* they enter us. Generally, they are so accustomed to coming right in, since they find such affinity in us, that we do not even feel them coming; the process of appropriating and identifying with them is instantaneous. But our practice of silence has now created a transparency within us that gradually allows us to see them coming, stop them on their way in, and reject them. After we have rejected them, they sometimes remain in the circumconscient,* circling round and round, waiting for an opportunity to reenter—we can very distinctly feel anger, desire or depression *prowling* around us—but through continued nonintervention these vibrations will gradually lose their strength and eventually leave us alone. We will have severed the connection between them and us. Then one day, we will happily notice that certain vibrations which had seemed inescapable no longer touch us; they are as if drained of their power and merely flash by as if on a movie screen; interestingly, we can even see in advance the little mischief trying one more time to perpetrate its trick. Or else, we will find that certain psychological states hit us at fixed times, or recur in cycles (this is what Sri Aurobindo and Mother call a *formation*, an amalgam of vibrations that, through sheer repetitions, tends to take on a kind of personality of its own); once we pick it up, we will see this formation unwind itself from beginning to end, like *a gramophone record*.[4] It is up to us to decide whether we want to "go along" or not. There are thousands of possible experiences, a whole world of observations. But the essential discovery we make is that there is very little of "us" in all this, except *a habit of response*.[5] As long as, out of ignorance, we falsely identify with the vital vibrations, we cannot expect to change anything in our nature, except through amputation; but from the moment we understand how it really works, everything can change, because we can choose *not to respond*, using silence to dissolve the troublesome vibrations and tuning in elsewhere, as we please. Hence, contrary to all the old saws, human nature *can* be changed. Nothing in our consciousness or nature is fixed once and for all; everything is a play of forces or vibrations, which gives the illusion of "natural" necessity by virtue of repetition. This is why Sri Aurobindo's yoga envisions *the possibility of an entire reversal of the ordinary rule of the reacting consciousness.*[6]

---

* Unless they sink into the subconscient, a process we will discuss later when studying that zone.

Having brought this mechanism to light, we will have found, at the same time, the true method toward vital mastery, which is not surgical but calming; the vital predicament is not overcome by struggling vitally against it, which can only exhaust our energies without exhausting its universal existence, but by taking another position and neutralizing it through silent peace: *If you get peace,* Sri Aurobindo wrote to a disciple, *then to clean the vital becomes easy. If you simply clean and clean and do nothing else, you go very slowly for the vital gets dirty again and has to be cleaned a hundred times. The peace is something that is clean in itself, so to get it is a positive way of securing your object. To look for dirt only and clean is the negative way.*[7]

The Adverse Forces

There is yet another difficulty. The vibrations coming from people or from the universal vital are not the only ones trying to disturb the seeker (actually, distinguishing between these two kinds is hardly possible since individuals are merely *ground stations*[8] for the universal vital or the universal mind, and vibrations weave endlessly from the one to the other). There is another type of vibrations, remarkable for their suddenness and violence; the seeker will literally feel these vibrations sweep over him massively; within seconds he becomes "a different person," having totally forgotten his main purpose, his efforts, his goal, as if everything had been swept away, left devoid of meaning, disintegrated. These are what Sri Aurobindo and Mother call *the adverse forces.* They are highly conscious forces whose sole aim, apparently, is to discourage the seeker and divert him from the path he has chosen. The first sign of their presence is easily perceptible: joy is clouded, consciousness is clouded, everything becomes shrouded in an atmosphere of melodrama and gloom. Personal distress is a sure sign of the enemy's presence. Melodrama is a favorite haunt of these forces; that is how they are able to create the greatest havoc, because they play with a very old teammate within us, who cannot help loving melodrama even as he cries out for relief. First, they generally make a point of forcing us into sudden, extreme, and irrevocable decisions in order to take us as far away as possible from our path—a pressing, exacting vibration that demands *immediate* compliance; or else, they take apart, with remarkable skill, the whole system of our quest to prove that we are deluding ourselves and that our efforts will come to nothing; more often, they bring about a state of depression, playing with another well-known teammate within us whom Sri Aurobindo calls *the man of sorrows: a fellow . . . covering himself with a sevenfold overcoat of tragedy and gloom, and he would not feel his existence justified if he couldn't be colossally miserable.*[9] All the vibrations of disorder that we call "our" sorrow or "our" troubles have the immediate result of weakening or disintegrating our protective "field of snow," which means that the door is wide open to the adverse forces. They have a thousand and one ways of attacking us—for we are indeed under attack—and the more determined we are, the more relentless they become. This may seem like an exaggeration, but only one who has never tried to make progress would doubt it. As long as we move with the common herd, life is relatively easy, with its moderate ups and downs; but the moment we want to get out of the rut, a thousand forces rise up, suddenly very interested that we should behave "like everyone else," then we realize how well organized the imprisonment is. We even realize that we can go as far downward as we can ascend, that our downward movements are in exact proportion to our capacity of ascent; many scales fall from our eyes. If we are a little honest with ourselves, we see that we are capable of anything, and that, as Sri Aurobindo says, our *virtue is a pretentious impurity.*[10] Only those who have never gone beyond the frontal personality can still harbor any illusion about themselves.

These adverse forces have been given all sorts of devilish and "negative" names throughout the world's spiritual history, as if their sole aim were to damn the seeker and give decent people a hard time. The reality is somewhat different, for where is the devil if not in God? If he is not in God, then there is not much left in God, because this world is evil enough, as are quite a few other worlds, so that not much would remain that is pure, except perhaps for a dimensionless and shadowless mathematical point. In reality, as experience shows, these disturbing forces have their place in the universe; they are disturbing only at the scale of our constricted momentary consciousness, and for a specific purpose. Firstly, they always catch us with our defenses down—yet were we firm and one-pointed, they could not shake us for a second. In addition, if we look into ourselves instead of whining and blaming the devil or the world's wickedness, we find that each of these attacks has exposed one of our many virtuous pretenses, or, as Mother says, has pulled off *the little coats we put on to avoid seeing.* Not only do the little, or big, coats conceal our own weaknesses, they are everywhere in the world, hiding its small deficiencies as well as its enormous conceit; and if the perturbing forces yank the coats a bit violently, it is not at random or with wanton malice, but to open our eyes and compel us to a perfection we might otherwise resist, because as soon as we have grasped hold of a grain of truth or a wisp of ideal, we have the unfortunate tendency to lock it up in an hermetic and impregnable construction, and to refuse to budge from there. For the individual as for the world, these rather ungracious forces are instruments of progress. "By what men fall, by that they rise," says the Kularnava Tantra in its wisdom. We protest against the apparently useless and arbitrary "catastrophe" that strikes our heart or our flesh, and we blame the "Enemy," but *is it not possible that the soul itself—not the outward mind, but the spirit within has accepted and* chosen *these things as part of its development in order to get through the necessary experience at a rapid rate, to hew through,* durchhauen, *even at the risk or the cost of much damage to the outward life and the body? To the growing soul, to the spirit within us, may not difficulties, obstacles, attacks be a means of growth, added strength, enlarged experience, training for spiritual victory?* [11] We complain against evil, but if it was not there to besiege and defy us, we would long ago have seized the eternal Truth and turned it into a nice, tidy piece of platitude. Truth moves on; it has legs; and the princes of darkness are there to make sure, however brutally, that it does not slumber. *God's negations are as useful to us as His affirmations,*[12] says Sri Aurobindo. *The Adversary will disappear only when he is no longer necessary in the world,* remarked Mother. *He is undoubtedly necessary, as is the touchstone for gold, to make sure we are true.*

Indeed, God may not be a pure mathematical point, external to this world; perhaps He is all this world and all this impurity laboring and suffering to become perfect, and to remember Itself here on earth.

The method for dealing with these adverse forces is the same as for the other vibrations: silence, inner stillness that lets the storm blow over. We may not succeed the first time in dissolving these attacks, but more and more they will seem to take place on the surface of our being; we may be shaken, upset, yet deep down we will feel the "Witness" in us, unscathed and unaffected—he is *never* affected. We fall and get back up again, each time becoming stronger. The only sin is discouragement. In practice, the seeker of the integral yoga will be far more exposed than others (Sri Aurobindo often said his yoga was a *battle* [13]), because he seeks *to embrace everything in his consciousness,* without rejecting anything, and because there is not just one passage to open up to the bliss above, not just one guardian of the treasure to subdue, but many passages, to the right and the left and below, at every level of our being, and more than one treasure to discover.

The True Vital

Thus, there is a kind of threshold to be crossed if we want to find the true life force behind the troubled life of the frontal man. According to traditional spiritual teachings, this crossing involves mortifications and renunciations of all sorts (which, by the way, serve mainly to enhance the ascetic's high opinion of himself), but we are after something quite different. We do not seek to leave life but to widen it; we do not want to give up oxygen for hydrogen, or vice versa, but to study the chemical composition of consciousness and to see under what conditions it will yield a clearer water and a more efficient operation. Yoga is *a greater art of life,*[14] proclaimed Sri Aurobindo. *The attitude of the ascetic who says "I seek nothing" and that of the worldly man who says "I want this thing" are the same,* remarks Mother. *The one may be as attached to his renunciation as the other is to his possession.* Actually, as long as we need to renounce anything at all, we are not ready; we are still submerged in dualities. Yet, without any special training, anyone can make the following observations. First, all we have to do is tell the vital, "You have to renounce this or to abandon that," for it to be seized with the opposite desire; or if it does agree to renounce something, we can be certain it will expect to be paid back a hundredfold, and it would just as soon deal with a big renunciation as a small one, since in either case it is at the center of the show, negatively or positively: both sides are equally nourishing it. If we unmask this simple truth, we will have understood the whole functioning of the vital, from top to bottom, namely, its utter indifference to our human sentimentalism; pain appeals to it as much as joy, deprivation as much as abundance, hatred as much as love, torture as much as ecstasy. It thrives in every case. This is because it is a Force, the same Force in pain as in pleasure. We are thus bluntly confronted with the absolute *ambivalence* of all the feelings that make up the niceties of our frontal personality. Every one of our feelings is the reverse of another; at any moment it may change into its "opposite": the disillusioned philanthropist (or, rather, the disillusioned vital in the philanthropist) becomes a pessimist, the zealous apostle retires to the desert, the staunch unbeliever becomes a sectarian, and the virtuous man is scandalized by all the things he does not dare to do. Here we uncover another feature of the surface vital: it is *an incorrigible charlatan,*[15] a shameless impersonator. (We are not even sure that our own mother's death escapes its pleasure.) Each time we cry in disapproval or in pain (any crying at all), there is a monkey snickering in us. We all know this, yet we remain as sentimental as ever. To top it all, the vital excels in befogging everything. It is fog incarnate; it mistakes the force of its feelings for the force of truth, and *substitutes for the heights a smoky volcano summit in the abyss.*[16]

Another observation, which follows from the first, becomes plainly apparent: that of the utter powerlessness of the vital to help others, or even simply to communicate with others, except when there is a meeting of egos. There is not a single vital vibration emanating from us, or relayed by us, that cannot immediately change into its opposite in the other person. We need only wish someone well for the corresponding ill feeling or resistance or opposite reaction to awaken automatically, as if it were being received at the same time as the other; the process seems as spontaneous and inevitable as a chemical reaction. Indeed, the vital does not seek to help, it always seeks to take, in every possible manner. All our feelings are tainted with grabbing. Our feeling of sadness—any sadness—at a friend's betrayal, for example, is the sure sign of our ego's involvement, for if we truly loved people for themselves, and not for ourselves, we would love them in any circumstances, even as adversaries; we would feel the joy of their existence in all cases. Our sorrows and sufferings are actually always the sign of a mixture, and therefore always deceitful. Joy alone is true. Because only the "I" within us that embraces all existences and all possible opposites of existence is true. We suffer because we put things outside ourselves. When all is inside, all is joy, because there is no longer any gap anywhere.

"But what about the 'Heart'?" we may protest. Well, isn't the heart in fact the most ambivalent place of all? It tires easily, too. And this is our third observation: Our capacity for joy is small, as is our capacity for suffering; we soon grow indifferent to the worst calamities. What waters of oblivion have not flowed over our greatest sorrows? We can contain very little of the great Force of Life—*we cannot withstand the charge,* as Mother says; a mere breath beyond the limit, and we cry out with joy or pain, we weep, dance, or faint. It is always the same ambiguous Force that flows, and before long overflows. The Force of Life does not suffer; it is not troubled or exalted, evil or good—it just is, flowing serenely, all-encompassing. All the contrary signs it assumes in us are the vestiges of our past evolution, when we were small and separate, when we needed to protect ourselves from this living enormity too intense for our size, and had to distinguish between "useful" and "harmful" vibrations, the ones getting a positive coefficient of pleasure or sympathy or good, the others a negative coefficient of suffering or repulsion or evil. But suffering is only a too great intensity of the same Force, and too intense a pleasure changes into its painful "opposite": *They are conventions of our senses,*[17] says Sri Aurobindo. *It only takes a slight shift of the needle of consciousness,* says the Mother. *To cosmic consciousness in its state of complete knowledge and complete experience all touches come as joy,* Ananda.[18] It is the narrowness and deficiency of consciousness that cause all our troubles, moral and even physical, as well as our impotence and the perpetual tragicomedy of our existence. But the remedy is not to starve the vital, as the moralists would have us do; it is to widen it; not to renounce, but to accept more, always more, and to extend one's consciousness. For such is the very sense of evolution. Basically, the only thing we must renounce is our ignorance and narrowness. When we frantically cling to our small frontal personality, to its put-ons and sticky sentimentality and saintly sorrows, we are not really "human"; we are the laggards of the Stone Age; we *defend our right to sorrow and suffering.*[19]

The seeker will no longer be fooled by the dubious game going on in his surface vital, but for a long time he will keep the habit of responding to the thousands of small biological and emotional vibrations circling around him. The transition takes time, much as the transition from the word-mongering mind to mental silence did, and it is often accompanied by spells of intense fatigue, because our organism loses the habit of renewing its energy at the common superficial source (which soon appears crude and heavy once we have tasted the other type of energy), yet it still lacks the capacity to remain constantly connected to the true source, hence some "gaps." But here again the seeker is helped by the descending Force, which powerfully contributes to establish a new rhythm in him. He even notices, with ever-renewed astonishment, that if he takes but one small step forward, the Help from above will take ten toward him—as if he were expected. It would be quite wrong to believe that the work is only negative, however; naturally the vital likes to think that it is making huge efforts to struggle against itself, which is its skillful way of protecting itself on all fronts, but in practice the seeker does not follow an austere or negative rule; he follows a positive need within his being, because he is truly growing out of yesterday's norms and yesterday's pleasures, which now feel to him like a baby's diet. He is no longer content with all that; he has better things to do, better things to live. This is why it is so difficult to explain the path to one who has never tried it, for he will see only his own current perspective or, rather, the loss of his perspective. Yet if we only knew how each loss of perspective is a step forward, how greatly life changes when we pass from the stage of closed truths to that of open truths—a truth like life itself, too great to be confined within limited perspectives, because it embraces them all and sees the usefulness of each thing at each stage of an infinite development; a truth great enough to deny itself and move endlessly to a higher truth.

Behind this childish, restless, easily exhausted vital, we will find a quiet and powerful vital—what Sri Aurobindo calls *the true vital*—that contains the very essence of the Life Force devoid of its sentimental and painful byproducts. We enter a state of peaceful, spontaneous concentration, like the sea beneath the movement of the waves. This underlying stillness is not a dulling of the nerves, any more than mental silence is a numbing of the brain; it is a basis for action. It is a concentrated power capable of initiating any action, of withstanding any shock, even the most violent and prolonged, without losing its poise. Depending on the degree of our development, all kinds of new capacities can emerge from this vital immobility, but first of all we feel an inexhaustible energy; any fatigue is a sign that we have fallen back into the superficial turmoil. The capacity for work or even physical effort increases tenfold. Food and sleep are no longer the single and all-absorbing source of energy renewal. (The nature of sleep changes, as we will see, and food can be reduced to an hygienic minimum, without the bloated feeling and diseases it usually entails.) Other powers, often considered "miraculous," may also manifest, but they are miracles *with a method*; we will not attempt to discuss them here, as it is better to experience them directly. Let us simply say that one who has become capable of controlling a certain vital vibration in himself is automatically capable of controlling the same vibration anywhere he meets it in the world. Further, in this stillness, another sign will appear permanently: the absence of suffering and a kind of inalterable joy. When an ordinary person receives a blow, whether physical or moral, his immediate reaction is to double up in pain; he contracts and begins to seethe inside, increasing the pain tenfold. On the contrary, the seeker who has established some immobility within himself will find that this immobility dissolves all shocks, because it is *wide;* because the seeker is no longer a small constricted person, but a consciousness overflowing the limits of its body. Like the silent mind, the quieted vital universalizes itself spontaneously: *In yoga experience the consciousness widens in every direction, around, below, above, in each direction stretching to infinity. When the consciousness of the yogi becomes liberated, it is not in the body, but in this infinite height, depth and wideness that he lives always. Its basis is an infinite void or silence, but in that all can manifest— Peace, Freedom, Power, Light, Knowledge, Ananda.*[20] The least pain, of any kind, is the immediate sign of a contraction in the being and of a loss of consciousness.

A very important corollary follows upon this widening of the being, which will make us appreciate the absolute necessity of vital immobility, not only for the sake of clarity of communications, efficiency in action, and joy in life, but simply for our own safety.

As long as we live in the small frontal person, the vibrations are small, the blows are small, the joys are small; we are protected by our very smallness. But when we emerge into the universal Vital, we find the same vibrations, or forces, on a gigantic, universal scale, for these are the very forces that move the world as they move us; and if we have not acquired a perfect *equanimity* or inner immobility, we are blown away. This is true not only of the universal Vital but of all the planes of consciousness. Indeed, one can, one must (at least the integral seeker) realize the cosmic consciousness on all levels: in the Superconscient, the mind, the vital, and even in the body. When he rises into the Superconscient, the seeker will find out that the intensities of the Spirit also can be overpowering (it is actually always the same divine Force, the same Consciousness-Force above or below, in Matter or in Life, in the Mind or higher up, but the farther it descends, the darker, more distorted and broken up it becomes by the medium it has to pass through), and if the seeker, just emerging from his heavy density, tries to rise too rapidly, to skip some stages without having first established a clear and firm foundation, he may well burst like a boiler. Vital clarity, therefore, is not a matter of morality, but a technical or even organic requirement, one could say. In practice, the great Solicitude is always there to keep us from premature experiences; perhaps we are narrow and small only as long as we need to be narrow and small.

Finally, when we have mastered vital immobility, we find that we can begin to help others with some effectiveness. For helping others has nothing to do with sentimentality or charity; it is a matter of power, of vision, of joy. In this tranquillity, we possess not only a contagious joy but a vision that dispels the shadows. We spontaneously perceive all vibrations; and distinguishing what they are enables us to manipulate them, quiet them, avert or even alter them. *Tranquillity*, says Mother, *is a very positive state; there is a positive peace which is not the opposite of strife—an active and contagious and powerful peace, which subdues and calms, straightens and puts things in their place.* We will give an example of this "contagious peace," although it belongs to a somewhat later stage in Sri Aurobindo's life. It was in Pondicherry, many years ago, in the season when tropical rains and sometimes cyclones sweep down suddenly and bring devastation. Doors and windows have to be barricaded with thick bamboo laths. That night, a cyclone erupted with torrents of rain, and Mother hurried to Sri Aurobindo's room to help him shut his windows. He was seated at his table, writing (for years Sri Aurobindo spent twelve hours a day writing, from six in the evening till six in the morning, then eight hours walking up and down "for the yoga"). The windows were wide open, but not a drop of rain had come inside his room. The peace that reigned there, recalls Mother, was so solid, so compact, that the cyclone could *not* enter.

CHAPTER 7

The Psychic Center

We are not the mind, since all our thoughts come from a universal Mind vaster than ours; we are not the vital, or our feelings or actions, since all our impulses come from a universal Vital larger than ours; and we are not this body either, for its parts are made of Matter, which obeys universal laws greater than ours. What, then, is the element in us that is not our environment, not our family, not our traditions or marriage or job, that is not the play of universal Nature in us or of circumstances, yet gives us a sense of self, even if everything else collapses—and especially when everything else has collapsed, at *our* hour of truth?

In the course of our exploration, we have encountered various centers or levels of consciousness, and we have seen that a consciousness-force was alive behind each of these centers, connecting our various states of being (the prime result of mental silence and of quieting the vital has even been to separate this consciousness-force from the mental and vital activities in which it is usually embroiled), and we have felt this current of force, or consciousness, as the fundamental reality of our being behind our various states. But this consciousness-force must be the consciousness of *someone*. Who or what is conscious in us? Where is the center, the master? Are we merely the puppets of some universal Being, who is our true center, since all the mental, vital and physical activities are in fact universal ones? The truth is twofold, but in no way are we puppets, except when we insist on mistaking the frontal being for our self, for it *is* a puppet. We do have an individual center, which Sri Aurobindo calls the *psychic being*, and a cosmic center or *central being*. Step by step, we must recover the one and the other, and become Master of all our states. For the moment, we will try to discover our individual center, the psychic being, which others call the soul.

It is at once the simplest thing in the world and the most difficult. The simplest, because a child understands it, or rather *lives* it, spontaneously; he is a king, he is on top of the world! He lives in his psychic being.* The most difficult, because this spontaneity is soon covered by all sorts of ideas and feelings; we start speaking of "soul," which means we've lost it. All the pain of adolescence is but the story of a slow imprisonment of the psychic being. We speak of "growing pains," but perhaps there are only choking pains, maturity being achieved when suffocation has become a natural state. All the seeker's difficulties, then, are the reverse journey of a gradual disentanglement from the various mental and vital admixtures. But, as we will see, it is not really a reversal; one never goes backward, and the psychic child one uncovers at the end of the journey (an end that is always a beginning) is not a momentary caprice but a *conscious* royalty. The psychic is a *being*; it grows. It is the miracle of eternal childhood in an ever vaster kingdom. It is "within as a child to be born," says the Rig Veda (IX.83.3).

The Psychic Birth

The first signs of psychic opening are love and joy—a joy that may be extremely intense and powerful, but without any exaltation and without object, as calm and deep as the sea. Psychic joy does not

---

* There are exceptions and degrees, almost visible to the naked eye.

need anything in order to be; it just is; even in a prison it cannot help being, for it is not a feeling but a state, like a river sparkling wherever it flows, whether over mud or rocks, across plains or mountains. It is a love that is not the opposite of hate, and it needs nothing to sustain itself; it simply *is*, burning steadily regardless of what it encounters, in all it sees and all it touches, simply because it cannot help loving, for that is its nature. Nothing is low for it, or high, or pure, or impure; neither its flame nor its joy can be tarnished. Other signs may also reveal its presence: It is light, nothing is a burden to it, as if the whole world were its playground; it is invulnerable, nothing can touch it, as if it were forever beyond all tragedies, already saved from all accidents; it is a seer, it sees; it is calm, so calm, a tiny breath in the depths of the being; and vast, as vast as the eternal sea itself. Indeed, it is eternal. And it is free; nothing can entrap it, neither life nor men, nor ideas, nor doctrines, nor countries—it is beyond, forever beyond, and yet innumerably present in the heart of everything, as if it were one with all, for it is God within us.

To a seeing eye, this is how the psychic being appears: *When you look at someone who is conscious of his soul and lives in his soul,* says Mother, *you feel you are going deep, deep down into the person, far, very far within. While generally, when you look into people's eyes (there are eyes you cannot go into, they are like closed doors, but some eyes are open, and you can enter), well, very close to the surface, you encounter something that vibrates, and sometimes shines and sparkles. You may misidentify this and say to yourself, "Oh, he has a living soul!" but that's not it. It is his vital. To find the soul you must withdraw from the surface, withdraw deep inside, enter far within, go deep, deep down, into a very deep, silent, and still cavity; and there is something warm, quiet, of a rich substance, very still and very full, and exceedingly soft—that is the soul. If you insist and are conscious yourself, you experience a feeling of plenitude and fullness, something with unfathomable depths. You feel that if you entered there, many secrets would be revealed; it's like the reflection of something eternal upon a calm, peaceful surface of water. Time ceases to exist. You feel you have always been and will be for all eternity.*

But these are only signs, an external translation of something that exists in itself, and that we would like to experience for ourselves. How does one open the doors of the psychic being, for it is well hidden? It is primarily hidden by our ideas and feelings, which steal from it and imitate it shamelessly; we have so many ideas about what is high or low, pure or impure, divine or undivine; we are locked in so many sentimental stereotypes about what is lovable or unlovable that the poor psychic being does not have much chance to manifest itself, since the place is already filled with this clutter. The moment it appears, it is instantly snatched up by the vital, which uses it for its own brilliant flights of exaltation, its own "divine" and tumultuous emotions, its possessive loves, its calculated generosities or gaudy aesthetics; or it is corralled by the mind, which uses it for its own exclusive ideals, its infallible philanthropic schemes, its straitjacketed moralities—not to mention churches, countless churches, which systematize it in articles of faith and dogma. Where is the psychic being in all that? It is there, nonetheless, divine, patient, striving to pierce through each and every crust and actually making use of everything that is given to it or imposed upon it. It "makes do" with what it has, so to speak. Yet that is precisely the problem: when it comes out of hiding, if even for a second, it casts such a glory upon everything it touches that we tend to mistake the circumstances of the revelation for its luminous truth. Someone who experiences the revelation of his psychic being while listening to Beethoven might say: "Music, nothing but music is true and divine on this earth"; another, who feels his soul in the middle of the ocean's immensity, may make a religion of the open seas; still another will swear by his own prophet, his church, or his gospel. Each one builds his own structure around his own particular nugget of experience. But the psychic being is *free*, marvelously free of everything! It needs *nothing* to exist; it is Freedom incarnate, and it uses each of our greater or lesser pieces of music, our sublime or less sublime scriptures, simply to bore a hole in our armor in order to emerge into the open. It lends its power and its love, its joy, its light, and its irresistible open Truth to all our ideas, all our feelings and doctrines, because this is its only chance to manifest openly, its only means of expression. In return, these emotions, ideas and doctrines derive from it their self-assurance; they appropriate and enshroud it, drawing from this element of pure Truth their indisputable assertions, their exclusive depths, their one-way universalities, such that *the very strength of the element of truth increases the strength of the element of error.*[1] Ultimately, the psychic becomes so thoroughly entangled and mixed in with the rest that we can no longer tell the difference and remove the counterfeit without destroying the very fabric of truth itself. Thus the world goes on, burdened with half-truths far heavier than falsehoods. Indeed, the real difficulty may not be to free ourselves from evil, which we can recognize easily enough if we are a bit sincere, but to free ourselves from that good which is the other side of evil yet has always annexed a partial element of truth.

If we want to experience the psychic being directly, in its so marvelously fresh and crystalline purity, as it exists irresistibly outside all the traps we set for it, outside all our ideas, feelings, and pronouncements, we must create a transparency within ourselves. Beethoven, the sea, or our churches were only instruments for achieving that transparency. Because it is always the same: the moment we are clear, Truth, vision, joy emerge spontaneously; it is all there without the least effort, because Truth is the most natural thing in the world; it's the rest that clouds everything—the mind and vital with their unruly vibrations and erudite complications. All spiritual disciplines worthy of the name, all *tapasya,* must ultimately tend toward that completely natural point where no effort is necessary; for effort is yet another clouding, another layer of complication. So the seeker will not attempt to enter the muddle of the moral mind, or try the impossible task of sorting out good from evil in order to bring the psychic to light, for, actually, the purpose of good *and* evil is intimately linked to their mutual harmfulness. (*My lover took away my robe of sin and I let it*

*fall, rejoicing; then he plucked at my robe of virtue, but I was ashamed
and alarmed and prevented him. It was not till he wrested it from me
by force that I saw how my soul had been hidden from me.*[2]) He will
simply try to let everything settle in the silence, for silence is clean
in itself; it is lustral water. "Do not try to wash off one by one the
stains on the robe," a very ancient Chaldean tradition exhorts,
"change it altogether." This is what Sri Aurobindo calls a *change
of consciousness.* In that transparency, the old habits of the being
will indeed quietly lose their hold, and we will feel a new poise of
consciousness within ourselves—not an intellectual poise, but a
new center of gravity. At heart level, but deeper than the vital
center of the heart (which covers and imitates the psychic), we will
feel a region of concentration more intense than the others, as if
they had all converged there; this is the *psychic center.* We had
already felt the onset of a current of consciousness-force within
us, taking on a life of its own, moving in the body, and becoming
increasingly intense as it gradually freed itself from its mental and
vital activities. Now, simultaneously something akin to a fire
breaks out at the center—*Agni.* This is the true self in us. We say
that we "need to know," "need to love," but *who* in us really needs?
To be sure, not the small ego, so satisfied with itself, nor the mental
chap who turns in circles, nor the vital chap who only wants to
take and take. But in the background there is this undying fire;
this is what needs, because it remembers something else. People
speak of a "presence," but it is more like a poignant absence, like
a living hole within us that grows hot and blazes up and presses
more and more, until it becomes reality—the only reality in a
world where one wonders if people are alive or just pretending to
be. This is the self of fire, the one true self in the world, the only
thing that does not fail us: "A conscious being is at the center of
the self, who rules past and future; he is like a fire without smoke.
. . . That, one must disengage with patience from one's own body,"
says the Upanishad.* It is "the child suppressed in the secret

---

*   *Katha Upanishad* IV.12,13; VI.17.

cavern" of the Rig Veda (V.2.1), "the son of heaven by the body of the earth" (III.25.1), "he that is awake in those who sleep" (*Katha Upanishad* V.8). "He is there in the middle of the house" (*Rig Veda* I.70.2); "He is like the life and the breath of our existence, he is like our eternal child" (I.66.1); he is "the shining King who was hidden from us" (I.23.14). This is the Center, the Master, the place where everything communicates:

The sunlit space where all is for ever known.[3]

If, even for one second in a lifetime, we have felt this Sun within, this flame, this living life—for there are so many dead lives—then everything changes for us; all memories pale before that memory. It is *the* Memory. If we are faithful to this burning *Agni*, it will grow ever stronger, like a living being in our flesh, like a relentless need. It will feel increasingly compact within us, pressing, poignant, like something that cannot burst out: *A terrible sensation that something restricts your sight and your movements; you try to force the passage, only to find yourself before a wall. So you push and push and push, but to no avail*, says Mother. Then, one day, through sheer need, sheer resolve, or sheer agony of feeling that imprisonment, the psychic tension will reach its breaking point, and we will have the experience: *The pressure becomes so great, the intensity of the question so strong that something in the consciousness shifts. Instead of being outside looking in, you are inside; and the moment you are inside, absolutely everything changes completely. All that used to appear true, natural, normal, real, tangible, at once appears totally grotesque, funny, unreal, and absurd. You have touched something supremely true and eternally beautiful; and this, you will never again lose.* "O Fire, when thou art well borne by us thou becomest the supreme growth and expansion of our being, all glory and beauty are in thy desirable hue and thy perfect vision. O Vastness, thou art the plenitude that carries us to the end of our way; thou art a multitude of riches spread out on every side." (*Rig Veda* III.1.12) True life awakens as if we had never seen the light of day before: *Place the prism on one side*, says Mother, *and the light is white; turn it over, and the light is broken up. Well, this is exactly what happens; you restore the white. In the ordinary consciousness everything is broken up, and now you restore the white.* Mother also described the experience in this way: *You are seated before a closed door, as it were, a heavy bronze door, and you are there wishing it would open to let you pass to the other side. So all your concentration, all your aspiration is gathered up in a single beam, which begins to push and push against that door, to push harder and harder, with increasing energy, until suddenly the door gives way. And you enter, as if thrust into the light.*

Then one is truly born.

Psychic Growth

Of all the feelings one experiences when the psychic door opens, the most immediate and irresistible is that of having always existed and of existing forever. We emerge into another dimension in which we see we are as old as the world, and eternally young—this life being *one* experience, *one* link in an unbroken chain of experiences that stretches far back into the past and loses itself in the future. Everything expands to the scale of the earth. What individual have we not been? What fault have we not borne? All values are turned upside down; which among these instances of pettiness, or greatness, is not a part of us? Where is the stranger? The traitor? The enemy? O divine understanding, absolute compassion! And everything becomes lighter, as if we had moved from life in a cave to life in high altitudes; everything comes together and dovetails, as if the old riddle were dissolved in a breath of light. Death is no more; only the ignorant can die. How could there be death for that which is conscious? *Whether I live or die, I am always.*[4] "Old and outworn, he grows young again and again," says the Rig Veda (II.4.5). "It is not born nor dies," says the Bhagavad Gita, "nor is it that having been it will not be again. It is unborn, ancient, everlasting; it is not slain with the slaying of the body. As a man casts from him his worn-out garments and takes others that

are new, so the embodied being casts off its bodies and joins itself
to others that are new. Certain is the death of that which is born
and certain is the birth of that which dies."*

What is ordinarily known as reincarnation is not unique to Sri
Aurobindo's teaching; all the ancient wisdoms have spoken of it,
from the Far East to Egypt to the Neo-Platonists,** but Sri
Aurobindo gives it a new meaning. From the moment we emerge
beyond the narrow momentary vision of a single life cut short by
death, two attitudes are possible: either we agree with the exclusive
spiritualists that all these lives are but a painful and futile chain
from which we had better free ourselves as soon as possible in order
to rest in God, in Brahman, or in some Nirvana; or we believe
with Sri Aurobindo—a belief founded upon experience—that the
sum of all these lives points to a growth of consciousness that
culminates in a fulfillment *upon the earth.* In other words, there is
evolution, an evolution of consciousness behind the evolution of
the species, and this spiritual evolution is destined to result in an
individual and collective realization upon the earth. One may ask
why the traditional spiritualists, enlightened as they are, have not
foreseen this earthly realization. First of all, the oversight concerns
only the relatively modern spiritualists; it does not apply to the
Veda (whose secret Sri Aurobindo rediscovered) and perhaps to
other, still misunderstood traditions. In fact, it would be appropriate to say that the spirituality of our modern era is marked by
a dimming of consciousness commensurate with its mental development. Furthermore, the spiritualists could hardly have reached
a conclusion different in nature from their premises. Having
started from the idea that the earthly world is an illusion, or an
intermediate realm more or less surrendered to the flesh and the
devil, they could only arrive where their premises took them: they
typically sought liberation and salvation outside the world. Instead
of patiently exploring all the human resources—mental, vital,

---

*   *Bhagavad Gita* II. 18, 20, 22, 27.
** Interestingly, the Fathers of the Church had also discussed the possibility
    of accepting reincarnation at the Alexandrian Council.

physical, and psychic—to free them from their sclerosis and to widen them, that is, divinize them as the Vedic sages had done (perhaps also the sages of the ancient Mysteries, not to mention Sri Aurobindo), they rejected everything and sought *to shoot at once from pure mind to pure spirit.*[5] So naturally they could not see what they would not see. The materialists, too, are guilty of evasion, but in a reverse way: they have explored a speck of physical reality and rejected everything else; starting from the idea that matter alone is real and the rest is hallucination, they, too, could only end up where their premises took them. However, if we start in all simplicity, without prejudices, as Sri Aurobindo did, armed with an open truth and total confidence in the integral possibilities of man, we may achieve an integral knowledge, and therefore an integral life.

Seen from the viewpoint of an evolution of consciousness, reincarnation ceases to be the futile round some have seen in it, or the delirious fantasy others have painted. With typical Western clarity, Sri Aurobindo rids us of the *spiritual fairy tale*, as Mother calls it, into which much serious knowledge has degenerated since the end of the Age of Mysteries; and he invites us to a clear-sighted, rather than clairvoyant, experimentation. The point is not to "believe" in reincarnation but to experience it, and first of all to understand the conditions in which the experience is possible. This is a practical question that concerns our integral development through time. Actually, it is not the small frontal personality that reincarnates, even if this comes as a disappointment to those who picture themselves as eternally the same Mr. Smith, in a Saxon tunic, then in velvet breeches, and finally in synthetic jogging pants, not to mention how boring this would be. The meaning of reincarnation is both deeper and vaster. At the time of death, the whole external frontal being disintegrates; the array of mental vibrations that clustered around us through habitual repetition and formed our mental ego, or mental body, disintegrates and returns to the universal Mind; similarly, the vital vibrations that made up our vital ego, or vital body, disintegrate in the universal

Vital, just as the physical body disintegrates into its natural constituents in universal Matter. Only the psychic remains; it is eternal, as we have seen. Experiencing reincarnation, therefore, will depend on our discovering the Center, the psychic Master that carries its memories from one life to another, and on the degree of our psychic development. If our psychic has remained buried all our life beneath our mental, vital, and physical activities, it has no memories whatsoever to take with it; it returns to earth again and again, in order precisely to break out on the surface of our being and to become openly conscious. To remember, we first have to stop being amnesiac, obviously. It is therefore hardly possible to speak of reincarnation below a certain stage of development, for what is the use of knowing that the psychic has reincarnated if it is not conscious? To become conscious is the very meaning of evolution.

Life after life, the psychic silently grows behind the frontal being, through the thousand sensations of our body, the thousand stimuli of our feelings, the countless thoughts that stir within us. It grows as we rise and it grows as we fall, through our sufferings and our joys, our good and our evil; these are its antennas for experiencing the world. When all this external machinery dissolves, it retains only the *essence* of its experiences, the personality's broad tendencies which constitute the first embryo of a *psychic personality* behind the frontal being;* it takes with it certain consequences from the life just lived, for each of our actions has a dynamism that tends to perpetuate itself (what is called *karma* in India); certain imprints will translate in another life into

---

* The psychic personality, or true personality, expresses each person's unique destiny (perhaps we should say his unique angle) beneath his cultural, social, and religious layers. Thus, a person might be successively a navigator, a musician, a revolutionary, a Christian, a Moslem, and an atheist; yet through each life he would express the same angle of love, say, or of conquering energy, or joy, or purity, which would impart a unique nuance to everything he undertook. From lifetime to lifetime, this particular angle would become more prominent, refined, and extensive.

particular talents, special problems, innate affinities, inexplicable anxieties, irresistible attractions, and sometimes even particular circumstances that repeat themselves almost mechanically, as if to confront us with the same, unresolved problem. Each life, then, represents one type of experience (we may think we have many experiences, but it is always the same one), and through the accumulation of many types of experiences the psychic being gradually acquires an individuality, increasingly strong and conscious and vast, as if it really began to exist only after going through a whole range of human experiences. The more it grows, the more individualized the consciousness-force in us becomes, and the more the psychic tension will increase and push, until the day it no longer needs its frontal chrysalis, and it breaks out into the open. At that point, the psychic becomes directly aware of the world around it; it becomes the master of the nature instead of being its sleeping prisoner; consciousness becomes the master of its force instead of remaining embroiled in the force. Yoga is in fact that point of our development when we move from the endless meanderings of natural evolution to a self-conscious and controlled evolution; it is *a process of concentrated evolution.*

As we see, there are many degrees of development, from the ordinary man in whom the psychic is merely a latent possibility, to the fully awakened being. Without reincarnation, it would be hard to account for the dramatic difference of degrees among souls—for example, between that of a pimp and that of Dante or Francis of Assisi, or simply between that of a man who searches and an *economic philistine*, as Sri Aurobindo put it—unless one believes that spiritual development is merely a matter of education, environment, or heredity (which is obviously not the case, since this would imply that only the offspring of "respectable" families would have souls, while three-fourths of an "unenlightened" humanity would be doomed to eternal damnation). *The very nature of our humanity*, says Sri Aurobindo, *supposes a varying constituent past for the soul as well as a resultant [earthly] future.*[6] And if, despite the evidence, we persist in thinking that man has only one life at his disposal, we encounter an absurdity: *Plato and the Hottentot, the fortunate child of saints or Rishis* and the born and trained criminal plunged from beginning to end in the lowest fetid corruption of a great modern city have equally to create by the action or belief of this one unequal life all their eternal future. This is a paradox which offends both the soul and the reason, the ethical sense and the spiritual intuition.*[7] But even among awakened beings, there are vast differences. Some souls, some consciousness-forces have just been born, while others have already acquired quite distinct individualities; some souls are in the midst of their first radiant self-discoveries, but they do not know much outside their own resplendent joys (they do not even have any precise memory of their past, nor are they aware of the worlds they carry within), while other, rare souls seem replete with a consciousness as vast as the earth. Indeed, a man can be a luminous yogi or a saint living in his soul, yet still possess a crude mind, a repressed vital, a body he ignores or crassly mistreats, and a completely virgin superconscient. "Salvation" may be achieved, but not the fullness of an integral life.

The discovery of the psychic must therefore be followed by what could be called figuratively "a psychic colonization," or, more soberly, a *psychic integration.* Contemporary psychology also uses the word *integration,* but around what is that "integration" supposed to take place? Integrating requires a center. Do they propose to integrate around the turmoil of the mental or vital ego? One might as well try to moor a boat by fastening it to the tail of an eel. Having discovered the psychic kingdom within, we must patiently, gradually colonize and adjoin the outer kingdom to it. If we are interested in a realization here on earth, all our mental and vital activities, and, as we will see, even our entire physical nature, must be integrated around the new center. It is on this condition that they will survive: only those activities that are "psychicized" will participate in the psychic immortality. Any-

---

*   Sages of the Vedic Age, at once seers and poets, who composed the Veda.

thing that takes place outside the psychic being, in effect, takes place outside us and does not last beyond the life of our bodies. There are lives in which "nobody" is there. The psychic center needs to partake in our external activities in order to be able to remember external things; otherwise, it is like a blind king. Then, and only then, can we begin to speak of reincarnation and memories of past lives, which will not necessarily be memories of garish or glorious deeds (how many Napoleons and Caesars there have been if we believe the scribblers of reincarnation!), but memories of *soul-moments*,[8] because for the psychic nothing is glorious or inglorious, high or low; the conquest of Mount Everest is no greater than the daily walk to the subway, if it is done consciously. The psychic is glory itself.

These "soul-moments" can retain the imprint of the physical circumstances that accompanied them. We might remember a setting, a place, a garment we were wearing at the time, some insignificant detail that becomes imbued with eternity, as it were, at the same time as the inner revelation occurs. We have all known, in this very life, moments of pure transparency or of a sudden blossoming, and twenty or forty years later that picture is still alive, along with the exact hue of the sky, the stone along the path, or the insignificant gesture enacted on that day, as if all that had now become eternal. It is not even "as if"; it *is* eternal. These are the only moments we have lived, the only moments when a real "I" has broken through to the surface in thousands of hours of nonexistence. In tragic circumstances, also, the psychic can emerge, when the whole being is gathered up in such a poignant intensity that something in us is suddenly rent asunder; then we sense something like a presence behind, which makes us do things we would normally be incapable of doing. For this is the other face of the psychic: not only is it joy and sweetness, but also quiet strength, as if it were forever above every possible tragedy—an invulnerable master. In this case, too, the details of a scene can be indelibly engraved. But what passes on to the next life is not so much the details as the *essence* of the scene: we will be struck by certain repetitive patterns of events or deadlocked situations that have an air of déjà vu and seem surrounded by an aura of fatality—for what has not been overcome in the past returns again and again, each time with a slightly different appearance, but basically always identical, until we confront the old knot and untie it. Such is the law of inner progress.

Generally, however, the memory of actual physical circumstances does not remain, because, although our small surface consciousness makes much of them, they are, after all, of little significance. There is even a spontaneous mechanism that erases the profusion of useless past memories, just as those of the present life soon become eradicated. If we glance behind us, without thinking, what is actually left of our present life? A nebulous mass with perhaps two or three outstanding images; all the rest is blotted out. This is likewise the case for the soul and its past lives. The sifting process is quite extensive. Furthermore, this mechanism of oblivion is very wise indeed, because if we were to recall our former lives prematurely, chances are we would be constantly hobbled by these past memories. Our present life is already teeming with so many useless memories that stand in the way of our progress, because they fixate us in the same inner attitude, the same contraction, the same refusal or revolt, the same tendency. To grow we need to forget. If, in our hopelessly childish outer consciousness, we were to remember having once been a virtuous banker, for example, while we now find ourselves in the skin of an adept crook, we would be understandably confused! Perhaps we are still too young to understand that our soul needed to experience the opposite of virtue or, rather, that the abscess our virtue was concealing had to be punctured. Evolution has nothing to do with becoming more saintly or intelligent; it has to do with becoming more conscious. It takes a great many ages for one to be able to fruitfully bear the truth of past lives.

Everything, then, depends upon the degree of our development and the extent to which our psychic being has participated in our outer life; the more we have "colonized" the outside, the more memories we take with us. Unfortunately, we are often content to have a so-called inner life, while we live outer life in any old way, without paying much attention to it—but this is the opposite of an integral yoga. If, however, from the very beginning, we embrace everything in our search, all the levels of our being, all of life, instead of rejecting worldly activities for an exclusive quest of the soul, then we will achieve an integral and integrated life in which we are the same outside and inside. On the other hand, if we exclude everything to arrive at so-called spiritual goals, it becomes very difficult afterward to retrace our steps, to descend from our fragile heights, to widen and universalize the mind, to liberate and universalize the vital, to clean the subconscient and finally to labor in the physical grime in order to divinize it; we are far too comfortable above to stir up all that mud, and, in truth, we can *no longer* do it. In fact, we do not even contemplate it, for how could we even imagine undertaking such an enormous task if, from the start, we consider the mind, the vital and the body perishable, and aim only at escaping from life or gaining a celestial salvation?

The psychic realization or discovery of the soul is therefore not the end of the road for the seeker, but the beginning of another journey, traveled consciously instead of ignorantly, in an ever wider consciousness, for the more the psychic being grows and participates in our worldly activities, the more clear, precise and continuous from life to life its mental, vital and physical memories become, and the more concerted, self-willed, and effective its births become; we then really begin to understand what immortality means. We are free; we are forever awake. Death is no longer a grimacing mask reminding us that we have not found ourselves, but a calm transition from one mode of experience to another. Once and for all we have seized the thread of consciousness, and we move here or there as one crosses a border between two countries, and back again to the old earth, until the day when, as Sri Aurobindo announced it, we may have developed enough, not only to ensure the continuity of our mental and vital existence, but also to infuse enough consciousness into the body so that it, too, participates in the psychic immortality. For, with respect to our mental, vital, and physical life, as well as our sleep, our death, and our immortality, everything is always a matter of consciousness. Consciousness is the means, consciousness is the key, and consciousness is the goal.

CHAPTER 8

Independence from the Physical

After the mind and vital, the physical—the third instrument of the spirit in us—plays a special role in Sri Aurobindo's yoga, since without it no *divine life* is possible on this earth. We will only discuss now some points of preliminary experience, the very ones Sri Aurobindo discovered at the beginning of his yoga; indeed, the yoga of the body necessitates a far greater development of consciousness than the one we have envisioned up until now, for the closer we come down to Matter, the higher the powers of consciousness required, because the resistance increases in proportion. Matter is the place of the greatest spiritual difficulty, but also *the place of Victory*. The yoga of the body, therefore, lies well beyond the scope of our vital or mental powers; it is the province of a *supramental yoga*, which we will discuss later.

Independence from the Senses

Matter is the starting point of our evolution. It is confined in Matter that consciousness has gradually evolved; therefore the more consciousness emerges, the more it will recover its sovereignty and assert its independence. This is the first step (not the last, as we will see). We are, however, almost totally subservient to the needs of the body for our survival, and to the bodily organs for perceiving the world; we are very proud, and rightly so, of our machines, but when our own machine gets a little headache, everything becomes a blur, and when we are denied our array of telegraphs, telephones, televisions, etc., we become incapable of knowing what is happening next door or of seeing beyond the end of our noses. We are hypercivilized beings who have not physically gone beyond the condition of the savage. Perhaps our machines are not so much a symbol of mastery as of frightening impotence. The blame for this lies equally with the materialists, for their lack of faith in the power of the inner spirit, and with the spiritualists, for their lack of faith in the reality of matter. This impotence, however, is not irreversible, since it is based mainly on our belief that we *are* impotent; we are somewhat like a person who has inherited a pair of crutches from his ancestors, and hence has lost faith in his own legs. The point is to have faith in our own consciousness; not only does it have legs, but thousands of eyes and arms, and even wings.

Through the very process of our evolution, the consciousness, submerged in Matter, has grown accustomed to depending upon outer organs and antennas to perceive the world; and since we have seen the antennas appear before the master of the antennas, we have childishly concluded that the antennas have created the master, and that without antennas there is no master, no perception of the world. But this is an illusion. Our dependence upon the senses is *merely a habit*—true, a millenary one, but no more inescapable than the flintstone implements of the Chellean man: *It is possible for the mind—and it would be natural for it, if it could be persuaded to liberate itself from its consent to the domination of matter,—to take direct cognizance of the objects of sense without the aid of the sense-organs.*[1] We can see and feel across continents as if distances did not exist, because distance is an obstacle only to the body and its organs, not to consciousness, which can reach anywhere it wishes in a second, provided it has learned to expand itself; there is another, lighter space where all is together in a flash point. Here we might expect to receive some "recipe" for clairvoyance or ubiquity, but recipes are just another kind of machinery, which is why we are so fond of them. True, hatha yoga can be effective, as can many other kinds of yogic exercises, such as concentrating on a lighted candle *(tratak)*, evolving infallible diets, doing breathing exercises and choking scientifically *(pranayama)*. Everything is or can be useful. But all these methods take a long time, and their scope is limited; moreover, they are always uncertain and sometimes even dangerous when practiced by people insufficiently prepared or purified. It isn't enough to want power, the receptacle should not collapse when it receives it; it is not enough to "see," one should be ready to understand what one sees. In practice, our task will be made much easier if we can only realize that it is *consciousness* that uses all the methods and exercises, and works through them; we will therefore save a lot of time by going directly to consciousness, with the added advantage that consciousness does not deceive. Even with a wooden stick as its only method, consciousness would eventually turn this stick into a magic wand, but the merit would not rest with either the stick or the method. Even if consciousness were imprisoned in a dungeon, it would find a way out. Such, in fact, is the whole story of the evolution of consciousness in Matter.

For the integral seeker, the work on the body has been added naturally to his work on the mind and the vital. For convenience, we have described the various levels of being one after another, but everything works as a whole, and each victory, each discovery at any level has its repercussions on all the other levels. When we worked on establishing mental silence, we observed that several mental layers had to be silenced: a *thinking mind*, which makes up our regular reasoning process; a *vital mind*, which justifies our desires, feelings and impulses; there is also a far more troublesome *physical mind*, whose conquest is as important for physical mastery as the conquest of the thinking mind and the vital mind are for mental and vital mastery. It would indeed seem that the mind is the scapegoat in integral yoga, since it is being hunted down everywhere. Let us note that it has also been a very substantial aid in the course of our evolution, and it remains, for many, an indispensable agent, but any aid, however high or divine, eventually becomes an obstacle, because it is meant for one step only, and we have many steps to take and more than one truth to conquer. If we accepted this simple proposition throughout our entire value system, including the particular ideal we are currently cherishing, we would progress quite rapidly on the path of evolution. This physical mind is the stupidest of all, the vestige in us of the first appearance of Mind in Matter. It is a microscopic, stubborn, fearful, narrow, and conservative (this was its evolutionary purpose) mind, which sends us ten times to check if the door is locked when we know perfectly well we have locked it, which panics at the slightest scratch and anticipates the worst illnesses the minute something goes wrong, which is unwaveringly skeptical of anything new and sets up mountains of complications whenever it must change its routine ever so slightly; it just repeats and repeats inside us like a droning old mule. We have all made its acquaintance at one time or another, and it is embarrassing enough that we have to reprimand it, but it is still there, underneath, muttering on all by itself; only the din of our customary existence keeps us from hearing it. Once the thinking and vital minds have been silenced, however, we do detect its presence, and then we realize how terribly unyielding it is. And it is too stupid to be open to reason. Yet, ultimately, it will have to yield, because just as the thinking mind is an obstacle to the widening of our mental consciousness and the vital mind is an obstacle to the universalization of our vital consciousness, the physical mind puts up a massive wall against the expansion of our physical consciousness, an expansion that is the basis of all physical mastery. In addition, it jams all communications and invites all disasters; a fact we should never fail to underscore is that the moment we merely "think" of something or someone, we are instantly in contact (most often unconsciously) with all the vibrations representing this thing or this person, and hence receive all the consequences of these vibrations. Because of its ingrained fear, the physical mind constantly puts us in contact with the direst possibilities; it always contemplates the worst. This obsession has little importance in ordinary life, where the activities of the physical mind are lost in the general hubbub, and where we are, in fact, protected by our very lack of receptivity, but when we have worked systematically at fostering transparency within ourselves and at increasing our receptivity, the negative interference caused by the physical mind can become quite a serious, and even perilous, obstacle.

This mental, vital, and physical transparency is the key to a twofold independence. First, an independence from sensations: since the consciousness-force is no longer entangled at all the levels of our being but gathered into a maneuverable beam, as it were, it can be disconnected at will from a particular point—from cold, hunger, pain, etc. Secondly, an independence from the senses: since the consciousness-force is now released from its immediate absorption in our mental, vital and physical activities, it can extend beyond the bodily frame and, through a kind of inner projection, contact things, beings, and events at a distance. Generally, we have to be in a state of sleep or hypnosis to be able to see at a distance, whether in space or in time, and to be free from the surrounding sensations, but these primitive and cumbersome methods are wholly unnecessary when the mental turmoil has ceased and we control our consciousness. Consciousness is *the only organ.*[2] It is what feels, sees, and hears. Sleep and hypnosis are simply very elementary means of removing the veil of the surface mind. And this makes sense: if we are full of the noise of our desires or fears, what else can we really see or hear except the innumerably reflected images of those same desires and fears? Just as the silenced mind and quieted vital become universalized, the clarified physical universalizes itself spontaneously. We are only prisoners of ourselves; the whole world is waiting at our door, if only we would consent to pull aside the screen of our small constructions. To this capacity for expansion of the consciousness must naturally be added a capacity for concentration, so that the expanded consciousness may silently and quietly focus on the desired object, and *become* that object. But concentration and expansion are spontaneous consequences of inner silence. In inner silence, the consciousness sees.

Independence from Illnesses

Once we are freed from the tension and constant buzz of the thinking mind, from the tyranny and restlessness and endless demands of the vital mind, from the stupidity and fears of the physical mind, we begin to appreciate what the body is without all these exhausting encumbrances, and we discover that it is a marvelous instrument—docile, enduring, and full of unlimited goodwill. The body is the most misunderstood instrument of all, and also the most ill-treated. In this newly acquired clarification of our being, we observe, firstly, that the body is never ill; it only wears out—though even this wearing-out is perhaps not inevitable, as we will see, with the supramental yoga. It is not the body that falls ill; it is the consciousness that fails. As we advance in yoga, we see that each time we get sick or succumb to an external "accident," it is *always* the result of unconsciousness, a wrong attitude, or a psychological disorder. These observations are all the more fascinating because the moment we set foot on the path of yoga, something in us becomes *alerted,* constantly pointing out our mistakes, indicating the real cause of everything that happens to us, and leaving nothing in the dark, as if "someone" were taking our search in earnest. Thus we come to witness, at times with amazement, a perfect correlation between our inner state and the outer circumstances (such as illnesses, for example, or "accidents") that befall us, as if life were no longer unfolding from outside in but from inside out, the inward molding the outward, to the most trivial circumstances; though in fact, nothing is trivial anymore, and everyday life appears as a network filled with signs waiting to be recognized. Everything is connected. The world is a miracle.

We may make a childish mistake when we imagine spiritual life to be full of visions and apparitions and "supernatural" phenomena. The Divine is nearer to us than we think, the "miracle" less pompous and more profound than all this primitive imagery. Once we have deciphered one of those little signs that pass us by, or even once seen the imperceptible link that ties all things, we are closer to the great Miracle than if we had touched some heavenly manna. Indeed, perhaps the real miracle is that the Divine is also natural, but we do not know how to look.

Thus, the seeker will become aware of this reversal of the life current, from the inside out (indeed, since the psychic Master has come out of its confinement); he will read these everyday signs and see that his inner attitude has the power to mold outer circumstances in both directions, good and bad. When we are in a state of harmony and our action conforms to the deeper truth of our being, nothing seems to resist—even "impossibilities" dissolve, as if another law came to supersede the "natural" one. (This is actually the true "nature" emerging from beneath the mental and vital complications.) Then we begin to enjoy a royal freedom. But when there is inner disorder, whether mental or vital, we notice that this disorder irresistibly *invites* detrimental outward circumstances, some accident or illness. The reason for this is simple: when something goes wrong within us, we send out a particular type of vibration that automatically elicits and contacts all other vibrations of the same type, at every level of our being; there is total jamming, and all external circumstances are upset and disrupted. Not only does the negative inner state create chaos, but it also weakens the circumconscious protective envelope mentioned earlier, which means that we are no longer protected by a certain intensity of vibration; we are open, vulnerable—for there is nothing like a vibration of disorder to poke holes in our protective envelope, or to disintegrate it—and then anything whatsoever can enter. We should also remember that a bad inner state is contagious; associations with certain people always tend to attract accidents or troubles. After we have had the same experience ten times or a hundred times—which might be anything from catching a cold to tripping on the stairs to having a serious accident, depending upon our inner state—we will finally realize that neither our own self nor so-called chance has anything to do with all this, and that the remedy lies not with any drug, but with restoring the true attitude, the inner order—in other words, with consciousness. If the seeker is conscious, he can live in the midst of an epidemic or drink all the filth of the Ganges River if he pleases; nothing will touch him, for what could touch the awakened Master? We have isolated bacteria and viruses, but we have not understood that these are only external agents; the illness is not caused by the virus but by the force *behind* that uses the virus. If we are clear, all the viruses in the world cannot do anything to us, because our inner force is stronger than that force; the vibration of our being has too high an intensity for that lower vibration to enter. Only like can enter like. Perhaps cancer will be cured or will disappear the way other medieval diseases have, but we still will not have eradicated the *forces* of illness, which will simply use something else, another agent, another virus, once their present vehicle has been exposed. Our medical science touches only the surface of things, not the source. The only disease is unconsciousness. At a later stage, when the inner silence is well established and we are capable of perceiving mental and vital vibrations as they enter our circumconscient, we will similarly be able to feel the vibrations of illness and drive them out before they can enter us: *If you can become conscious of this environmental self of yours,* Sri Aurobindo wrote to a disciple, *then you can catch the thought, passion, suggestion or force of illness and prevent it from entering into you.*[3]

There are two other categories of illness that need mentioning, which are not directly related to any fault of ours: those that result from subconscious resistance (we will discuss them later with the purification of the subconscient) and those that may be called "yogic illnesses," which result from an uneven development between the higher levels of consciousness and our physical consciousness. For instance, our mental or vital consciousness may widen considerably and receive new intensities, while our physical consciousness still lags behind in old vibratory movements and cannot withstand this increased intensity. This leads to a loss of equilibrium that may bring on illnesses, not through the intrusion of any outer agent, microbe or virus, but through a disruption in the normal relationship among the inner parts of our being; such illnesses may include allergies, colloidal disorders of the blood, and nervous and mental disorders. Here we are touching the problem of matter's receptivity to the higher forces of consciousness, one of the major problems of the supramental yoga. This is also one of the reasons why Sri Aurobindo and Mother insist so much on the development of our physical body; without it, we may be able to go into ecstasy and soar straight into the Absolute, but we are unable to bring the intensity and plenitude of the Spirit down to our "lower" kingdom—the mental, vital, and material realm—in order to create a divine life there.

Independence from the Body

Thus, consciousness can be independent of the sense organs, independent of illnesses, and, to a large extent, independent of food and sleep, once it has discovered the inexhaustible reservoir of the great Force of Life; it can even be independent of the body. When the current of consciousness-force in us is sufficiently individualized, we find that we can detach it not only from the senses and the objects of the senses, but also from the body. First in our meditations, which are the primary training ground prior to natural mastery, we observe that the consciousness-force becomes particularly homogeneous and compact, and, after freeing itself from the mind and vital, it slowly withdraws from the humming of the body, which becomes very still, like a transparent and weightless mass taking up no space, something almost nonexistent; breathing subsides and the heartbeat grows fainter; then, suddenly, there is a sharp release, and we find ourselves "else-where," outside the body. This is what is called "exteriorization" in technical language.

There are all kinds of "elsewheres," as many as there are planes of consciousness, and we can go out at one point or another, depending upon where we have focused our consciousness (the universal Mind and universal Vital have already been mentioned), but the most immediate elsewhere, the one that borders on our physical world and resembles it except for a greater intensity, is what Sri Aurobindo calls *the subtle physical.* This knowledge is as ancient as the world and not unique to Sri Aurobindo's yoga, but it is part of our integral development, preparing us for the day when we leave our body for a longer period in what men igno-rantly call "death." To make it clearer, let us listen to a young disciple describe his experience in the subtle physical, when he left his body for the first time: "I was stretched out on my couch, concentrated, when I suddenly found myself at my friend's house; he was playing music with several others. I could see everything quite clearly, even more clearly than in the physical world, and I moved very quickly, without obstacle. I stayed there for quite a while, watching; I even tried to draw their attention, but they were not conscious. Then, suddenly, something pulled me, an instinct: 'Now I must return.' I had the sensation of a sore throat. I remember that in order to get out of their room, which was completely closed except for a small opening near the ceiling, my form seemed to vaporize (I still had a form but it wasn't like regular matter, it was more luminous, less opaque), and I went out like a trail of smoke through the open window. Then I found myself back in my room, near my body, and realized that my head was all crooked, stiff against the pillow, and I was breathing with difficulty. I tried to reenter my body, but I couldn't. I got scared. I would enter through the legs, and, having come as far as the knees, I would slip back out. It happened two or three times: the consciousness would rise up, then slip back out again like a spring. I thought, 'If only I could knock over this stool (there was a small

stool under my feet), it would make noise and I would wake up!'
But nothing doing. And I was breathing more and more heavily.
I was terribly afraid. Suddenly I remembered Mother and I called
out: 'Mother! Mother!' And I found myself back in my body, wide
awake, with a stiff neck."*

Thus, after many cycles of confinement and awakening, after
innumerable shocks that force consciousness to remember itself
and emerge into the open, then shut itself up again in order to
grow under cover, it finally becomes a fully formed individuality,
breaks through its outer shell, and asserts its independence. This
independence, writes Sri Aurobindo, *will come to be so much the
normal attitude of the whole being to the physical frame that the latter
will feel to us as if something external and* detachable *like the dress
we wear or an instrument we happen to be carrying in our hand. We
may even come to feel that the body is in a certain sense non-existent
except as a sort of partial expression of our vital force and of our*

---

* Three comments might be made. First, because of a rather amusing lack
of experience this boy was trying to reenter his body "through the legs";
no wonder he had trouble! It is generally through the heart center that
one leaves and reenters. One can also go out through the top of the head,
but this is scarcely recommended. When yogis leave their bodies for good
(what is called *iccha-mrityu* in India, or willed death), they go out
through the top of the head. Secondly, during the exteriorization, the
body grows cold, and the circulation is reduced to a minimum; this
temperature drop can even become complete catalepsy with all the outer
signs of death, depending on how "removed" the consciousness is from
the physical level. This is an opportunity to verify concretely that when
consciousness withdraws, force withdraws, because they are one and the
same thing. When we faint, the consciousness withdraws also, because
we are unable to withstand certain degrees of intensity, and since we have
not built a conscious bridge between our various states of being, this
involuntary withdrawal results in a void for us. Finally, we notice that
remembering his Master, in this case the Mother, was enough to restore
order in the disorder of fear, and to enable the young disciple to make
the correct movement for reentering his body. By thinking of Mother,
he instantly tuned in to the right vibration, which set everything right.
This is, roughly speaking, one of the mechanisms of protection or help
from Master to disciple.

mentality. These experiences are signs that the mind is coming to a right poise regarding the body, that it is exchanging the false viewpoint of the mentality obsessed and captured by physical sensation for the viewpoint of the truth of things.[4] For the true viewpoint is always that of the Master, the psychic, the spirit in us. Each time we feel an impossibility, a limitation, or a barrier, we can be sure that this represents tomorrow's victory, because without perceiving the obstacle we could not conquer it; we are created to conquer all and live all our dreams, for it is the spirit in us that dreams. In a world where constraints are closing in on us like an iron network, the first of these dreams is perhaps to be able to sail out in the open, unhampered by the body and by boundaries. Then we will no longer need passports; we will be stateless, the visa-less heirs to all the nations of the world. Then we will be able to enjoy a marvelous expansion of life and freedom: "O Vastness. . . " says the Rig Veda.

CHAPTER 9

Sleep and Death

The Planes of Consciousness

Not everyone is capable of consciously leaving his body, or consciously widening his mind and vital, but many of us do so unconsciously, in sleep, just when the little I's of the frontal being are less noisome and less engrossed in their superficial preoccupations. These sundry I's express a fraction of reality, the reality seen by the naked eye, but immense realms stretch beyond them. We have already mentioned a universal Mind, a universal Vital, and a subtle Physical behind this physical shell; now we must try to recover our entire universal reality. There are three methods or stages for achieving this. The first, available to everyone, is sleep. The second, less common, involves conscious exteriorization or deep meditation. The third, in which everything becomes simple, requires a more advanced degree of development: without recourse to sleep or meditation, it is indeed possible to see in every manner, with eyes wide open and in the very midst of other activities, as if all the levels of universal existence were present before us, and accessible through mere shifts of consciousness, rather as if we were adjusting our eyesight from a nearby object to a distant one. Sleep, then, is a first tool; it can become conscious, increasingly conscious, ultimately reaching a point of development where we will become continuously conscious, whether on this side of the veil or the other, where sleep, as well as death, will no longer be a return to a quiescent state or a dispersion into our natural constituent parts, but merely a transition from one mode of consciousness to another. Because, although the line we have drawn between sleep and waking, life and death, may agree with external appearances, it has no more essential reality than our national borders have in terms of physical geography, or the external colors and fixed appearance of an object have in terms of nuclear physics. Actually, there is no separation anywhere, *except for our lack of consciousness;* the two worlds (or, rather, this one and countless others) coexist constantly, are constantly intermingled, and it is only a particular way of perceiving *the same thing* that makes us say, in one case, "I live," and in the other, "I sleep" or "I am dead" (provided we are conscious enough to realize this), just as we can experience the same object differently, depending on how we look at it, at the subatomic, atomic, molecular, or purely external level. "Elsewhere" is everywhere in this reality. We have attached a unique and exclusive value to the various symbols that form our outer physical life because they are right before our eyes, but they are no more or no less valid than the other symbols that make up our extraphysical life. The atomic reality of an object does not cancel or contradict its external reality, nor is it separate from it, and vice versa. Not only are other symbols as valid as our physical ones, but we cannot really understand our physical symbols unless we understand *all* non-physical symbols. Without the knowledge of the other degrees of existence, our knowledge of the ordinary human world remains as incomplete and false as would be a study of the physical world that would exclude the knowledge of molecules, atoms, and particles. Nothing is understood unless everything is understood.

Thus, there is an infinite gradation of coextensive, simultaneous realities, upon which sleep opens a natural window. Indeed, if we set aside the superficial life-death-sleep classification in favor of a more essential classification of the universe, we see that, from top to bottom (if there is such a thing as top and bottom), this universe is but a continuum of consciousness-force or, as Sri Aurobindo puts it, a gradation of *planes of consciousness* ranging without break from pure Matter to pure Spirit—Subtle Physical, Vital, Mind, Supermind (we may use another terminology, if we like, but the fact remains)—and everything occurs on these planes: our life, our sleep, our death. Everything occurs within those planes; everything coexists there, without any separation. Life, death, and sleep are simply different *positions* of consciousness within this one gradation. When we are awake, we receive mental or vital vibrations, which are translated in us by certain symbols, certain ways of seeing, understanding, or living. When we are asleep, or "dead," we receive the *same* mental, vital or other vibrations, which are translated in us by other symbols, other ways of seeing, understanding, or living *the same reality*. In each case, the key to our existence, here or elsewhere, is always our capacity of consciousness; if we lack consciousness in life, we will lack consciousness in every other way: death will really be death, and sleep really a stupor. To become aware of these different planes of reality is therefore our fundamental work. Once we have done this work integrally, the artificial boundaries that separate our different modes of existence will crumble: we will move without break, without any gap of consciousness, from life to sleep to death. More precisely, death and sleep will cease to exist as we understand them, to be replaced by different manners of continuously perceiving the total Reality, and perhaps ultimately by an integral consciousness that will perceive everything simultaneously. Our evolution is far from over. *Death is not a denial of Life but a process of Life.*[1]

This physical life in this physical body has, therefore, a special prominence among all our modes of existence, because it is here that we can become conscious; this is *the field of work*, as the Mother says, the meeting-point of all the planes in one body. This is the field of work because it is the starting, or almost starting, point of evolution; through this body, slowly, after countless undifferentiated lives, a "self" takes on an individuality by coming in contact with higher and higher planes of consciousness, and vaster and vaster reaches of consciousness on each plane. Hence, there are as many different kinds of death or sleep as there are lives, because they are the same thing; everything depends upon the degree of our evolutionary development; there are all possible degrees in sleep and death, as in life, from the complete zombie to the fully awake and individualized consciousness. Therefore, there are no general rules regarding sleep and death, because everything is possible, just as it is in our physical waking state. We can at most outline some general features.

As mentioned earlier, we are made up of several centers of consciousness, ranging from above the head to the bottom. Each of these centers is somewhat like a radio receiver tuned in to particular wavelengths, and is linked with different planes of consciousness from which we constantly receive, most often unknowingly, all sorts of vibrations—subtle physical, vital or mental, higher or lower—that account for our way of thinking, feeling and living, with our individual consciousness acting as a filter and picking up certain vibrations rather than others, in accord with its own social environment, tradition, education, etc. As a general rule, in sleep or in death, we go by affinity to those places or planes with which we have already established a relationship. This is the elementary stage when the consciousness is not truly individualized; although it may be mentally refined and cultivated, it thinks more or less like everyone else, feels like everyone else, and lives like everyone else: it is merely a temporary aggregate whose continuity does not extend beyond the body in which everything is centered. When this bodily center dies, everything scatters into small vital, mental, and other fragments, which return to their respective realms, since they no longer have a center. And when the center is asleep, everything is more or less asleep, since the nonphysical mental and vital elements exist only in relation to, and to serve, the bodily life. In this primary state, whenever the consciousness falls asleep, it slips back into the subconscient (we use the word *subconscient* as Sri Aurobindo used it, in the etymological sense, meaning that which is historically sub-conscious, not below the level of our waking consciousness but below the conscious stage in the evolutionary sense, as in the animal or the plant);[2] in other words, the consciousness returns to its evolutionary past, which may bring out an array of chaotic images made by random associations of many fragments of memories and impressions, unless it carries on its waking activities in a more or less incoherent way. From there, the consciousness sinks further into a vegetable or larval past, which is its actual sleep, like the sleep of plants and animals. Many stages are necessary before the true center, the psychic and its consciousness-force, are formed and impart some coherence and continuity to this volatile mixture. But from the moment the body ceases to be the main center, and one begins to have an inner life independent of physical circumstances and physical life, and especially when one does yoga, which is a process of accelerated evolution, life truly changes, as do death and sleep; one begins to exist. Actually, the first thing one notices is the special nature of certain dreams, as if visible, outward changes were preceded by inner mutations of a subtler order, affecting our dreams. We go from animal sleep to conscious sleep, or *sleep of experience*, and from a death that rots to a death that lives. The partitions that divided our integral life crumble. Instead of living in total dispersion for lack of a center, we have found the Master and seized upon the thread of consciousness-force that links together all the planes of universal reality.

Sleep of Experience

Depending on the development of our consciousness, there are many degrees in this new type of sleep, from the rare spasmodic flashes we may have on one plane or another to a continuous and self-governing vision, capable of moving freely throughout the entire range of planes. Here again, everything depends upon our waking consciousness. By affinity we normally go to the planes with which we have established a connection. The vital, mental or other vibrations we have accepted, which have become ideas, aspirations, desires, base or noble reactions, constitute this connection, and when we leave our body, we simply go to the source of these vibrations—an extraordinarily vivid and striking source, next to which our mental and vital translations in the physical world seem pallid and virtually empty. Then we begin to become aware of the immense and countless worlds that suffuse and envelop and overshadow our little earthly planet, determining its destiny and ours. It is obviously impossible to describe these worlds in a few pages or even in several volumes; it would be like trying to describe the earth on the basis of a glimpse of Long Island. We will simply give a few clues to help the seeker check his own experience. The first requirements for this exploration, as Sri Aurobindo has often insisted, are a *clear austerity*, the absence of desire, and a silent mind; otherwise we may fall prey to all kinds of illusions. Patiently, through repeated experiences, we first learn to identify the plane on which our experience has taken place, then the level within each plane. This process of situating our experience is as important for our quest as knowing which road we are traveling and which state or country we are crossing when we explore the earth. Then we learn to understand the meaning of our experiences; this is a foreign language, even several languages, which we must decipher without any interference from our own mental language. Indeed, one of the main difficulties is that mental language is the only language we know, so as we wake up, its own transcriptions will tend unconsciously to interfere with and to distort the purity of the experience. Without a knowledgeable guide to unravel this tangle, we must learn to remain as mentally silent as possible upon awakening, and to feel, intuitively, the meaning of these other languages; this occurs fairly rapidly as our consciousness develops and our experiences multiply. At first, it is like a jungle or a Chinese marketplace: everything looks the same. Then, over the months and years, one eventually makes out paths and faces, places and signs, and a more vivid proliferation than on earth.

But how to remember one's sleep? For most people it is a total blank—a link is missing. There are in fact many links, or *bridges*, as the Mother puts it, as if we were made of a series of countries connected to one another by bridges. Thus, we may easily remember some parts of our being and their travels, while others are forgotten for lack of a bridge to the rest of our consciousness. When crossing this void, or untrained part of the consciousness, we forget (which generally happens to those who fall into "ecstasy," a subject we will return to). Usually, a sufficiently developed person travels through the whole range of planes of consciousness in his or her sleep and goes right to the supreme Light of the Spirit—*Sat-Chit-Ananda*—most often unconsciously, but those few minutes are the true sleep, true repose in the absolute relaxation of Joy and Light. Sri Aurobindo used to say that the real purpose of sleep is to return spontaneously to the Source and reimmerse oneself in it. From there we come down slowly through each plane—the Mind, Vital, Subtle Physical, and Subconscient (the last one is remembered the most easily)—where each part of our being has its own corresponding experiences. There are also many zones within each plane, each with its own particular bridge. The major difficulty is in building the first bridge, the connection with the external waking consciousness. The one and only way to do this is to remain perfectly motionless and silent upon awakening. If we turn over or move, everything vanishes or, rather, the great lake of sleep is instantly covered with little ripples, which keep us from seeing anything. If we begin to think, then the ripples turn into swirls of mud that totally obscure everything; thought has no place in this process, neither can the mind help us to remember. Instead, we must gaze steadily upon the vast, quiet lake, in a very sustained but objectless contemplation, as if the sheer pointedness of our gaze were going to pierce the dark blue depths. If we persevere long enough, we will see an image suddenly emerge before our eyes, or just a faint outline, like the scent of a faraway land, laden with fragrance and very familiar, yet still elusive. At that point, we should not leap at the image, for it would immediately vanish, but let it gradually become clearer, assume its own shape, and eventually a whole scene will emerge. Once we have seized hold of the thread, it is usually enough to pull it gently, without trying to think or understand (understanding will come later; if we begin interpreting prematurely, we will cut off all communications), and that thread will take us from one country to another, from one memory to another. We may sometimes remain stuck for years at the same point on the way, as if there were a memory lapse somewhere, a gap in the road. To build the missing connection, we must be patient and just persevere; through obstinacy, a path will eventually open, as in the jungle. To try to recall dreams is not the only method, however; we can also concentrate at night, before going to sleep, with a will to remember and to wake up once or twice, at fixed intervals, in order to catch the thread at different points along the way. This method is particularly effective. We know how we only have to want to wake up at a given time for the inner clock to work precisely, almost to the minute; this is called "making a formation." These formations are like little vibratory nodules issued by the will and which then acquire an existence of their own, discharging their duties very effectively.* We can make more or less powerful, and more or less durable, formations (that can be periodically recharged) for all sorts of purposes, and in particular for remembering to awaken at regular intervals during our sleep. If we persevere for months, or years if necessary, eventually each time a significant event takes

---

* We all make formations, unwittingly, through our desires and thoughts (good and bad), then we forget them. But the formations do not forget; they return two years or ten years later, their work done—the particular desire or thought has been fulfilled, certain circumstances have been rearranged—while we have long stopped thinking about them; we do not even recognize the result as originating from ourselves. We are thus besieged by all sorts of small living entities that go on seeking realization, even while we no longer want them.

place on some plane of our sleep, we will be automatically alerted. We will only need to stop in the middle of the sleep, repeat the event two or three times to ourselves to record it, then go back in again.

In this enormous field of experience we can stress only a few general practical points, which may strike the seeker at the beginning of his investigation. First, a clear distinction must be drawn between ordinary subconscious dreams and actual experiences. Experiences are not dreams, though we are in the habit of mixing them together; they are real events, on one plane or another, in which we have participated. They are distinguished from ordinary dreams by their striking intensity: any event in the outer physical world, however exceptional, seems dull next to them. They leave a deep impression in us, and the memory of them is *more vivid* than any physical memory, as if we had touched a richer mode of existence—not necessarily richer in its external aspect or color, although it may be strikingly bright (especially in the Vital), but in its content. When the seeker awakens with an overwhelming sensation, as if he had bathed in a world replete with signs having more than one meaning at a time (the events of our physical world rarely mean more than one thing at a time), which are so filled with invisible ramifications and depths that he could contemplate them for a long time and not exhaust their meaning, or when he has watched and participated in scenes that seem infinitely more real than physical scenes (which are always flat, as if they rested against a hard, somewhat photographic background), he will know he has had a real experience and not a dream.

> *Unreal-seeming yet more real than life,*
> *. . .truer than things true*
> *If dreams these were or captured images,*
> *Dream's truth made false earth's vain realities.*[3]

There is yet another remarkable phenomenon: as we ascend the scale of consciousness, the quality of the surrounding light changes— differences in luminosity are a *sure* indication of where we are and even of the meaning of the scene. There is indeed a whole spectrum, from the muddy shades of the subconscient (gray, brown, black); the vibrant hues of the Subtle Physical; the bright colors of the Vital, which, we should note, always look somewhat artificial, flashy, and a bit hard (this region is particularly deceptive); to the lights of the Mind, which become increasingly powerful and pure as one rises toward the Origin. From the Overmind and above (we will discuss the Overmind later), a radical change occurs in the nature of the vision: the objects, beings and things we see no longer seem to be illumined from the outside, flatly (as is the Earth by the sun), but they are *luminous in themselves*, and ultimately there is no longer anyone "outside" looking in, but only ecstasy in a still, resplendent Light, utterly free of the clatter and sensational happenings of the lower planes. To come into contact with that Light, if only for a few minutes, is to feel as rested as after eight hours of sleep. This is how yogis can live without sleep, and also how a few minutes of concentration in the day can refresh us as much as a long walk in the countryside. Our body is unbelievably resilient; psychological turmoil is what tires us.

Aside from participating in events of a universal character, we find that sleep is a gold mine of information about our own individual condition. All the levels of our being stand out during sleep, as if we had been deaf and dumb, made of cardboard, during our waking hours, and suddenly everything in us awakens to a life truer than life. These various inner levels of our being may appear in sleep as rooms, or houses, in which the slightest detail is significant: *When one sets out to explore one's inner being*, explains the Mother, *and the different parts that form it, one often has the impression of entering a hall or a room; according to the color, the atmosphere, and the objects it contains, one gets a very clear feeling of the part being visited. Then one may even move into deeper and deeper rooms, each with its own character.* Sometimes, instead of rooms, we may encounter all kinds of beings—an entire family or even a menagerie—which represent the forces and vibrations we are accustomed to harboring in us, and which make up "our" nature.

These are not beings of "dream"; they are the real beings we harbor. Forces are conscious, vibrations are conscious; beings and forces, consciousness and force, are two simultaneous sides of the same reality. Then we see very vividly what we want to keep, or no longer keep, within ourselves.

Something else will strike the seeker by its almost daily recurrence. He will find, after the fact, that he has had, during the night, the exact premonition of all the important *psychological* events that will take place the next day. First, he may believe this is pure coincidence, or deny the connection between one event and the other, but after the same thing has reoccurred hundreds of times, he will begin to be on guard; and finally, once he has completely awakened to the fact, he will use this foreknowledge to take protective measures beforehand. For example, we may have a spell of depression that day, or go into a rage, or feel a movement of rebellion inside us, or a sexual impulse, etc., or even, to take another example of a seemingly different nature, we may trip on the stairs two or three times and almost fall headlong, or contract a violent fever; then we notice that each of these small, very trivial daytime incidents corresponds exactly to another incident, most often symbolic in nature (symbolic, because it is not the fact itself, but a mental transcription when we wake up in the morning), which we experienced the night before: either we were attacked in a "dream" by an enemy, or we were involved in an unhappy turn of event, or else we saw, sometimes very precisely, all the details surrounding the psychological scene that would take place the next day. It would seem that "someone" is perfectly awake in us and very concerned with helping us identify all the why's and hidden mechanisms of our psychological life, all the reasons for our falls as well as progress. For, conversely, we may have a premonition of all the happy psychological movements that will translate the next day into a progress, an opening of consciousness, a feeling of lightness, an inner widening; we remember that the night before we saw a light, an ascent, or a wall or house crumbling (symbolic of our resistance or the mental constructions that were confining us). We are also very struck by the realization that these premonitions are usually not associated with events *we* deem important on our physical plane, such as the death of a parent or some worldly achievement (although these premonitions also may occur), but with very trivial details, bearing no external importance, yet always very meaningful for our inner progress. This is a sign of the development of our consciousness. Instead of unconsciously accepting mental, vital or other vibrations, which shape our life without our knowledge and which we naively assume to be our own (we say: this is *my* anger, *my* depression, *my* sexual impulse, *my* fever), we begin to see them coming into us. This is visible proof, supported by hundreds of experiences night after night, that all the play of our frontal nature originates outside ourselves, in a universal Mind, a universal Vital, or even higher regions if we are capable of tuning in to them. This is the beginning of mastery, because once we have seen, or foreseen, something we can change the course of circumstances. Earthly life is simultaneously the place of the most rigorous and the most blind determinism, and of conquered freedom—it all depends upon our consciousness. A disciple once wrote to Sri Aurobindo relating his "dreams," emphasizing the rather bizarre coincidence that seemed to occur between nocturnal events and waking. This was the answer he received: *Understand that these experiences are not mere imaginations or dreams but actual happenings. . . . It is a mistake to think that we live physically only, with the outer mind and life. We are all the time living and acting on other planes of consciousness, meeting others there and acting upon them, and what we do and feel and think there, the forces we gather, the results we prepare have an incalculable importance and effect, unknown to us upon our outer life. Not all of it comes through, and what comes through takes another form in the physical—though sometimes there is an exact correspondence; but this little is at the basis of our outward existence. All that we become and do and bear in the physical life is prepared behind the veil within us. It is therefore of immense importance for a yoga which aims at the transformation of life to grow conscious of what goes on*

*within these domains, to be master there and be able to feel, know
and deal with the secret forces that determine our destiny and our
internal and external growth or decline.*[4]

Sleep of Action

We have gone from animal sleep to conscious sleep or sleep of
experience; we can now go to a third type of sleep, sleep of action.
For a long time, our sleep, however conscious it may be, remains
indeed a passive kind of state. We are only the witness of things,
a helpless spectator of something happening in this or that part of
our being. It should be stressed that it is always *a part* of our being
that undergoes a particular experience, although at the time we
may have the impression that our whole being suffers, fights, or
travels, etc., just as we may have the impression, when discussing
politics or philosophy with a friend, that our whole self participates in the discussion, when it is merely a mental or vital fraction
of it. As sleep becomes more conscious, we go from impressions
to naked realities. We realize that we are made up of a medley of
mental, vital, and other fragments, each with a separate existence
and separate experiences on its own particular plane. At night,
when the bond of the body and the tyranny of the mental mentor
have vanished, this independence becomes remarkably alive. All
the vibrations we have gathered in us, and which make up "our"
nature, become so many little entities running here and there, and
we discover all sorts of strangers in us whose existence we had never
suspected. In other words, these fragments are not integrated
around the true center, the psychic, and because they are not
integrated, we cannot bring them under control and change the
course of circumstances. We are passive, because the real "we" is
the psychic, and most of these fragments are not connected with
the psychic.

Hence the necessity of integration rapidly becomes imperative
if we wish to control circumstances here, there, and everywhere.

For example, when we leave our body and go into the regions of the lower Vital (corresponding to the area of the navel and sex centers), the part of our being that is exteriorized in this region often goes through very unpleasant experiences; it is attacked by all sorts of voracious forces, giving rise to what is commonly called a "nightmare," from which we escape by returning as quickly as possible into our body, where we are safe. Now, if that particular part of our being has accepted to become integrated around the psychic center, it can safely go out into these rather infernal regions because it possesses the psychic light (the psychic is a fragment of the great original Light), and when under attack, it needs only remember this light (or the Master, which is the same) for all adverse forces to vanish. By remembering, it calls upon the true vibration, which has the power to dissolve or disperse all vibrations of a lesser intensity. There is even an interesting transitory stage in which we helplessly participate in terrifying pursuits, for instance, and suddenly that fragment of ourselves remembers the light (or the Master), thus abruptly reversing the situation. On these planes we can also meet many people, known or unknown, near or far away, living or dead—*the ever-living whom we name as dead*,[5] as Sri Aurobindo says—who are on the same wavelength, and we can be the witness or helpless partner of their misadventures (which may translate into unpleasant happenings on earth, as we have seen; all the blows received there will be received here; each occurrence there prepares something here). But if the fragment of ourselves having the experience with the corresponding fragment of that friend or stranger or "dead" person is able to remember the Light (that is, if it is integrated around the psychic), it becomes capable of reversing the course of events, of assisting a friend or stranger in distress, of helping a disembodied being go through a difficult passage, get out of a dangerous place, or free himself from some unhealthy associations (there are so many places where we are prisoners). The following is an example of such an experience, chosen deliberately in negative terms and as simply as possible: X "dreams" that she is walking with a friend along the shore of a lake with seemingly marvelously clear waters, when suddenly a snake springs up from the bottom of the lake and bites her friend on the throat. She makes several attempts to protect her friend, but becomes frightened herself, is pursued by the snake, and runs "back home" (into her body). The next day she learns that her friend is ill and has completely lost her voice. She herself experiences throughout the day a series of small abortive incidents, within and without. If she had been actively conscious, centered, nothing would have happened, and the adverse force would have fled. There are contrary examples where accidents have been "miraculously" averted because they were overcome on the previous night by a conscientious friend, if not by oneself. Thus, we can usefully participate in many activities that prepare our own tomorrows, or more extensive tomorrows, depending upon our capacities. "A conscious being, no larger than a man's thumb, stands in the centre of our self; he is Master of the past and the present . . . he is today and he is tomorrow," says the Katha Upanishad. (IV.12,13) We need to have numerous experiences, with actual verifications whenever possible, before we can appreciate to what extent these dreams are not dreams. There are some prisons that cannot be unlocked here until we have unlocked them there. The problem of action is thus intimately connected with that of integration.

This integration is all the more necessary when we no longer have a body, i.e., when we are supposedly dead, because these fragments no longer have the recourse of returning to the body for protection. If they are not integrated, they suffer a great deal of unpleasantness. This is probably the origin of all the stories about hell, which—this cannot be repeated enough—concern *only* some lower parts of our nature. For the lower planes (notably the lower Vital, corresponding to the navel and sex centers, the most difficult regions to integrate) are full of ravenous forces. As a young disciple who had died prematurely said when describing his journey to a friend during sleep: "Just behind your world there is no law and order"—a proper British laconism for hell. And he added: "I had Mother's light (the Master) with me, and I crossed over." Since this experience is typical of many deaths, it should be noted that the two friends met in lovely colored gardens, typical of the higher vital regions (corresponding to the heart center), which constitute some of the countless so-called paradises of the other world—though not so lofty paradises, to be sure. Generally, the disembodied person remains there as long as he wishes; then, after he grows tired of it, he moves to the place of true rest, in the original Light, with his soul, to await the time of return. To say that a person will go to "eternal hell" is a cruel absurdity. How could the soul, which is pure Light, ever be a prisoner of those lower vibrations? It would be like saying that infrared light controls the ultraviolet. Like goes with like, always and everywhere, whether here or on the other side. And what could ever be "eternal," truly, except the soul, except joy? *If there were an unending Hell, it could only be a seat of unending rapture,* said Sri Aurobindo, *for God is joy,* Ananda, *and than the eternity of His bliss there is no other eternity.*[6]

As our being becomes integrated around the psychic, it thus goes from passive to active sleep, if one may still speak of "sleep," and from a troublesome death to an interesting journey or another form of work. But, depending on the breadth of our consciousness, there are also many degrees in this experience, from a limited action that does not extend beyond the small circle of living or dead acquaintances, or the worlds familiar to us, to the universal action of a few great beings whose psychic has in a sense colonized vast stretches of consciousness, and who protect the world with their silent light.

Let us conclude these brief generalities, which are at best trail markers for the seeker, with a final observation concerning premonitions. We should again emphasize that having a premonition about something is the sign that this "something" already exists on some plane before taking place here; it does not hang in midair. We are extremely scrupulous and precise regarding physical reality, yet we treat the happenings of nonphysical worlds as if they were incoherent or vague, perhaps because the vagueness is in our own mind. We find through experience, however, that everything is perfectly rational, if not always reasonable: not only does the luminosity intensify as we ascend the scale of consciousness, but time accelerates, covering a wider range of space, as it were, or more distant events (both in the future and in the past), and ultimately we emerge into that motionless Light where everything *is.* As a consequence, we realize that the fulfillment on earth of our premonitory vision takes place sooner or later in time, depending on the plane of consciousness where the vision has occurred. For example, when we see in the subtle Physical, which borders our world, the earthly transcription is almost immediate, a few hours or a day away; we see an accident, and the next day, it takes place. Moreover, the vision is very precise, down to the slightest detail. The higher we rise on the scale of consciousness, the later the fulfillment of the vision and the more universal its scope; the details of realization are less precise, as if the happening itself were unavoidable (provided our vision is sufficiently free of egoism), with a margin of uncertainty concerning the actual facts of its realization—though in a sense, this margin accounts for the changes or distortions suffered by a higher truth as it descends from plane to plane to its earthly realization. All kinds of interesting conclusions can be derived from this observation, in particular that the more conscious we are on earth, or the higher we are capable of rising on the scale of consciousness and approaching the Origin, the closer we bring the earth to the Origin by annuling the distorting determinisms of the intermediary planes. This can have important consequences not only in an individual sense, for mastering and transforming our own life, but also in global terms, for the transformation of the world. A great deal has been written about determinism versus individual freedom, but the problem is too often seen from the wrong perspective. It is not a question of freedom versus determinism, but of freedom *and* many determinisms. We are subject, Sri Aurobindo says, to a series of *superim-*

posed determinisms—physical, vital, mental and higher—and the determinism of each plane can change or cancel the determinism of the plane immediately below it. For instance, good health and a given life-span in a person can be modified by the vital determinism of "his" passions or various psychological disorders, which in turn can be modified by the mental determinism of his willpower and his ideal, which can then be modified by the greater law of the psychic, and so on. Freedom means to move to a higher plane. And the same applies to the earth, because the very same forces drive the individual and the collective. As individual meeting points of all these determinisms in matter, if we are capable of rising to a higher plane, we automatically help change all the lower determinisms and give the earth access to a greater freedom, until the day when, with the help of the pioneers of evolution, we can lift ourselves to a *supramental* plane, which will change the present destiny of the world as the Mind once changed its destiny around the Tertiary Era. And in the end—if there is an end—perhaps the earth will attain the supreme Determinism, which is supreme Freedom and perfect accomplishment. Through our work on consciousness, each of us contributes to resisting the fatalities that assail our world, and acts as a leavening agent for the earth's freedom and divinization. Indeed, the evolution of consciousness has a supreme meaning for the earth.

CHAPTER 10

The Revolutionary Yogi

Such are the mental, vital, physical and psychic discoveries that Sri Aurobindo pursued alone, step by step, between the ages of twenty and thirty, simply by following the thread of consciousness. The remarkable thing is that he practiced yoga in circumstances and places where one would usually not do yoga: while giving his lectures in French or English at the State College of Baroda, during his work at the court of the Maharaja, and more and more in the midst of his secret revolutionary activities. The hours of the night that were not devoted to studying his mother tongue or Sanskrit or to political work were spent writing poetry. "Aurobindo had the habit of writing poetry till late into the night," his Bengali teacher recalls, "and consequently he did not get up very early in the morning. . . . He would concentrate for a minute before starting, then the poetry would flow from his pen like a stream." From writing poetry, Sri Aurobindo would pass to his experimental sleep. In 1901, at the age of twenty-nine, he married Mrinalini Devi and tried to share his spiritual life with her. *I am experiencing all the signs and symptoms*, he wrote to her in a letter found in the archives of the British police. *I should like to take you with me along this path.* But Mrinalini did not understand him, and Sri Aurobindo would remain alone. We could search Sri Aurobindo's life in vain for those moving or miraculous anecdotes that adorn the lives of great sages and mystics, in vain for sensational yogic methods; everything seemed so ordinary, apparently, that nothing attracted one's attention, just as in life itself. Perhaps he had found more miracles in the ordinary than in the extraordinary: *With me all is different, all is uncommon,* he wrote in a letter to Mrinalini. *All is deep and strange to the eyes that see.*[1] And perhaps that is what he wants us to discover through his example, his work, his yoga—all those unknown riches beneath the ordinary crust. *Our lives [are] a deeper mystery than we have dreamed.*[2] If we only knew how hollow our so-called miracles are, without breadth, like a magic show for adults—the moment we have two cents' worth of knowledge we can see how it is made!—and how simple the Truth is compared to all that supernatural imagery. As he progressed in his yoga, Sri Aurobindo left all the imagery for what he called *spiritual realism,*[3] not because he disliked pretty images—he, the poet!—but because he saw that these images would be prettier still if they were to assume a physical reality upon the earth, if the supraphysical were to become our normal physical, visible to the naked eye. This naturalization of the beyond, and the calm mastery of life, that Sri Aurobindo achieved were possible only because he never separated the two worlds: *My own life and my yoga have always been since my coming to India both this-worldly and other-worldly without any exclusiveness on either side,* he wrote in a letter to a disciple. *All human interests are, I suppose, this-worldly and most of them have entered into my mental field and some, like politics, into my life, but at the same time, since I set foot on the Apollo Bunder in Bombay, I began to have spiritual experiences, but these were not divorced from this world but had an inner and infinite bearing on it, such as a feeling of the Infinite pervading material space and the Immanent inhabiting material objects and bodies. At the same time I found myself entering supraphysical worlds and planes with influences and an effect from them upon the material plane, so I could make no sharp divorce or irreconcilable opposition between what I have called the two ends of existence and all that lies between them. For me all is Brahman and I find the Divine everywhere.*[4]

The Problem of Action

It is first in his revolutionary activities that we find Sri Aurobindo's spiritual realism. A program had soon been drawn up, consisting of four points: to awaken India to the concept of independence, for which newspaper articles and political speeches would suffice; to keep people's minds in a state of constant rebellion—at the turn of the century Sri Aurobindo was certainly one of the first, with another of India's great heroes, Tilak, to speak of total liberation, passive resistance, and noncooperation (Gandhi would not come on the Indian political scene until fifteen years later); to transform the Indian Congress party and its timid demands into an *extremist movement* unambiguously promoting the ideal of complete independence; and finally to secretly prepare an armed insurrection.

With his younger brother, Barin, he began to organize guerrilla groups in Bengal under the cover of athletic or cultural programs; he even sent an emissary to Europe, at his own expense, to learn how to make bombs. When Sri Aurobindo declared, *I am neither an impotent moralist nor a weak pacifist,*[5] he meant every word of it. He had studied enough French history, as well as the Italian and American revolutions, to know that sometimes armed revolt can be justified; neither Joan of Arc nor Mazzini nor Washington were apostles of "nonviolence." In 1920, when Gandhi's son went to visit him in Pondicherry to discuss nonviolence, Sri Aurobindo answered with this simple, and still applicable, question: "What would you do if tomorrow the Northern Frontiers were overrun?" Twenty years later, in 1940, Sri Aurobindo and Mother publicly took the side of the Allies, while Gandhi, undoubtedly in an outburst of praiseworthy feelings, sent an open letter to the British people urging them not to take up arms against Hitler and to use only "spiritual force" instead. It would therefore be appropriate to explain Sri Aurobindo's spiritual position with regard to violent action.

War and destruction, he wrote, *are not only a universal principle of our life here in its purely material aspects, but also of our mental and moral existence. It is self-evident that in the actual life of man intellectual, social, political, moral, we can make no real step forward without a struggle, a battle between what exists and lives and what seeks to exist and live and between all that stands behind either. It is impossible, at least as men and things are, to advance, to grow, to fulfill and still to observe really and utterly that principle of harmlessness which is yet placed before us as the highest and best law of conduct. We will use only soul-force and never destroy by war or any even defensive employment of physical violence? Good, though until soul-force is effective, the Asuric force in men and nations tramples down, breaks, slaughters, burns, pollutes, as we see it doing today, but then at its ease and unhindered, and you have perhaps caused as much destruction of life by your abstinence as others by resort to violence. . . . It is not enough that our own hands should remain clean and our souls unstained for the law of strife and destruction to die out of the world; that which is its root must first disappear out of humanity [our emphasis]. Much less will mere immobility and inertia unwilling to use or incapable of using any kind of resistance to evil, abrogate the law; inertia, tamas, indeed, injures much more than can the [dynamic] rajasic principle of strife which at least creates more than it destroys. Therefore, so far as the problem of the individual's action goes, his abstention from strife and its inevitable concomitant destruction in their more gross and physical form may help his own moral being, but it leaves the Slayer of creatures unabolished.*[6]

The whole evolution of Sri Aurobindo's thought and of his practical attitude toward war, from his underground activity in Bengal to his retreat in Pondicherry in 1910, revolves around the question of *methods*: how to strike most effectively at this "Slayer of creatures," "the Eater," as the Vedic rishis called it. And from the independence of India, Sri Aurobindo went on to the independence of the world. Indeed, as he advanced in his yoga, he became increasingly aware, through experience, that hidden forces are not only behind our personal psychological disorders, but behind the world disorders as well—everything comes from somewhere else, as we have said—and that if our abstaining leaves the

Slayer of creatures standing, our wars do not destroy it either, although in practice it may still be necessary for us to soil our hands in wars. In the very midst of the First World War, Sri Aurobindo observed with prophetic force: *The defeat of Germany . . . could not of itself kill the spirit then incarnate in Germany; it may well lead to a new incarnation of it, perhaps in some other race or empire, and the whole battle would then have to be fought over again. So long as the old gods are alive, the breaking or depression of the body which they animate is a small matter, for they know well how to transmigrate. Germany overthrew the Napoleonic spirit in France in 1813 and broke the remnants of her European leadership in 1870; the same Germany became the incarnation of that which it had overthrown. The phenomenon is easily capable of renewal on a more formidable scale.*[7] We now know that the old gods are capable of transmigrating. Seeing all the years of nonviolence ending in the terrible violence that marked the partition of India in 1947, Gandhi himself said with a touch of sadness just before his death, "The attitude of violence we have secretly harbored comes back on us, and we fly at each other's throats when the question of distribution of power arises. . . . Now that the yoke of subjection is lifted, all the forces of evil have come to the surface." For neither violence nor nonviolence goes to the root of Evil. Right in the middle of the Second World War, while Sri Aurobindo was taking a public stand in favor of the Allies,* because it was the only *practical* thing to do, he wrote to a disciple: *You write as if what is going on in Europe were a war between the powers of the Light and the powers of Darkness—but that is no more so than during the Great War. It is a fight between two kinds of Ignorance. . . . The eye of the yogin sees not only the outward events and persons and causes, but the enormous forces which precipitate them into action. If the men who fought were instruments in the hands of rulers and financiers, etc., these in turn were mere puppets in the clutch of these forces. When one*

---

* At the risk of incurring the censure of his compatriots (it must be remembered that India had suffered enough under British rule not to be uninterested in the fate of Britain under German attack).

is habituated to see the things behind, one is no longer prone to be touched by the outward aspects—or to expect any remedy from political, institutional or social changes.[8] Sri Aurobindo had become aware of these "enormous forces" behind, of the constant infiltration of the supraphysical into the physical. His energies were not focused on a moral problem—violence versus nonviolence—which after all would be rather superficial, but on a problem of effectiveness. He saw clearly, again through experience, that in order to cure the world's evil it is first necessary to cure "what is at its roots in man." Nothing can be cured outside if it is not first cured inside, nothing can be controlled outside if it is not controlled inside, for inside and outside are the same thing. We cannot transform the external substance without transforming our inner substance, for they are again the same thing. There is but one Nature, one world, one substance, and as long as we approach problems outwardly, we will get nowhere. And if we find this solution too difficult for us, then there is no hope for man or the world, because all our outward panaceas and saccharin moralities are ultimately doomed to annihilation and destruction by those hidden inner powers: *The only way out,* Sri Aurobindo wrote, *is through the descent of a consciousness which is not the puppet of these forces but is greater than they are and can force them either to change or disappear.*[8] It was toward this new, supramental consciousness that Sri Aurobindo was progressing in the midst of his revolutionary work.

> *. . . We may find when all the rest has failed*
> *Hid in ourselves the key of perfect change.*[9]

Nirvana

In 1906 Sri Aurobindo left Baroda to plunge into the heart of political turmoil in Calcutta. The blunders of Lord Curzon, the governor of Bengal, had led to student unrest; the time was ripe. With another great nationalist, Bepin Pal, Sri Aurobindo launched an English daily, *Bande Mataram* ("I bow to Mother India"), the first newspaper to publicly advocate the goal of total independence, which would become a powerful instrument of India's awakening. He founded an *Extremist Party* and drew up a national action program—boycott of British goods, boycott of British courts, boycott of British schools and universities. He became the principal of the first "National College" in Calcutta and created so much commotion that less than a year later a warrant was issued for his arrest. Unfortunately for the British, Sri Aurobindo's articles and speeches were legally unassailable; he neither preached racial hatred, nor even attacked the government of Her Majesty; he simply proclaimed the right of all nations to independence. The charge against him was dismissed for lack of evidence; only the printer, who didn't know a word of English, was sentenced to six months in jail. This aborted arrest made Sri Aurobindo famous; he was henceforth the recognized leader of the nationalist party; he came out from behind the scenes, where he would have preferred to remain. *I do not care a button about having my name in any blessed place,* he wrote later; *I was never ardent about fame even in my political days; I preferred to remain behind the curtain, push people without their knowing it and get things done.*[10] But it would be wrong to imagine Sri Aurobindo as a fanatic; all his contemporaries were struck by this "calm young man who with a single word could silence a tumultuous meeting." It was in the midst of this external turmoil, between political meetings and the newspaper to get out every morning (and under constant threat from the secret police) that, on December 30, 1907, Sri Aurobindo met a yogi by the name of Vishnu Bhaskar Lele, who was to bring a paradoxical experience into his already paradoxical life.

It was the first time, after thirteen years in India, that Sri Aurobindo voluntarily met a yogi! It shows how much he distrusted asceticism and spiritualists. His first question to Lele was typical: *I want to do Yoga but for work, for action, not for sannyasa (renouncing the world) and Nirvana.*[11] Lele's reply was strange and deserves attention: "It would be easy for you as you are a poet."

The two men retired to a quiet room for three days. From then on, Sri Aurobindo's yoga would assume a different direction, seemingly away from action, but actually to the secret of action and of changing the world. *The first result,* Sri Aurobindo wrote, *was a series of tremendously powerful experiences and radical changes of consciousness which he had never intended . . . and which were quite contrary to my own ideas, for they made me see with a stupendous intensity the world as a cinematographic play of vacant forms in the impersonal universality of the Absolute Brahman.*[12]

> *In the enormous spaces of the self*
> *The body now seemed only a wandering shell. . . .*[13]

Sri Aurobindo's entire integral yoga was shattered. All his efforts of mental, vital and physical transformation, as well as his faith in a fulfilled earthly life, were swept away, swallowed up in a stupendous Illusion—nothing remained except empty forms. *It threw me suddenly into a condition above and without thought, unstained by any mental or vital movement; there was no ego, no real world—only when one looked through the immobile senses, something perceived or bore upon its sheer silence a world of empty forms, materialized shadows without true substance. There was no One or many even, only just absolutely That featureless, relationless, sheer, indescribable, unthinkable, absolute, yet supremely real and solely real. This was no mental realization nor something glimpsed somewhere above,—no abstraction,—it was positive, the only positive reality—although not a spatial physical world, pervading, occupying or rather flooding and drowning this semblance of a physical world, leaving no room or space for any reality but itself, allowing nothing else to seem at all actual, positive or substantial. . . . What it [this experience] brought was an inexpressible Peace, a stupendous silence, an infinity of release and freedom.*[14] Sri Aurobindo had gone straight into what the Buddhists call Nirvana, what the Hindus call the Silent Brahman or That; the Tao of the Chinese ; the Transcendent, the Absolute, or the Impersonal of the Westerners. He had reached that famous "liberation" *(mukti),* which is considered the "peak" of all spiritual life—what could there be beyond the Transcendent? Sri Aurobindo could tangibly verify the words of the great Indian mystic Sri Ramakrishna: "If we live in God, the world disappears; if we live in the world, God exists no longer." The gulf he had tried to bridge between Matter and Spirit had split open again before his unveiled eyes. The Western and Eastern spiritualists were right in assigning a life beyond as the sole destination of man's effort: paradise, Nirvana, or liberation—elsewhere, elsewhere, but not in this vale of tears or illusion. Sri Aurobindo's experience was there, irrefutable, before his very eyes.

But this experience, which is generally considered the final stage, was to be, for Sri Aurobindo, the starting point of new, higher experiences integrating the truth of the world and the truth of the beyond into a total, continuous and divine Reality. This is indeed a fundamental consideration, the understanding of which is central to the very meaning of our existence, for there are only two alternatives: either the supreme Truth is not of this world, as all the world religions have proclaimed, and we are wasting our time with futilities; or there is something else besides everything we have been told. The consideration is all the more relevant since it is not a theory but a practical experience. Here is what Sri Aurobindo reported: *I lived in that Nirvana day and night before it began to admit other things into itself or modify itself at all . . . in the end it began to disappear into a greater Super-consciousness from above. . . . The aspect of an illusionary world gave place to one in which illusion is only a small surface phenomenon with an immense Divine Reality behind it and a supreme Divine Reality above it and an intense Divine Reality in the heart of everything that had seemed at first only a cinematic shape or shadow. And this was no reimprisonment in the senses, no diminution or fall from supreme experience, it came rather as a constant heightening and widening of the Truth. . . . Nirvana in my liberated consciousness turned out to be the beginning of my realization, a first step towards the complete thing, not the sole true attainment possible or even a culminating finale.*[15]

What kind of Transcendent was this, which seemed to stand

not at the summit but at midpoint? To use a rather simple but correct analogy, we could say that sleep represents a transcendental state with respect to waking, but it is no higher or truer than waking, nor is it less true. It is simply another state of consciousness. The moment we withdraw from mental and vital activity, obviously everything vanishes, much as taking an anesthetic dulls all sense of feeling. Indeed, we have a natural tendency to think that this immobile and impersonal Peace is superior to our turmoil, but after all, the turmoil is usually of our own making. The superior or inferior has nothing to do with going into another state, but with the quality or poise of our consciousness within a given state. Hence, Nirvana is not the top of the ladder, any more than sleep or death are. It can be experienced at *any level of our consciousness* through concentration—in the mind, in the vital, and even in the physical consciousness. The hatha yogi bent over his navel, or the Basuto dancing around his totem, can suddenly pass elsewhere, if such is their destiny, into another, transcendental dimension where all this world is reduced to nothingness. The same can happen to the mystic concentrated in his heart, or to the yogi concentrated in his mind. For one does not actually go *higher* as one enters Nirvana; one merely opens a passageway and goes out. Sri Aurobindo had not gone beyond the mental plane when he experienced Nirvana: *I myself had my experience of Nirvana and silence in the Brahman long before there was any knowledge of the overhead spiritual planes.*[16] It is after ascending to higher, superconscious planes that he had experiences superior to Nirvana, where the illusionary, immobile and impersonal aspect merged into a new Reality, simultaneously embracing this world and the beyond. Such was Sri Aurobindo's first discovery. *Nirvana cannot be at once the ending of the Path with nothing beyond to explore . . . it is the end of the lower Path through the lower Nature and the beginning of the Higher Evolution.*[17]

From another perspective, we might also ask ourselves if the goal of evolution is really to get out of it, as is believed by the followers of Nirvana and of all the religions that see the beyond as the goal of our efforts. If we put aside our emotional reasons for our belief or disbelief, and look only at the evolutionary process, we must acknowledge that Nature could easily have arranged that "exit" when we were still at an early mental stage, still living as instinctively intuitive beings, open, malleable. The Vedic age, the Mysteries of ancient Greece, or even the Middle Ages, would have been more appropriate for that "exit" than as we are now. If such was the goal of evolutionary Nature, and assuming evolution does not proceed haphazardly but according to a Plan, that is the type of man Nature would have fostered; it would have been easy, then, to *outleap the intellect*,[18] as Sri Aurobindo writes in his *Human Cycle*, and pass from the instinctively intuitive phase to an other-worldly spiritualism. The intellect is an utterly useless outgrowth if the goal of evolution is merely to get out of it. It appears, however, that Nature worked against that primitive intuition and deliberately covered it with ever thicker mental layers, increasingly complex and universal, and increasingly useless in terms of getting out; we all know how the wonderfully intuitive efflorescence of Upanishadic India at the beginning of this story, or of NeoPlatonic Greece at the beginning of this era, was leveled to be replaced by a human intellect that was inferior and denser, to be sure, but more general. We can only raise the question without trying to answer it. We wonder if the meaning of evolution is to indulge in the luxury of the mind, only to destroy it later and regress to a submental or nonmental religious stage or, on the contrary, to develop the mind to the utmost,* as we are being driven to do, until it exhausts its own narrowness and superficial turmoil and rises to its higher, superconscious regions, at a spiritual and supramental level where the Matter-Spirit contradiction will vanish like a mirage, and where we will no longer need to "get

---

* We must again emphasize that Sri Aurobindo's yoga, which seeks to go beyond the mind, is supposed to begin *after* the intellect has run its full course and would be impossible, as we shall see, if all the intermediate steps were not completed. "Mental silence" would obviously make no sense to an aboriginal of the Fiji Islands or to a back-country peasant.

out" because we will be everywhere Within.

Nevertheless, It would be wrong to believe that the experience of Nirvana is a false experience, a kind of illusion of the illusion; first, because there are no false experiences but only incomplete experiences, and then because Nirvana actually frees us from an illusion. Our usual way of seeing the world is deficient. It is like a very realistic optical illusion, as realistic as the broken appearance of a stick dipped in water, and just as erroneous. We must "cleanse the doors of perception," as William Blake said, and Nirvana helps us to do just that, albeit a bit radically. Usually, we see a three-dimensional world with a multitude of objects and beings *separated* from one another, the way the two parts of the stick appear in water, but the reality is quite different when we ascend to a higher plane, to the Superconscient, just as it is again different when we descend to the lower, atomic level. The one difference between the broken stick and our customary vision of the world is that one is merely an optical illusion, while the other is an earnest one. We insist on seeing as broken a stick which in reality is not. That this earnest illusion agrees with our present practical life and with the superficial level at which our existence unfolds may justify the illusion, but it is also the reason we are powerless to control life, for to see falsely is to live falsely. The scientist, who is not hampered by appearances, sees better and controls better, but his vision, too, is incomplete and his control uncertain; he has not truly mastered life, not even physical forces, but is merely using some of their most obvious effects. Therefore this problem of vision is not just one of personal satisfaction; it is not a matter of seeing better in order to have lovely visions in rose or blue, but of achieving a true mastery of the world and circumstances and ourselves, which are all the same thing since nothing is separate. Until now, those who have had access to that higher form of vision (there are many levels) have used it primarily for themselves, or they have not been capable of *incarnating* what they saw, since their main efforts were aimed precisely at getting out of this incarnation. But such ambiguous attitude is not inevitable, as Sri Aurobindo will show us.

He had not prepared this whole physical, vital, mental, and psychic foundation for nothing.

Nirvana is thus a useful (but not indispensable) intermediate stage in the transition from ordinary vision to the other vision. It helps us get rid of the complete illusion in which we ordinarily live. "As if by an enchantment they see the false as the true," says the Maitri Upanishad (VII.10). Sri Aurobindo does not use the word *illusion*; he simply says that we live in *Ignorance*. Nirvana frees us from our Ignorance, only to lead us into another kind of Ignorance, because an eternal problem with human beings is that they go from one extreme to another; they feel they must deny one thing in order to accept another, and therefore mistake an intermediate stage as being an end in itself, just as many great spiritual experiences have been mistaken for ends in themselves. There is actually no end, but only *a constant heightening and widening of the Truth.*[19] We could say that, inasmuch as it opens upon the beyond, the nirvanic or religious stage in general represents a first stage of evolution that takes us away from a false vision of the world, and that its purpose is essentially educational. But one who is awakened and truly born must prepare for the next evolutionary stage, and leave the religious focused on the other world for the spiritual focused on the Totality. Then nothing is excluded, everything widens. The integral seeker must therefore be on his guard, for any inner experience touching our being's intimate substance always feels irrefutable and final when it occurs; it is dazzling at any level—we may recall Vivekananda speaking of Nirvana: "An ocean of infinite peace, without a ripple, without a breath"—and there is great temptation to remain there, as if that were the ultimate haven. We will simply mention this advice of the Mother to all seekers: *Whatever the nature, the power or the marvel of an experience, you must never be dominated by it to the point of its overwhelming your whole being. . . . Whenever you enter in some way in contact with a force or a consciousness that is beyond your own, instead of being entirely subjugated by this consciousness or force, you must always remember that this is but one experience among thousands and thousands of others, and conse-quently it is by no means absolute. No matter how beautiful it is, you can and you must have better ones; no matter how exceptional it is, there are others that are even more marvelous; and no matter how high it is, you can always rise higher in the future.*

Sri Aurobindo lived for several months in this Nirvana before reaching elsewhere. What is strange is that, while in this state, he was still able to continue publishing a daily newspaper, attend secret meetings, and even make political speeches. The first time he had to speak in public in Bombay, he expressed his difficulty to Lele: *He asked me to pray, but I was so absorbed in the Silent Brahman consciousness that I could not pray. He replied that it did not matter; he and some others would pray and I had simply to go to the meeting and make Namaskar [bow] to the audience as Narayan and wait and speech would come to me from some other source than the mind.*[20] Sri Aurobindo did exactly as he was told and *the speech came as though it were dictated. And ever since all speech, writing, thought and outward activity have so come to me from the same source above the brain-mind.*[21] Sri Aurobindo had come in contact with the Superconscient. The speech delivered at Bombay was in fact quite interesting: *Try to realize the strength within you,* he said to the nationalist militants, *try to bring it forward; so that everything you do may be not your own doing but the doing of that Truth within you. . . . Because it is not you, it is something within you. What can all these tribunals, what can all the powers of the world do to That which is within you, that Immortal, that Unborn and Undying One, whom the sword cannot pierce, whom the fire cannot burn? . . . Him the jail cannot confine and the gallows cannot end. What is there that you can fear when you are conscious of Him who is within you?*[22]

On May 4, 1908, at dawn, Sri Aurobindo was pulled out of bed at gunpoint by the British police. He was thirty-six. An attempt on the life of a British magistrate based in Calcutta had just failed. The bomb used in the attempt had been manufactured in the garden where Barin, his younger brother, had been training "dis-ciples."

CHAPTER 11

Oneness

Sri Aurobindo was to spend a whole year in the Alipore jail awaiting the verdict. He had had no hand in the unsuccessful assassination attempt; organizing the rebellion had nothing to do with isolated acts of terrorism. *When I was arrested and hurried to the Lal Bazar police station I was shaken in faith for a while, for I could not look into the heart of His intention. Therefore I faltered for a moment and cried out in my heart to him, "What is this that has happened to me? I believed that I had a mission to work for the people of my country and until that work was done, I should have Thy protection. Why then am I here and on such a charge?" A day passed and a second day and a third, when a voice came to me from within, "Wait and see." Then I grew calm and waited. I was taken from Lal Bazar to Alipore and was placed for one month in a solitary cell apart from men. There I waited day and night for the voice of God within me, to know what He had to say to me, to learn what I had to do. . . . I remembered then that a month or more before my arrest, a call had come to me to put aside all activity, to go into seclusion and to look into myself, so that I might enter into closer communion with Him. I was weak and could not accept the call. My work [for the liberation of India] was very dear to me and in the pride of my heart I thought that unless I was there it would suffer or even fail and cease; therefore I would not leave it. It seemed to me that He spoke to me again and* said, *"The bonds you had not the strength to break, I have broken for you, because it is not my will nor was it ever my intention that that should continue. I have had another thing for you to do and it is for that I have brought you here, to teach you what you could not learn for yourself and to train you for my work."*[1] This "work" was to realize cosmic consciousness, or Oneness, and to explore the planes of consciousness above the ordinary mind, i.e., the Super-conscient, which was to put Sri Aurobindo on the track of the Great Secret. *What happened to me during that period I am not impelled to say, but only this that day after day, He showed me His wonders. . . . That knowledge He gave to me day after day during my twelve months of imprisonment.*[2]

Cosmic Consciousness

Sri Aurobindo had lived for months in a sort of phantasmagoric and empty dream set against the sole background of the Transcendent's static Reality. Strangely enough, however, it is in the midst of this Void, and as if issuing from it, that the world burst forth again with a new face, as if each time everything had to be lost in order to be found again at a higher level: *Overpowered and subjugated, stilled, liberated from itself, the mind accepts the Silence itself as the Supreme. But afterwards the seeker discovers that all is there for him contained or new-made . . . then the void begins to fill, there emerges out of it or there rushes into it all the manifold Truth of the Divine, all the aspects and manifestations and many levels of a dynamic Infinite.*[3] When we have seen only a static Infinite, we have seen only one face of God, Whom we have excluded from this world (though a world we claim to be empty of God may be better than a world filled with a solemn and judgmental God), but once the Silence has washed away our solemnities, great and small, leaving us for a time filled with pure whiteness, we find the world and God together again at every level and in every point, as if they had never been separated except through an excess of materialism or spiritualism. It was in the Alipore courtyard, during the exercise period, that this new change of consciousness took place: *I looked at the jail that secluded me from men and it was no longer by its high walls that I was imprisoned; no, it was Vasudeva* who surrounded me. I walked under the branches of the tree in front of my cell, but it was not the tree, I knew it was Vasudeva, it was Sri Krishna* whom I saw standing there and holding over me his shade. I looked at the bars of my cell, the very grating that did duty for a door and again I saw Vasudeva. It was Narayana* who was guarding and standing sentry over me. Or I lay on the coarse blankets that were given me for a couch and felt the arms of Sri Krishna around me, the arms of my Friend and Lover.... I looked at the prisoners in the jail, the thieves, the murderers, the swindlers, and as I looked at them I saw Vasudeva, it was Narayana whom I found in these darkened souls and misused bodies.*[4] That experience would never again leave Sri Aurobindo. During the six months the trial lasted, with its two hundred-odd witnesses and four thousand pieces of evidence, Sri Aurobindo was locked every day in an iron cage in the middle of the courtroom, but it was no longer a hostile crowd or judges that he saw: *When the case opened ... I was followed by the same insight.* He said to me, "*When you were cast into jail, did not your heart fail and did you not cry out to me, where is Thy protection? Look now at the Magistrate, look now at the Prosecuting Counsel.*" *I looked and it was not the magistrate whom I saw, it was Vasudeva, it was Narayana who was sitting there on the bench. I looked at the Prosecuting Counsel and it was not the Counsel for the Prosecution that I saw; it was Sri Krishna who sat there and smiled. "Now do you fear?" he said, "I am in all men and overrule their actions and their words.*"[5] Indeed God is not outside His world, He did not "create" the world—He *became* the world, as the Upanishad says: "He became knowledge and ignorance, He became the truth and the falsehood.... He became all this whatsoever that is." (*Taittiriya Upanishad* II.6) "This whole world is filled with beings who are

---

*   One of the names of the Divine.

His members," says the Swetaswatara Upanishad (IV.10). *All to the eye that sees is One, to a divine experience all is one block of the Divine.*[6]

We may think that this is an altogether mystical vision of the universe, with very little in common with our daily reality; at every step we encounter ugliness and evil; this world is riddled with pain, saturated with strangled cries. Where is the Divine in all this? Is the Divine that barbarism ever ready to open its torture camps? Or that pervading egoism? Or that villainy, concealed or flaunted? God is innocent of all these crimes. He is perfect. He cannot be a party to this—*neti neti*—God is so pure that He is not of this world. There is simply no place for Him in all this suffocating squalor! *We must look existence in the face if our aim is to arrive at a right solution whatever that solution may be. And to look existence in the face is to look God in the face; for the two cannot be separated. . . . This world of our battle and labor is a fierce dangerous destructive devouring world in which life exists precariously and the soul and body of man move among enormous perils, a world in which by every step forward, whether we will it or no, something is crushed and broken, in which every breath of life is a breath too of death. To put away the responsibility for all that seems to us evil or terrible on the shoulders of a semi-omnipotent Devil, or to put it aside as a part of Nature, making an unbridgeable opposition between world-nature and God-nature, as if Nature were independent of God, or to throw the responsibility on man and his sins, as if he had a preponderant voice in the making of this world or could create anything against the will of God, are clumsily comfortable devices. . . . We erect a God of Love and Mercy, a God of good, a God just, righteous and virtuous according to our own moral conceptions of justice, virtue and right-eousness, and all the rest, we say, is not He or is not His, but was made by some diabolical Power which He suffered for some reason to work out its wicked will or by some dark Ahriman counterbalancing our gracious Ormuzd, or was even the fault of selfish and sinful man who has spoiled what was made originally perfect by God. . . . We have to look courageously in the face of the reality and see that it is God and* *none else who has made this world in His being and that so He has made it. We have to see that Nature devouring her children, Time eating up the lives of creatures, Death universal and ineluctable and the violence of the Rudra* forces in man and Nature are also the supreme Godhead in one of his cosmic figures. We have to see that God the bountiful and prodigal creator, God the helpful, strong and benignant preserver is also God the devourer and destroyer. The torment of the couch of pain and evil on which we are racked is his touch as much as happiness and sweetness and pleasure. It is only when we see with the eye of the complete union and feel this truth in the depths of our being that we can entirely discover behind that mask too the calm and beautiful face of the all-blissful Godhead and in this touch that tests our imperfection the touch of the friend and builder of the spirit in man. The discords of the world are God's discords and it is only by accepting and proceeding through them that we can arrive at the greater concords of his supreme harmony, the summits and thrilled vastness of his transcendent and his cosmic Ananda. . . .** For truth is the foundation of real spirituality and courage is its soul.*[7]

Then the wound is healed that seemed forever to divide the world between Satan and Heaven, as if there were nothing else but Good and Evil, with us in between like *an infant coddled and whipped into virtuous ways.*[8] All duality is a vision based on Ignorance. There is nothing but *the innumerable One*[9] everywhere, and "God's discords" to help the Godhead grow within us. Even so, quite a gap remains between this perhaps divine imperfection and the ultimate Perfection. Is not this cosmic Divine a lesser Divine? Should we not try to find elsewhere an untarnished, transcendent, and perfect Divine? *If there is an opposition between the spiritual life and that of the world, it is that gulf which he [the integral seeker] is here to bridge, that opposition which he is here to change into a harmony. If the world is ruled by the flesh and the devil, all the more reason that the children of Immortality should be here to conquer it for God and the Spirit. If life is an insanity, then there are*

---

*   One of the forms of the Divine.

** Divine joy.

so many million souls to whom there must be brought the light of divine reason; if a dream, yet it is real within itself to so many dreamers who must be brought either to dream nobler dreams or to awaken; or if a lie, then the truth has to be given to the deluded.[10]

But we are not entirely satisfied. We may accept that God is in all this evil and suffering, we may understand that the hidden Enemy who torments us is really the builder of our strength, the secret shaper of our consciousness; indeed, we may be the "warriors of the Light" in this dark world, like the rishis of old, but why the darkness in the first place? Why has He, Whom we conceive as eternally pure and perfect, become this world so scarcely divine in its appearances? What did He need Death and Falsehood and Suffering for? If this is only a mask, then why the mask? If it is only an illusion, then why this cruel game? Perhaps it is a blessing after all that the Lord did not make the world according to our idea of perfection, because we have so many ideas about what is "perfect," about what God should be, and especially about what He should not be, that there would be nothing left in our world after we had whittled away everything that protrudes, except for one big Zero that would not tolerate even the impurity of our own existence—or perhaps a military camp. *Virtue,* the Mother observed, *has always suppressed elements of life; if all the virtues of the different countries in the world were joined together, there would be hardly anything left of life.* Indeed, we still know only one kind of perfection, that which eliminates, not that which embraces all; yet perfection is *totality.* Because we see only one instant of Eternity at a time, and because that instant fails to contain what we wanted to see or to have, we complain and declare this world erroneously built; but when we emerge from our instantaneity and enter the Totality, everything changes, and we see Perfection in the making. This world is not finished; it is *becoming.* It is a progressive conquest of the Divine by the Divine for the Divine, on its way to becoming *the endless more that we must be.*[11] Our world is in evolution, and evolution has a spiritual meaning:

Earth's million roads struggled towards deity.[12]

What do we really know of the great earthly journey? To us, it appears tortuous, cruel, impure, but we have only just been born! We have hardly emerged from Matter, muddy, small, pain-ridden, like a god buried in a tomb who no longer sees, searching right and left, bumping into everything. But who knows what other birth, what recovered memory, what regained power await us farther along our path? This world is in the making, and we do not yet know the full story.

> *Seek Him upon the earth. . .*
> *For thou art He, O King. Only the night*
> *Is on thy soul*
> *By thy own will. Remove it and recover*
> *The serene whole*
> *Thou art indeed. . .*[13]

The Central Being. The Universal Person

"Thou art He"—such is the eternal truth. *Tat tvam asi*, thou art That. This is the Truth the ancient Mysteries taught and the later religions forgot. Having lost the central secret, they fell prey to all the aberrant dualisms, substituting obscure mysteries for the great, simple Mystery. "I and my Father are one," Jesus Christ said (John 10,30); "I am He,"—so'ham—the sages of India say; indeed, this is the truth *all* liberated men discover, whether they be from the East or the West, from the past or the present. This is the eternal Fact we must all discover. This "I," the self who asserts its identity with God, is not that of a privileged individual—as if there were any room left for a little personal and exclusive self in that triumphant blossoming, or as if the sages of the Upanishads, the Vedic rishis, or Christ had once and for all monopolized every divine relationship. This is in fact the voice of all men fused into a single cosmic consciousness, and we are all the sons of God.

There are two ways of making this Discovery, or two stages. The first one is to find the soul, the psychic being, eternally one with the Divine, the little light from that great Light: "The Spirit who is here in man and the Spirit who is there in the Sun, lo, it is One Spirit and there is no other," says the Upanishad*; "whoever thinks 'Other is he and I am other,' he knows not."** Some six or seven thousand years ago the Veda called this discovery of the Spirit within "the birth of the Son": "The red glowing mass of him is seen: a great god has been delivered out of the darkness." (*Rig Veda* V.1.2) In strikingly powerful words the Vedic rishis affirmed the eternal identity of Son and Father, and the divine transmutation of man: "Rescue thy father, in thy knowledge keep him safe, thy father who becomes thy son and bears thee." (*Rig Veda* V.3.9).

The moment we are born, we see that this soul within us is the same in all human beings, and not only in all beings but also in things, in a latent, unrevealed state. "He is the child of the waters, the child of the forests, the child of things stable and the child of things that move. Even in the stone he is there." (*Rig Veda* I.70.2). All is one because all is the One. Did Christ not say, "This is my body, this is my blood," of two most material, most earthly symbols—bread and wine—to convey that Matter, too, is the body of the One, the blood of God?‡ If He had not been already there in the stone, how would He have come to be in man, through what miraculous intervention? We are the result of an evolution, not of a sequence of arbitrary miracles. *All the earth-past is there in [our human nature] . . . the very nature of the human being presupposes a material and a vital stage which prepare his emergence into mind and an animal past which moulded a first element of his complex humanity. And let us not say that this is because material Nature developed by evolution his life and his body and his animal mind, and only afterwards did a soul descend into the form so created . . . for that supposes a gulf between soul and body, between soul and life, between*

---

*   *Taittiriya Upanishad* X.

**   *Brihadaranyaka Upanishad* I.4.10

‡   See Sri Aurobindo, *Eight Upanishads*, X.XI.

soul and mind, which does not exist; there is no body without soul, no body that is not itself a form of soul; Matter itself is substance and power of spirit and could not exist if it were anything else, for nothing can exist which is not substance and power of the Eternal. . . .[14] *The dumb and blind and brute is That and not only the finely, mentally conscious human or the animal existence. All this infinite becoming is a birth of the Spirit into form.*[15]

Once we have opened the doors of the psychic, a first phase of cosmic consciousness is unveiled. But the growing psychic, the consciousness-force growing increasingly alive and compact and strong inside, is no longer satisfied with a narrow individual form. Feeling itself one with That, it wants to be as vast as That, as universal as That, and to rediscover its innate Totality. *To be and to be fully is Nature's aim in us . . . and to be fully is to be all that is.*[16] We need totality because we *are* the Totality. The ideal that beckons us, the goal that guides our steps, is not really in front; it does not draw us, but pushes us; it is behind—as well as in front and inside. Evolution is the eternal blossoming of a flower that was always a flower. Without this seed in the depths nothing would move, because nothing would need anything. This is the world's Need—this is our *central being.* This is our brother of light, who sometimes emerges when all seems lost, the sunlit memory that churns us again and again and will not leave us in peace until we have recovered all our Sun. This is our cosmic center, as the psychic was our individual center. But this central being is not located in a particular point; it is in all points, inconceivably at the heart of each thing and embracing all things at the same time. It is supremely *within,* as it is supremely above and below and everywhere—it is a *giant point.*[17] When we have found it, all is found, and all is there. The adult soul recovers its origin, the Son recovers the Father or, rather, the Father, who became the Son, becomes Himself again: *There is a pushing back and rending or a rushing down of the walls that imprisoned our conscious being; there is a loss of all sense of individuality and personality, of all placement in Space or Time or action or law of Nature; there is no longer an ego, a person definite and definable, but only consciousness, only existence, only peace and bliss; one becomes immortality, becomes eternity, becomes infinity. All that is left of the personal soul is a hymn of peace and freedom and bliss vibrating somewhere in the Eternal.*[18]

We believed ourselves to be small and separated from one another, one person plus another person in the midst of separate things. We needed this separation to grow under our separate shells, lest we remained some undifferentiated mass of the universal plasma, a member of the flock without a life of his own. Through this separation we have become conscious. We are still incompletely conscious, and we suffer from being separated— separated from others, separated from ourselves, separated from things, because we stand outside the one point where everything unites.

> *The only way to set everything straight*
> *is to recover consciousness; and this is very simple.*
> *There is but one origin.*
> *This origin is perfection of the Truth,*
> *since it is the only truly existing thing.*
> *By manifesting outwardly, by projecting and scattering itself,*
> *it has produced what we see*
> *and lots of nice and brilliant little brains,*
> *in search of what they have not yet found;*
> *but they can find it,*
> *for what they seek is within them.*
> *The remedy is at the center of the ill.**

After we have suffered enough, through lives upon lives of this long evolution, after we have grown enough to realize that everything comes to us from outside, from a Life greater than ours, from a universal Mind and Matter vaster than ours, then the time comes to become consciously what we unconsciously always were—a universal Person: *Why shouldst thou limit thyself? Feel thyself also in the sword that strikes thee and the arms that embrace, in the blazing*

---

* The Mother, in a conversation with children.

of the sun and the dance of the earth . . . in all that is past and all that is now and all that is pressing forward to become. For thou art infinite and all this joy is possible to thee.[19]

Knowledge through Identity

We might suppose this cosmic consciousness to be a kind of poetic and mystical superimagination, something purely subjective and without any practical bearing. But first, we could try to clarify what we mean by "objective" and "subjective," because if we insist on using so-called objectivity as the sole criterion for truth, then this entire world is likely to escape us altogether—as our art, our painting, and even our science have been shouting to us for the last fifty years—leaving us merely with a few sure crumbs. It is true that roast beef is more universally verifiable and, therefore more objective, than the joy in Beethoven's last quartets; but that is a lessening of the world, not an enrichment. Actually, this is a false opposition. Subjectivity is really an advanced or preparatory stage for objectivity; once everyone verifies the reality of cosmic consciousness, or simply the joy in Beethoven's quartets, we may attain an objectively less barbarous universe.

Sri Aurobindo was not a man to be satisfied with cosmic dreaming. The authenticity of the experience and its practical relevance can be immediately verified by a very simple test, which reveals a new mode of knowledge through identity: we know a thing because we *are* that thing. Consciousness can move to any point of *its* universal reality, focus on any being, any event, and know it immediately and intimately, as one knows the beating of one's own heart, because everything now takes place within; nothing is outside or separate anymore. As the Upanishad long ago stated: "When That is known, all is known."* The first signs of this new consciousness are quite tangible: *One begins to feel*

---

* *Shandilya Upanishad,* II.2.

others too as part of oneself or varied repetitions of oneself, the same self modified by Nature in other bodies. Or, at the least, as living in the larger universal self which is henceforth one's own greater reality. All things in fact begin to change their nature and appearance; one's whole experience of the world is radically different from that of those who are shut up in their personal selves. One begins to know things by a different kind of experience, more direct, not depending on the external mind and the senses. It is not that the possibility of error disappears, for that cannot be so long as mind of any kind is one's instrument for transcribing knowledge, but there is a new, vast and deep way of experiencing, seeing, knowing, contacting things; and the confines of knowledge can be rolled back to an almost unmeasurable degree.[20]

This new mode of knowledge is not really different from ours. Indeed, any experience, any knowledge, of whatever order, from the most physical level to metaphysical heights, is secretly a knowledge through identity: we know because we *are* what we know. *True knowledge*, Sri Aurobindo said, *is not attained by thinking. It is what you are; it is what you become.*[21] Without that secret identity, that underlying total oneness, we would be unable to know anything about the world and beings. Ramakrishna crying out in pain and bleeding from the cuts of the whip that lashed the ox nearby, the psychic knowing that an object is hidden in a particular place, the yogi curing a sick disciple hundreds of miles away, or Sri Aurobindo preventing the cyclone from entering his room, are only a few striking illustrations of a natural phenomenon. What is natural is not separation, not differentiation, but the indivisible oneness of all things. If beings and objects were different from us, really separate from us, if we were not in essence this cyclone or that ox, this hidden treasure or that sick disciple, not only would we be unable to act upon them, feel them, or know them, but they would be invisible and nonexistent to us. Only like can know and feel like; only like can act upon like. We can know only what we are: *Nothing can be taught to the mind which is not already concealed as potential knowledge in the unfolding soul of the creature. So also all perfection of which the outer man is capable, is only a realizing of the eternal perfection of the Spirit within him. We know the Divine and become the Divine, because we are That already in our secret nature. All teaching is a revealing, all becoming is an unfolding. Self-attainment is the secret; self-knowledge and an increasing consciousness are the means and the process.*[22]

We have become separated from the world and other beings through the millennia of our evolution. We have formed egos, have hardened a few atoms of the Great Body, and have proclaimed "I" against all others, similarly hardened under an egoistic crust. Once separated, we could no longer see anything of what *we* were, formerly, in the great Mother-Unity. So we have invented eyes, hands, senses, and a mind to join with what we had excluded from our great Being, and we now believe that without these eyes, fingers, and heads, we can know nothing; but this is only our separatist illusion; our present indirect knowledge conceals and hides from us an immediate recognition without which our eyes, fingers, heads, and even our microscopes would not perceive nor understand anything, nor even work. Our eyes are not organs of vision but organs of division; when the Eye of Truth opens in us, those lenses or crutches are no longer needed. Ultimately, our evolutionary journey is a slow reconquering of what we had exiled, a revival of Memory. Our progress is not measured by the amount of inventions we create, which are merely artificial means of recovering what we have estranged from ourselves, but by the amount of the world that we are able to reintegrate and recognize as ourselves.

And this is joy—*Ananda*—because to be all that is is to have the joy of all that is.

The bliss of a myriad myriads who are one.[23]

"Whence shall he have grief, how shall he be deluded, who sees everywhere the Oneness?"*

---

* *Isha Upanishad,* 7.

CHAPTER 12

The Superconscient

The Riddle

A triple change of consciousness, then, charts our journey on earth: the discovery of the psychic being or immanent Spirit, the discovery of Nirvana or transcendent Spirit, and the discovery of the central being or cosmic Spirit. This is probably the real meaning of the Father-Son-Holy Ghost trinity of the Christian tradition. Our purpose is not to decide which experience is better than the other, but to verify them for ourselves: *Philosophies and religions dispute about the priority of different aspects of God and different Yogins, Rishis and Saints have preferred this or that philosophy or religion. Our business is not to dispute about any of them, but to realize and become all of them, not to follow after any aspect to the exclusion of the rest, but to embrace God in all His aspects and beyond aspect* [1]—this is the very meaning of an integral yoga. Still, we wonder if there is nothing beyond this triple discovery, because however supreme each of them may seem when we experience it, none gives us the integral fulfillment to which we aspire, at least if we consider that both the earth and the individual must participate in this fulfillment. Discovering the psychic being, for instance, is a great realization—we become aware of our divinity—but it remains limited to the individual and does not extend beyond

the personal walls that confine us. Discovering the central being
is a very encompassing realization—the world becomes our own
being—but we lose the sense of individuality; indeed, it would be
a mistake to think of a Mr. Smith sitting in the middle of his
cosmic consciousness and enjoying the view—for there is no more
Mr. Smith. Discovering the Transcendent is a very lofty realization, but we lose both the individual and the world—there is
nothing left but That, forever outside of the human play. In
theory, we can say that Father, Son, and Holy Ghost are one—in
theory we can say anything we like—but in practice, when we
experience them, each of these changes of consciousness seems to
be cut off from the others by a vast gulf. As long as we do not find
a practical way of reconciling that triple hiatus among pantheist,
individualist, and monist, there will be no fulfillment, neither for
the individual nor for the world. It is not enough to find our
individual center and leave out the totality of the world, or to find
the totality of the world and leave out the individual, and even
less so to find supreme Peace if both the world and our individuality are dissolved—"I do not want to be sugar," the great Ramakrishna exclaimed, "I want to eat sugar!" In this chaotic and
harried world where we have to act, to confront things, to become,
we need primordially to *be*. Without this being, our becoming is
squandered in the prevailing chaos. But without this becoming,
our being dissolves into a *blissful Zero*.[2] And without an individuality, what do marvelous realizations really matter, since we are no
longer there? Such is the contradiction we must resolve, not in
philosophical terms, but in terms of life and power of action. Until
now, such a reconciling path has seemed nonexistent or unknown;
this is why all religions and spiritualities have placed the transcendent Father at the top of the hierarchy, outside this whole unfortunate chaos, urging us to search elsewhere for the totality to
which we aspire. Yet intuition tells us that if we, beings endowed
with a body, aspire to totality, then totality *must* be possible; it
must be possible in a body, otherwise we would not aspire to it.
There is no such thing as "imagination"; there are only deferred

realities, or truths awaiting their time. In his own way, Jules Verne testifies to this. Is there not something else to discover, then, a fourth change of consciousness that would change everything?

In his iron cage in the middle of the courtroom, Sri Aurobindo had reached the end of the road. One after another, he had realized the Immanent, the Transcendent, and the Universal—that cage scarcely held anything more than a body: in his consciousness, he was everywhere at will. But perhaps he was recalling an individual named Aurobindo, who since Cambridge and his years in the West had continuously accumulated consciousness in that body, and now the infinite Consciousness was a reality, but that body remained the same as millions of others, subject to the same laws of Nature, hungry, thirsty, and occasionally ill, like all the other bodies, and advancing slowly but surely towards disintegration. The consciousness is vast, luminous, immortal, but underneath everything remains the same. And because he was clear-sighted, because he was no longer fooled by all the masks added on by morality or decency, perhaps he was also espying, in the subconscient, the animal grimace beneath the infinite Consciousness, and the same material squalor intact beneath the lovely halo—for underneath everything continues as usual, and nothing is changed. Perhaps he was also looking, beyond the cage, at all his other selves who continued to judge and hate and suffer. Who is saved unless all is saved? And what did that infinite Consciousness *do* for all these people? It sees, it knows, but what can it *do*? Had he not left Baroda to act, to do something concrete? There he was, watching everything in his infinite consciousness, experiencing the immense joy above, feeling *joy laugh nude on the peaks of the Absolute*,[3] but what could his joy do if the above were not also everywhere below? Below, everything continues as before, suffering, and dying. He was not listening to the judges, or even answering the questions on which his life depended; he was only hearing the Voice repeating: *I am guiding, therefore fear not. Turn to your own Work for which I have brought you to jail.* Thus Sri Aurobindo kept his eyes closed in that cage, searching within. Was there not a totality above that could be also the totality below? Had the road come to an end with this *golden impotence*?[4] What was the sense of this whole journey?

The soul, which for some inexplicable reason has come into this Matter, or becomes this Matter, evolves slowly over the ages; it grows, takes on an individuality through its senses, its mind, its experiences; more and more it recalls its lost or submerged divinity, its consciousness within its force, finally to recognize itself and return to its Origin, transcendent and nirvanic, or cosmic, depending upon its destiny and its inclinations. Is this whole saga, then, only a long and laborious trajectory from the Divine to the Divine through the dark purgatory of Matter? But why the purgatory? Why this Matter? Why ever enter it at all if it is only to get out? Some will say that the cosmic or nirvanic beatitudes of the end are well worth all the grievances of the journey. That may be so, but meanwhile the earth suffers; we may be beaming up there in supreme bliss, but torture, illness and death are still proliferating and thriving down here; our cosmic consciousness makes not an atom of difference in the earth's evolution, and our Nirvana still less. Some will say that every human being should do the same and awaken from his state of error—all right, but again why the earth if it is merely to awaken from the error of the earth? We speak of "the fall," of Adam and Eve, of some absurd original sin which ruined what God had made perfect in the beginning—yet everything is God! The serpent of paradise, if ever there were one, was God, and so were Satan and his Pomp and his Works. There is nothing but Him! Would He then be so clumsy as to fall unknowingly, so helpless as to suffer unwillingly, or so sadistic as to play at being at fault just for the fun of getting Himself out of His fault? Is the earth just a mistake? For if this earth does not have a meaning *for the earth*, if the suffering of the world does not have a meaning *for the world*, if it is only a place of transit to purge ourselves of some absurd mistake, then nothing and no one, neither supreme bliss nor ultimate ecstasy, will ever excuse this useless interlude—God did not need to enter Matter if it was to get out of it; God did not need Death and Suffering and Ignorance, unless this Suffering, Death, and Ignorance bear their *own* meaning, unless this earth and this body are ultimately the place of a Secret that changes everything, and not merely instruments of purgation or escape.

> *I climb not to thy everlasting Day*
> *Even as I have shunned thy eternal Night. . .*
> *Thy servitudes on earth are greater, king,*
> *Than all the glorious liberties of heaven. . .*
> *Too far thy heavens for me from suffering men.*
> *Imperfect is the joy not shared by all.*[5]

Yet, if we look more closely at this enigma, at this kernel of soul around which the whole mystery revolves, we must admit that the soul does not need in the least to be "saved"; it is forever free and pure, forever saved in its own light. The moment we enter the soul with our eyes wide open, we see that it is exquisitely divine and light, untouched by all the mud flung at it. It is the earth that must be saved, because it is overburdened; it is life that must be saved, because it is dying. Where is the seed that can perform that Deliverance? Where is the Power that will deliver? Where is the world's true salvation? The spiritualists are right in wanting us to taste the supreme lightness of the soul, but so too are the materialists, who churn Matter and seek to bring out wonders from that denseness. But they do not have the Secret. No one has the Secret. The wonders of the former have no body, and those of the latter no soul.

The body, yes, the body, which at first had seemed to be only an obscure instrument for the liberation of the Spirit, may be precisely, paradoxically, the place of an unknown totality of the Spirit: *These seeming Instrumentals are the key to a secret without which the Fundamentals themselves would not unveil all their mystery.*[6] "Turn to your own Work," said the Voice. This Work was not to bask in cosmic bliss, but to find here, in this body and for the earth, a new path that would integrate within a single form of consciousness the freedom of the Transcendent, the living immensity of the Cosmic, and the joy of an individual soul on a fulfilled earth and in a truer life. For *the true change of consciousness*, the Mother says, *is one that will change the physical conditions of the world and make of it a new creation.*

The Conditions of the Discovery

If we wish "to change the physical conditions of the world," that is, the so-called natural laws that rule our life and the world, and if we want to implement this change through a power of consciousness, then two conditions are required. First, we must work in our own individual body without seeking any escape in the beyond, since this body is the very point of insertion of consciousness into Matter; and secondly, we must seek to discover the principle of consciousness that will have the power to transform Matter. So far, as we can readily see, none of the forms of consciousness or levels of consciousness known to humanity has had the power to bring about this change, neither mental consciousness nor vital consciousness nor physical consciousness. True, through sheer discipline some individuals have managed to defy natural laws and to overcome gravity, cold, hunger, illness, etc. But, first, these were individual changes that could never be passed along, and secondly, they do not really transform Matter: the laws governing the body remain essentially the same, while certain special effects, supernatural in appearance, are superimposed more or less temporarily over nature. Here we can recall the example of another revolutionary yogi, a companion of Sri Aurobindo's, who was once bitten by a rabid dog. Using his power of consciousness, he immediately blocked the effects of the virus and went on with his life as if nothing had happened (let us note in passing that had this yogi been in a perfect state of consciousness, he could *not* have been bitten in the first place). But one day, during a particularly stormy political meeting, he lost his temper and flew into a rage at one of the speakers. A few hours later he was dying in the terrible throes of rabies. His power came only from the *control* of his consciousness, and the instant his consciousness faltered, everything returned as it was before, because the laws of the body had not been changed, only muzzled. Therefore, the kind of change Sri Aurobindo and Mother envision has nothing to do with acquiring more or less temporary "supernatural" powers and draping them over our natural powers, but with changing man's very nature as well as his physical conditioning; it is not control but actual transformation. Furthermore, if we seek an earth-wide realization, this new principle of existence, which Sri Aurobindo calls supramental, must definitively *establish* itself among us, at first in a few individuals, then, by contagion, in all those who are ready—much as the mental principle and the life principle have become naturally and definitively established on earth. In other words, it involves creating a divine superhumanity on earth, which will no longer be subject to the laws of ignorance, suffering, and decay.

The undertaking may seem formidable or chimerical, but this is only because we see things on the scale of a few decades. Actually, it would be very much in keeping with the evolutionary process itself. Indeed, if we take all this earthly evolution to be an evolution of the Spirit in forms, all these human births to be a growth of the soul and Spirit in man, we may doubt whether the Spirit will always be satisfied with human narrowness, just as we may ask why It should, at the end of the journey, simply return to Its supraterrestrial Glory and Joy, which It did not need to leave in the first place; after all, the Light is already there, eternally, immutably, and it hardly represents a conquest for the Spirit! But Matter . . . there is a heaven to be built! Perhaps It seeks to experience the same Glory and Joy in conditions seemingly contrary to Its own, in a life besieged by death, ignorance, and obscurity, in the multitudinous diversity of the world, instead of in a blank unity. Then this life and this Matter would at least have a meaning; no longer a purgatory or an empty transition to the beyond, but a *laboratory* where step by step—through matter, plants, animals, and then an increasingly conscious human being—the Spirit evolves the superman, the god: *The soul has not finished what it has to do by merely developing into humanity; it has still to develop that humanity into its higher possibilities. Obviously, the soul that lodges in a Caribbee or an untaught primitive or an Apache of Paris or an American gangster, has not yet exhausted the necessity of human birth, has not developed all its possibilities or the whole meaning of humanity, has not worked out all the sense of Sachchidananda in the universal Man; neither has the soul lodged in a vitalistic European occupied with dynamic production and vital pleasure or in an Asiatic peasant engrossed in the ignorant round of the domestic and economic life. We may reasonably doubt whether even a Plato or a Shankara marks the crown and therefore the end of the outflowering of the spirit in man. We are apt to suppose that these may be the limit, because these and others like them seem to us the highest point which the mind of man can reach, but that may be the illusion of our present possibility. . . . The soul had a prehuman past, it has a superhuman future.*[7]

Sri Aurobindo is not a theoretician of evolution; he is a practitioner of evolution. Whatever he said or wrote on evolution came to him through actual experience. We have jumped ahead in this discussion merely to shed some light upon his groping progress in the Alipore jail. He could see that that cosmic and blissful vastitude was not the place where any work could be done, that one had to come back down into the body, humbly, and search there. Yet, we may ask, if "the transformation" is to take place through a power of consciousness and not by some external machinery, what consciousness higher than the cosmic consciousness can there be? Is that not the top of the ladder and therefore the limit of power? The question is relevant if we wish to understand the practical process of the discovery, and eventually experience it ourselves. We might answer with two observations. First, it is not enough to attain higher powers of consciousness; there must be *someone* to embody them, otherwise we are like a hunter discovering fabulous treasures—through binoculars. Where is the "someone" in the cosmic consciousness? There is no one left. A present-day analogy may explain this better: we can send a rocket into the sun, thus reaching the apex of the world, but not the apex of man, who has not moved an inch in the process. The rocket has gone *out* of the earth's range. Similarly, the yogi concentrates on *one* point of his being, gathers all his energies like the cone of a rocket, breaks through his outer carapace, and emerges elsewhere, in another cosmic or nirvanic dimension.

*He mounted burning like a cone of fire.**

But *who* has realized cosmic consciousness? Not the yogi; the yogi goes on drinking, eating, sleeping, being ill at times like all human animals, and dying. It is not he, but a tiny point of his being that is experiencing cosmic consciousness, the very one on which he so earnestly concentrated to break through his carapace. The rest of his being, all the human and earthly nature that he has excluded from the experience, which he has repressed or mortified in order to better concentrate on that single point of escape, does not share in his cosmic consciousness, except through indirect radiation. Sri Aurobindo was therefore making this first important observation, that a linear realization, in one point, is not enough, but that a *global realization,* in all points—one that embraces the individual's entire being—is necessary. *If you want to transform your nature and your being, and participate in the creation of a new world,* the Mother says, *that aspiration, that one-pointed and linear push is no longer enough; you must embrace everything and contain everything in your consciousness.* Hence the integral yoga or "full yoga," *purna yoga.* We sought to get rid of the individuality as a burden preventing us from fluttering at will in the spiritual and cosmic expanses, but without it we can do nothing for the earth; we cannot draw below the treasures from above: *There is something more than the mere self-breaking of an illusory shell of individuality in the Infinite.*[8] Thus, with Sri Aurobindo, we are led to this first

---

* *Savitri* 28:80.

conclusion: *The stifling of the individual may well be the stifling of the god in man.*[9]

A second, even more important observation commands our attention. To return to the rocket analogy: the rocket can break through the earth's atmosphere at any point, taking off either from New York or from the equator, and still reach the sun. There is no need to climb Mt. Everest to set up the launching pad! Similarly, the yogi can realize cosmic consciousness in any point, or at any level, of his being—in his mind, in his heart, and even in his body—because the cosmic Spirit is everywhere, in every point of the universe. The experience can begin anywhere, at any level, by concentrating on a rock or a sparrow, an idea, a prayer, a feeling, or what people scornfully call an idol. Cosmic consciousness is not the highest point of human consciousness; we do not go above the individual to reach it, but outside. It is hardly necessary to ascend in consciousness, or to become Plotinus, in order to attain the universal Spirit. On the contrary, the less mental one is, the easier it is to experience it; a shepherd beneath the stars or a fisherman of Galilee has a better chance at it than all the philosophers of the world put together. What, then, is the use of all this development of consciousness if folk-like mysticism works better? We must admit that either we are all on the wrong track, or else those mystical escapades do not represent the whole meaning of evolution. On the other hand, if we accept that the proper evolutionary course is that of the peak figures of earthly consciousness—Leonardo da Vinci, Beethoven, Alexander the Great, Dante—we are still forced to acknowledge that none of these great men has been able to transform life. Thus, the summits of the mind or the heart do not give us, any more than the cosmic summits, the key to the riddle and the power to change the world: another principle of consciousness is required. But it must be another principle *without any break in continuity* with the others, because if the line is broken or if the individual is lost, we fall back into cosmic or mystical dispersion, thereby losing our link with the earth. To be conscious of Oneness and of the Transcendent is certainly an indispensable basis for any realization (without which we might as well try to build a house without foundations), but it must be done in ways that respect evolutionary continuity; it must be an evolution, not a revolution. In other words, we must get out without getting out. Instead of a rocket that ends up crashing on the sun, we need a rocket that harpoons the Sun of the supreme consciousness and is able to bring it down to all points of our earthly consciousness: *The ultimate knowledge is that which perceives and accepts God in the universe as well as beyond the universe and the integral Yoga is that which, having found the Transcendent, can return upon the universe and possess it, retaining the power freely to descend as well as ascend the great stair of existence.*[10] This double movement of ascent and descent of the individual consciousness is the basic principle of the supramental discovery. But in the process Sri Aurobindo was to touch an unknown spring which would change everything.

The Ascent of Consciousness

It is not enough to describe Sri Aurobindo's discovery, we must also understand how it is accessible to us. It is very difficult to draw a diagram, however, and say, "Here is the way," because spiritual development is always adapted to the nature of each individual. And for good reason: this is not about learning a foreign language but about oneself, and no two natures are alike: *The ideal I put before our yoga does not bind all spiritual life and endeavor. The spiritual life is not a thing that can be formulated in a rigid definition or bound by a fixed mental rule; it is a vast field of evolution, an immense kingdom potentially larger than the other kingdoms below it, with a hundred provinces, a thousand types, stages, forms, paths, variations of the spiritual ideal, degrees of spiritual advancement.*[11] Therefore we can give only a few pointers, with the hope that each person will find the particular clue that will open his or her own path. One should always keep in mind that the true system of yoga is to capture the thread of one's *own* consciousness, the "shining thread" of the rishis [*Rig Veda*, X.53], to seize hold of it, and follow it right to the end.

Since cosmic consciousness and Nirvana do not give us the evolutionary key we are seeking, let us resume our quest, with Sri Aurobindo, where he had left it at Baroda prior to his two great experiences. The first step is the ascent into the Superconscient. As we have said, as silence settles in the seeker's mind, as he quiets his vital and frees himself from his absorption in the physical, the consciousness emerges from the countless activities in which it was indiscernibly commingled, scattered, and it takes on an independent existence. It becomes like a separate being within the being, a compact and increasingly intense Force. And the more it grows, the less it is satisfied with being confined in a body; we notice that it radiates outward, first during sleep, then during meditation, and finally with our eyes wide open. But this outward movement is not just lateral, as it were, toward the universal Mind, universal Vital, and universal Physical; the consciousness also seeks to go *upward.* This ascending urge may not even be the result of a conscious discipline; it may be a natural and spontaneous need (we should never forget that our efforts in this life are the continuation of many other efforts in many other lives, hence the unequal development of different individuals and the impossibility of setting up fixed rules). We may spontaneously feel something above our head drawing us, like an expanse or a light, or like a magnetic pole that is the origin of all our actions and thoughts, a zone of concentration above our head. The seeker has not silenced his mind to become like a slug; his silence is not dead, but alive; he is tuned in upward because he senses a life there. Silence is not an end but a means, just as learning to read notes is a means to capture music, and there are many kinds of music. Day after day, as his consciousness becomes increasingly concrete, he has hundreds of almost imperceptible experiences springing from this Silence above. He might think about nothing, when suddenly a thought crosses his mind—not even a thought, a tiny spark—and he knows exactly what he has to do and how he has to do it, down to the smallest detail, as if the pieces of a puzzle were suddenly falling into place, and with a sense of absolute certainty (below, everything is always uncertain, with always at least two solutions to every problem). Or a tiny impulse might strike him: "Go and see so-and-so"; he does, and "coincidentally" this person needs him. Or "Don't do this"; he persists, and has a bad fall. Or for no reason he is impelled toward a certain place, to find the very circumstances that will help him. Or, if some problem has to be solved, he remains immobile, silent, calling above, and the answer comes, clear and irrefutable. When he speaks or writes, he can feel very tangibly an expanse above his head, from which he draws his thoughts like the luminous thread of a cocoon; he does not move, simply remaining under the current and transcribing, while nothing stirs in his own head. But if he allows his mind to become the least involved, everything vanishes or, rather, becomes distorted, because the mind tries to imitate the intimations from above (the mind is an inveterate ape) and mistakes its own puny fireworks for true illuminations. The more the seeker learns to listen above and to trust these intimations (which are not commanding and loud but scarcely perceptible, like a breath, more akin to feelings than thoughts, and astonishingly rapid), the more numerous, accurate, and irresistible they will become. Gradually, he will realize that all his acts, even the most insignificant, can be unerringly guided by the silent source above, that all his thoughts originate from there, luminous and beyond dispute, and that a kind of *spontaneous knowledge* dawns within him. He will begin to live a life of constant little miracles. *If mankind only caught a glimpse of what infinite enjoyments, what perfect forces, what luminous reaches of spontaneous knowledge, what wide calms of our being lie waiting for us in the tracts which our animal evolution has not yet conquered, they would leave all and never rest till they had gained these treasures. But the way is narrow, the doors hard to force, and fear, distrust and scepticism are there, sentinels of Nature to forbid the turning away of our feet from less ordinary pastures.*[12]

Once the expanse above becomes concrete, alive, like a spread of light overhead, the seeker will feel impelled to enter into a more direct communication with it, to emerge into the open, for he will begin to feel, with painful acuteness, how narrow and false the mind and life below are, like a caricature. He will feel himself colliding everywhere, never at home anywhere, and finally feel that everything—words, ideas, feelings—is false, grating. That's not *it*, never *it*; it's always off the point, always an approximation, always insufficient. Sometimes, in our sleep, as a premonitory sign, we may find ourselves in a great blazing light, so dazzling that we instinctively shield our eyes—*the sun seems dark in comparison*, remarks the Mother. We must then allow this Force within us, the Consciousness-Force that gropes upward, to grow; we must kindle it with our own need for something else, for a truer life, a truer knowledge, a truer relationship with the world and its beings—our *greatest progress [is] a deepened need.*[13] We must dismiss all mental constructions that at every moment try to steal the shining thread. We must remain in a constant *state of openness* and be too great for ideas—for it is not ideas that we need, but space. *We must not only cut asunder the snare of the mind and the senses, but flee also beyond the snare of the thinker, the snare of the theologian and the church-builder, the meshes of the Word and the bondage of the Idea. All these are within us waiting to wall in the spirit with forms; but we must always go beyond, always renounce the lesser for the greater, the finite for the Infinite; we must be prepared to proceed from illumination to illumination, from experience to experience, from soul-state to soul-state. . . . Nor must we attach ourselves even to the truths we hold most securely, for they are but forms and expressions of the Ineffable who refuses to limit itself to any form or expression; always we must keep ourselves open to the higher Word from above that does not confine itself to its own sense and the light of the Thought that carries in it its own opposites.*[14] Then, one day, because of our burning need, after being like a mass of compressed gas, the doors will finally burst open: *The consciousness rises*, says the Mother,

*breaking the kind of hard carapace, there, at the top of the head, and
one emerges into the light.*

Above was an ardent white tranquillity.[15]

This experience of the breaking through into the Superconscient, the passage from a past that binds us hand and foot to a
seeing future, is the starting point of Sri Aurobindo's yoga. Instead
of being underneath, forever weighed down, we are above, breathing in the open: *The consciousness is no longer in the body or limited
by it; it feels itself not only above it but extended in space; the body is
below its high station and enveloped in its extended consciousness . . .
it becomes only a circumstance in the largeness of the being, an
instrumental part of it . . . in the definitive realization of a higher
station above there is really no more coming down except with a part
of the consciousness which may descend to work in the body or on the
lower levels while the permanently high-stationed being above presides
over all that is experienced and done.*[16]

Ecstasy?

Once this breakthrough has been achieved, we must proceed
slowly and systematically. Indeed, the first impulse of the consciousness is to soar straight up, as if drawn upward, giving a
rocket-like feeling of infinite ascent, which culminates in a sort of
luminous nirvana. The blissfulness that accompanies this blossoming on "top" (or what appears to us to be the top), or this
dissolving, is so irresistible that it would seem utterly incongruous
to wish to descend to intermediate levels and seek anything else;
it would seem like a fall; all we want is remain as still as possible
so as not to disturb that magnificent Peace. In fact, we do not even
notice any intermediate levels between the exit at the top of the
head and the merging "all the way on top"; somewhat dazzled,
like a newborn baby opening his eyes for the first time, the seeker
cannot recognize anything in that undifferentiated whiteness, or

bluish whiteness, and soon loses his footing, i.e., falls into a trance or state of "ecstasy," as they say in the West, or *samadhi*, as they say in India. When he returns from that state, however, he finds himself exactly as before. *In his haste to arrive . . . [the seeker] assumes that there is nothing between the thinking mind and the Highest, and, shutting his eyes in samadhi, tries to rush through all that actually intervenes without even seeing these great and luminous kingdoms of the Spirit. Perhaps he arrives at his object, but only to fall asleep in the Infinite.*[17]

Naturally, upon his return, the seeker will say that this is a marvelous, indescribable, supreme state. And he is right, but, as the Mother remarked, *You can say anything you like about it, since you do not remember anything. . . . As you go out of your conscious being and enter a part of yourself that is completely unconscious or, rather, a zone with which you have no conscious connection, you enter into samadhi. . . . You are in an impersonal state, that is, a state in which you are unconscious; and naturally, this is why you don't remember anything, because you have not been conscious of anything.* Sri Aurobindo used to say that ecstasy is simply a higher form of unconsciousness. It may turn out that what we call Transcendent, Absolute, or Supreme is not what has often been described as an ecstatic extinction, but only the limit of our *present* consciousness. It seems absurd to say: "Here is where the world ends and the Transcendent begins," as if there were a gap between the two. (For a pigmy, for instance, the Transcendent might begin at the rudimentary c-a-t=cat of reason and the world might vanish no higher than the intellect.) There really is no gap, except in our consciousness. Perhaps evolving means precisely to explore farther and farther reaches of consciousness within an inexhaustible Transcendent, which is not really "above" or elsewhere outside this world but everywhere here, gradually unveiling itself before our eyes. For, if the prehistorical Transcendent was once located right above the protoplasm, then above the amphibian, then the chimpanzee, and then man, this does not mean it left the world of protoplasm to recede higher and higher, in a sort of constant race to exclude itself; it is *we* who have left the primitive unconsciousness to live farther ahead in an omnipresent Transcendent.*

Therefore, instead of swooning on top (or what he feels as the top), and assuming his ecstasy to be a sign of progress, the seeker must understand that it is a sign of unconsciousness and strive to uncover the actual life hidden beneath his bedazzlement: *Strive to develop your inner individuality,* said the Mother, *and you will become able to enter those same regions fully conscious, to have the joy of communion with the highest regions without losing consciousness and returning with a zero instead of an experience.*** And Sri Aurobindo insisted: *It is in the waking state that this realization must come and endure in order to be a reality of life. . . . Experience and trance have their utility for opening the being and preparing it, but it is only when the realization is constant in the waking state that it is truly possessed.*[18] The goal we are seeking is a state of integral mastery, not that of spiritual escapism, and that mastery is possible only in a continuity of consciousness. When we fall into ecstasy, we lose the "someone" who could be the bridge between the powers above and the powerlessness below.

After breaking through the carapace at the top of the head in Alipore jail, Sri Aurobindo began methodically to explore the planes of consciousness above the ordinary mind, just as in Baroda he had explored the planes of consciousness below. He resumed where he had left off the ascent of the great ladder of consciousness, which extends without gap or ecstatic interlude from Matter

---

* At this stage of our search, it is not possible to say more on the subject. The supramental experience would be needed to acquire the key to this false opposition.

** "Ecstasy," some have thought, would be better termed "enstasy." Is one then "in oneself" only when outside oneself? For "ecstasy"—*ex-stare*—means literally to be outside one's body or outside the perception of the world. To put it simply, our goal is an "in-oneself" that is *not* outside ourselves. Only when the supreme experiences can take place within our body and in the midst of everyday life will we be able to speak of "enstasy"; otherwise the term is misleading, though it perfectly illustrates the gulf we have created between life and Spirit.

to that unknown point where he would truly discover something new. For *the highest truth, the integral self-knowledge is not to be gained by this self-blinded leap into the Absolute but by a patient transit beyond the mind.*[19]

Beings and Forces

Constantly and unknowingly, we receive influences and inspirations from these higher, superconscious regions, which express themselves inside us as ideas, ideals, aspirations, or works of art; they secretly mold our life, our future. Similarly, we constantly and unknowingly receive vital and subtle-physical vibrations, which determine our emotional life and relationship with the world every moment of the day. We are enclosed in an individual, personal body only through a stubborn visual delusion; in fact, we are porous throughout and bathe in universal forces, like an anemone in the sea: *Man twitters intellectually (=foolishly) about the surface results and attributes them all to his "noble self," ignoring the fact that his noble self is hidden far away from his own vision behind the veil of his dimly sparkling intellect and the reeking fog of his vital feelings, emotions, impulses, sensations and impressions.*[20] Our sole freedom is to lift ourselves to higher planes through individual evolution. Our only role is to transcribe and materially embody the truths of the plane we belong to. Two important points, which apply to every plane of consciousness, from the highest to the lowest, deserve to be underscored in order for us better to understand the mechanism of the universe. First, these planes do not depend upon us or upon what we think of them any more than the sea depends on the anemone; they exist *independently* of man. Modern psychology, for which all the levels of being are mixed together in a so-called collective unconscious, like some big magician's hat from which to draw archetypes and neuroses at random, betrays in this respect a serious lack of vision: first, because the forces of these planes are not at all unconscious (except to us), but very conscious, definitely more so than we are; and secondly, because these forces are not "collective," in the sense that they are no more a human product than the sea is the product of the anemone; it is rather the frontal man who is the product of that Immensity behind. *The gradations of consciousness are universal states not dependent on the outlook of the subjective personality; rather the outlook of the subjective personality is determined by the grade of consciousness in which it is organized according to its typal nature or its evolutionary stage.*[21] Naturally, it is only human to reverse the order of things and put ourselves in the center of the world. But this is not a matter of theory, always debatable, but of experience, which everyone can have. If we go out of our body and consciously enter these planes, we realize that they exist outside us, just as the entire world exists outside Manhattan, with forces and beings and even places that have nothing in common with our earthly world; entire civilizations have attested to this, stating it, engraving it, or painting it on their walls or in their temples, civilizations that were perhaps less ingenious than ours, but certainly not less intelligent.

The second important point concerns the conscious forces and beings that occupy these planes. Here we must clearly draw a line between the superstition, or even hoax, arising from our "collective" contribution, and the truth. As usual, the two are closely intermingled. More than ever, the integral seeker must be armed with that *clear austerity* Sri Aurobindo mentions so often. He must not confuse super-reason with unreason. In practice, whenever we enter these planes consciously, whether in sleep or meditation or through deliberate exteriorization, we see two sorts of things: impersonal currents of force, which can be more or less luminous, and personal beings. But they are two forms of the same thing: *The wall between consciousness and force, impersonality and personality becomes much thinner when one goes behind the veil of matter. If one looks at a working from the side of impersonal force one sees a force or energy at work acting for a purpose or with a result, if one looks from the side of being one sees a being possessing, guiding and using or else representative of and used by a conscious force as its instrument of specialized action and expression. . . . In modern science it has been found that if you look at the movement of energy, it appears on one side to be a wave and act as a wave, on the other as a mass of particles and to act as a mass of particles each acting in its own way. It is somewhat the same principle here.*[22]

Some seekers may therefore never see beings, but only luminous forces; others will see only beings and never any force; it all depends on their inner disposition, on their form of aspiration, on their religious, spiritual, or even cultural background. This is where subjectivity begins, and with it the possibility of confusion and superstition. But subjectivity should not undermine the experience itself; it is merely a sign that the same thing can be viewed and transcribed differently depending on our nature—have two artists ever seen the same landscape in the same way? According to the experts in natural or supernatural phenomena, the criterion for truth should be an unchanging consistency of experience, but this is perhaps more likely a criterion of monotony; the very multiplicity of experiences proves that we are dealing with a *living* truth, not a wooden substance like our mental or physical truths. Furthermore, these conscious—highly conscious—forces can take any form at will, not to deceive us but to make themselves accessible to the particular consciousness of the person who opens himself to them or invokes them. A Christian saint having a vision of the Virgin and an Indian having a vision of Durga may see the same thing; they may have entered in contact with the same plane of consciousness, the same forces; yet Durga would obviously mean nothing to the Christian. On the other hand, if this same force manifested itself in its pure state, namely, as a luminous, impersonal vibration, it would be accessible neither to the Virgin worshiper nor to the Durga devotee; it would not speak to their hearts. Devotion, too, has its place, for not everyone has the necessary development to feel the intensity of love contained in a simple little golden light without form. Still more remarkably, if a poet, such as Rimbaud or Shelley, came in contact with these *same* planes of consciousness, he would see something completely different again, yet still the same thing; obviously, neither Durga nor the Virgin is of particular concern to a poet, so he might perceive instead a great vibration, pulsations of light, or colored waves, which in him would translate into an intense poetic emotion. We may recall Rimbaud: "O happiness, O reason, I drew aside the azure of the sky, which is blackness, and I lived as a golden spark of *natural* light." This emotional translation may indeed come from the same plane of consciousness, or have the same frequency, we might say, as that of the Indian or Christian mystic, even though the poetic transcription of the vibration seems far removed from any religious belief. The mathematician suddenly discerning a new configuration of the world may have touched the same height of consciousness, the same revelatory vibration. For nothing happens "by chance"; everything comes from somewhere, from a particular plane, and each plane has its own wavelength, its own luminous intensity, its own frequency, and one can enter the *same* plane of consciousness, the *same* illumination in a thousand different ways.

Those who have exceeded, or think they have exceeded, the stage of religious forms will jump to the conclusion that all personal forms are deceptive, or of a lower order, and that only impersonal forces are true, but this is an error of our human logic, which always tries to reduce everything to a uniform concept. The vision of Durga is no more false and imaginary than Shelley's poem or Einstein's equations, which were confirmed ten years later. Error and superstition begin with the assertion that *only* the Virgin is true, or *only* Durga, or *only* poetry. The reconciling truth would be in seeing that all these forms come from the same divine Light, in different degrees.

But it would be another mistake to think of the so-called impersonal forces as some improved mechanical forces. They have an intensity, a warmth, a luminous joy that very much suggest a person without a face. Anyone who has experienced a flood of golden light, a sapphire-blue blossoming, or a sparkling of white light knows beyond a doubt that with that gold comes a spontaneous and joyful Knowledge; with that blue, a self-sustaining power; with that whiteness, an ineffable Presence. Some forces can sweep upon us like a smile. Then one truly understands that the opposition between personal and impersonal, consciousness and force, is a practical distinction created by human logic, without much relation to reality, and that one need not see any person to be in the presence of *the* Person.

Practically, the one essential thing is to open oneself to these higher planes; once there, each person will receive according to his or her capacity and needs or particular aspiration. All the quarrels between materialists and religious men, between philosophers and poets and painters and musicians, are the childish games of an incipient humanity in which each one wants to fit everyone else into his own mold. When one reaches the luminous Truth, one sees that It can contain all without conflict, and that everyone is Its child: the mystic receives the joy of his beloved One, the poet receives poetic joy, the mathematician mathematical joy, and the painter receives colored revelations—all spiritual joys.

However, "clear austerity" remains a powerful protection, for unfortunately not everyone has the capacity to rise to the high regions where the forces are pure; it is far easier to open oneself at the vital level, which is the world of the great Force of Life and desires and passions (well known to mediums and occultists), where the lower forces can readily take on divine appearances with dazzling colors, or frightening forms. If the seeker is pure, he will see through the hoax either way, and his little psychic light will dissolve all the threats and all the gaudy mirages of the vital melodrama. But how can one ever be sure of one's own purity? Therefore, not to pursue personal forms but only a higher and higher truth, and letting It manifest under any form It chooses, will help us avoid error and superstition.

We can now try to describe these superconscious levels, as they appear when one does not succumb to ecstatic unconsciousness, and as Sri Aurobindo experienced them. Certainly, what is closest to the universal truth has nothing to do with forms, which are always limited and related to a given tradition or age (though these forms have their place and their truth), but with luminous vibrations. By "vibrations," we do not mean any lifeless waves of quantum physics, but movements of light, inexpressibly filled with joy, love, knowledge, beauty, and all the qualities manifested by the best of human consciousness, whether they be religious or not:

> *A light not born of sun or moon or fire,*
> *A light that dwelt within and saw within*
> *Shedding an intimate visibility. . . .*[23]

The Planes of the Mind

Before reaching the supramental plane, which is the beginning of the *higher hemisphere* of existence, the seeker will go through several mental layers or worlds, which Sri Aurobindo has respectively called, in ascending order, the higher mind, the illumined mind, the intuitive mind, and the overmind. We may of course use a different terminology, but these four zones correspond to very specific experiences, verifiable by anyone who has the capacity to consciously undertake the ascent.

Theoretically, these four zones of consciousness belong to the Superconscient. We say *theoretically*, because the superconscious threshold varies with individuals: for some, the higher mind or even the illumined mind is not superconscious, but a normal part of their waking consciousness, while for others, the mere reasoning mind is still a remote possibility of inner development; in other words, the line dividing the superconscient from the rest tends to recede upward as our evolution progresses. If the subconscient is our evolutionary past, the Superconscient is our evolutionary future, gradually becoming our normal waking consciousness.

We will not attempt here to describe what these higher planes of consciousness are in themselves, independent of man. Each of them is a whole world of existence, vaster and more active than the earth, and our mental language is inadequate to describe them; we would need the language of the visionary or the poet—"another language," as Rimbaud said. This is what Sri Aurobindo has created in *Savitri*, his poetic epic, to which we refer the reader.

> *A million lotuses swaying on one stem,*
> *World after coloured and ecstatic world*
> *Climbs towards some far unseen epiphany.*[24]

But we can say what these planes bring to man, how they change our vision of the world when we ascend to them.

The ordinary mind, which we all know, sees things one at a time, in succession, linearly. It cannot take leaps, for that would create holes in its logic and cause it to lose its bearings: things would become "incoherent," irrational, or vague. It cannot see more than one thing at a time, or a contradiction would arise; if it accepts a particular truth or fact within its field of consciousness, it must automatically reject all that is different from that particular truth or fact; it works like a camera shutter, letting in one and only one image at a time. Anything that is not part of its momentary vision belongs to the limbo of error, falsehood, or darkness. All things, therefore, are part of an inexorable system of opposites: white versus black, truth versus falsehood, God versus Satan, and this ordinary mind moves along like a donkey on a road, glancing at one tuft of grass after another. In short, the ordinary mind keeps punching out little pieces of time and space. The more one goes down the ladder of consciousness, the smaller the pieces. We can suppose that to a beetle, whatever crosses its path comes from the future to its right, cuts the line of its present and disappears into the past to its left; a man standing astride the beetle, who can be on the right and on the left at the same time, is simply miraculous and untenable, unless he has one leg in truth and the other in falsehood, which is not possible, therefore man does not exist—he is impossible in beetle terms. For us, the shutter has grown a little wider; future and past are no longer to the right and left in space, but yesterday and tomorrow in time—we have gained a little time since the beetle. But there is another, supramental consciousness that can widen the shutter even more, gain even more time, and stand astride yesterday and tomorrow; it sees simultaneously present, past and future, black and white, truth and so-called falsehood, good and so-called evil, yes and no—for all opposites are the result of dividing time into little pieces. We speak of "error" because we do not yet see the good it is preparing, or of which it is the visible half; we speak of "falsehood" because we have not yet had enough time to see the lotus blossom out of the mud; we speak of "black," but our daylight is black to one who sees the Light! Our error was the necessary companion of good; *no* was the inseparable other half of *yes*; white and black and all the other colors of the rainbow were the various transcriptions of a unique light gradually unveiling itself. There are no opposites, only complements. The whole story of the ascent of consciousness is the story of a widening of the aperture, the passage from a linear and contradictory consciousness to a global one.

But Sri Aurobindo does say "global," does say higher *hemi-sphere* of consciousness when speaking of the Supramental, because the higher truth does not exclude the earth; it is not whole without its lower half. What is above does not annul what is below, but fulfills it; timelessness is not the opposite of time, any more than two embracing arms are the opposite of the person embraced. The secret, precisely, is to find timelessness amidst time, the infinite in the finite, and the encompassing wholeness of things in the lowliest fraction. Otherwise no one is embraced and no one embraces anything.

This ascent of consciousness is not only the conquest of time, but also the conquest of joy, love, and vastness of being. The lower evolutionary levels do not cut only time and space into pieces; they cut up everything. A progressive *law of fragmentation*[25] presides over the descent of consciousness from the Spirit down to the atom—fragmentation of joy, fragmentation of love and power, and naturally fragmentation of knowledge and vision. Everything is ultimately broken down into a cloud of minuscule tropisms, a hazy dust of *somnambulist consciousness*,[26] which is already a quest for the Light, or perhaps a memory of the Joy. *The general sign of this descent is an always diminishing power of intensity, intensity of being, intensity of consciousness, intensity of force, intensity of the delight in things and the delight of existence. So too as we ascend towards the supreme level these intensities increase.*[27]

a) The Ordinary Mind

The quality of light or the quality of vibrations is essentially what distinguishes one plane of consciousness from another. If we start at our own evolutionary level and consider consciousness in its aspect of light, from which all the other levels derive, the ordinary mind appears to the seeing eye as a grayish mass with many darker tiny spots or fairly obscure vibratory nodules, like a cloud of flies swarming about people's heads and representing their thousand and one thoughts; they come and go and swirl about endlessly, migrating from one person to the next. Occasionally, a little burst of light, a little joy, a little flame of love dancing amid this grayness, may descend from above. But this *ground of neutrality*, as Sri Aurobindo calls it, is so thick, so pervasive, that it swallows up and discolors everything, pulling down everything into its obscure gravitation; we cannot bear joy, or pain, for too long, cannot bear too much light; everything is small, spasmodic, soon quenched. And everything is subject to a thousand conditions.

b) The Higher Mind

This new degree is frequently found in philosophers and thinkers. It is less opaque, freer. The background is no longer so gray, or there is a bluish tinge to it, and the little descending bursts of light are less rapidly swallowed up. They are also more intense, more abundant and frequent. Joy tends to last longer; love tends to be more encompassing and less subject to the countless conditions of the lower levels: one begins to know what joy and love are in themselves, without cause. But the light is still cold, somewhat hard. It is still a heavy mental substance catching the light from above and mixing it with its own substance, covering it with a thinking layer without even being aware of it, and therefore understanding the light received only after a long process of logicalization, dilution, and fragmentation into pages, words or ideas. Further, the pages and paragraphs of the higher mind derive from a single point of light, or a small number of points (this is its own preset conclusion; a small drop of intuition hurriedly digested), and so it goes to a great deal of trouble to eliminate from its development anything that might contradict its conclusion. Indeed, it can open itself to higher planes and receive flashes, but this is not its normal altitude; its mental substance is designed to break down the light. It cannot understand unless it first explains.

c) The Illumined Mind

The illumined mind has a different nature. As the higher mind gradually accepts silence, it gains access to this region, meaning that its substance gradually clarifies, and what came one drop at a time now comes flowing in: *The ground is no longer a general neutrality but pure spiritual ease and happiness upon which the special tones of the aesthetic consciousness come out or from which they arise. This is the first fundamental change.*[28] The consciousness is filled with a flood of light, often golden, infused with colors that vary with the inner state; this is a *luminous irruption.* And simultaneously, a state of enthusiasm, in the Greek sense of the word, a sudden awakening as if the whole being were on the alert, immersed in a very fast rhythm and in a brand-new world, with new values, new perspectives, and unexpected associations. The smoke screen of the world is lifted. Everything is interconnected within a great, joyous vibration. Life becomes vaster, truer, more alive; little truths twinkle everywhere, wordlessly, as if each thing held a secret, a special sense, a special life. One bathes in an indescribable *state of truth*, without understanding anything about it—it just *is*. And it is marvelously. It is light, alive, loving.

This luminous flood will translate differently in different people (one is always too quick to give it a form instead of letting it quietly permeate the being and do its work of clarification). For some, there will be a sudden poetic blossoming, others will see new architectural forms, others will pursue new scientific discoveries, while still others will worship their God. Generally, the access to this new consciousness is accompanied by a spontaneous flowering of creative energies, particularly in the poetic field. It is interesting to note the number of poets of all languages—Chinese, Indian, English, etc.—among Sri Aurobindo's disciples, as if poetry and art were the first practical result of his yoga: *I have seen both in myself and others a sudden flowering of capacities in every kind of activity come by the opening of consciousness,—so that one who laboured long without the least success to express himself in rhythm becomes a master of poetic language and cadences in a day. It is a question of the right silence in the mind and the right openness to the Word that is trying to express itself—for the Word is there ready formed in those inner planes where all artistic forms take birth, but it is the transmitting mind that must change and become a perfect channel and not an obstacle.*[29]

Poetry is the most convenient means of conveying what these higher planes of consciousness are. In a poem's rhythm one can easily perceive vibrations. We will therefore use poetry to convey a sense of what these higher planes are, even though the Superconscient is not the sole privilege of poets. In his vast correspondence on poetry and in his *Future Poetry*, Sri Aurobindo has given numerous instances of poetry issuing from the illumined mind. It is naturally Shakespeare who would give us the most abundant examples, provided we let go of the external meaning and listen to what vibrates behind the words; for poetry and all the arts are ultimately a means of capturing a tiny ineffable note, a mere nothing, a "nothing" that still constitutes life's very essence:

> . . . that his virtues
> Will plead like angels, trumpet-tongued. . .
> And, pity, like a naked new-born babe
> Striding the blast, or heaven's cherubin, horsed
> Upon the sightless couriers of the air
> Shall blow the horrid deed in every eye
> That tears shall drown the wind.

A poem is not "illumined" because of its meaning; it is illumined because it embodies the particular note of that plane. We could find the same note in a painting by Rembrandt, a musical composition by César Franck, or simply in a friend's words; it is the touch of truth behind, the little vibration that goes straight to our heart, for which the poem, the canvas, or the sonata are only more or less adequate transcriptions. The higher one rises, the purer, more luminous, vast, and powerful is the vibration. When Wordsworth says:

> And beauty born of murmuring sound
> Shall pass into her face. . . ,

the vibration is almost palpable, so strong is its presence. Yet this is not an illumined vibration; it does not come from above the head but from the heart. Moreover, it has nothing to do with the meaning of the lines; the words are merely the garments of the vibration. Whereas this line by Francis Thompson issues straight from the illumined mind:

> The abashless inquisition of each star.

What essentially distinguishes the works that come from this plane is what Sri Aurobindo calls a *luminous sweep*, a sudden flooding of light. The vibration is unlike any other, always eliciting a kind of shock, and then something keeps vibrating long afterward, like a tuning fork. Nevertheless, it seldom remains pure through the entire work, for the movement of the work follows that of consciousness, with its highs and lows, unless it is created even through a special discipline. The last three lines in the

Shakespearean passage quoted above fall away from the illumined overhead inspiration; they contain some vital and also some ordinary mental consciousness.

Along with its beauty, we are also discovering the limits of the illumined mind: illumined poetry produces streams of images and revelatory words (because vision, and even hearing, often open at this stage), almost an avalanche of luxuriant, sometimes incoherent images, as if the consciousness were hard put to contain the flood of light and unaccustomed intensity; it is overwhelmed. Enthusiasm easily changes into exhilaration, and if the rest of the being has not been sufficiently prepared and purified, any of the lower parts can seize hold of the descending light and force and use them for their own ends; this is a frequent snare. Whenever the lower parts of the being, especially the vital, seize upon the luminous flood, they harden it, dramatize it, distort it. There is still power, but compelling and hard—while the essence of the illumined mind is joy. Here we could cite the names of many poets and creative geniuses.* Furthermore, the substance of the illumined mind is not truly transparent, but only translucent; its light is diffused, somewhat as if it could feel the truth everywhere without concretely touching it; hence the frequent instances of incoherence and vagueness. It is only the beginning of a new birth. Before going higher, more purification is necessary, and above all more peace, more natural equilibrium, and more silence. The higher we ascend in consciousness, the sturdier the equilibrium required.

---

* It may be worthwhile to stress the great difference between an individual who receives occasional inspirations or illuminations, often of an unreliable nature, and one who has systematically developed his consciousness, so that he can settle at will on any level of consciousness, remain there as long as he wishes, and receive without distortion the corresponding inspirations and illuminations. This is the task of the integral yoga.

d) The Intuitive Mind

The intuitive mind differs from the illumined mind by its clear transparency. It is quicksilver, skipping barefoot from rock to rock. Unlike the higher mind, it is not hampered by the mental orthopedic braces that shackle us to the ground, as if knowledge forever depended upon the ponderous volume of our reflections. Knowledge is a flash bursting forth from the silence. It is right there, not really higher or deeper, but just before our eyes, waiting for us to become a little clear. It is not so much a matter of raising ourselves as of clearing our obstructions. In spring, the rice fields of India stretch before the eye, quiet and green, laden with sweet fragrance, beneath a heavy sky; suddenly, with a single cry, thousands of parrots take flight. Yet we had seen nothing. It so sudden, lightning-fast—like the incredible rapidity with which the consciousness clears up. One mere detail, one sound, one drop of light, and a whole magnificent, overflowing world appears—thousands of imperceptible birds in the flash of a wing. Intuition reproduces, on our scale, the original mystery of a great Gaze: a mighty glance that has seen all, known all, and that delights at seeing bit by bit, slowly, successively, temporally, from a myriad points of view, what It had once wholly embraced in a fraction of Eternity.

An eternal instant is the cause of the years.[30]

With intuition comes a very special joy, different, it seems, from the illumined joy. No longer is there the sense of a flow coming from outside, but a kind of recognition, as if there were always two of us, a brother of light living in the light and a brother of shadow, ourself, living below, groping awkwardly in the darkness, repeating all the gestures and movements of the brother of light, imitating his knowledge and his great adventure, but in a shabby, stunted, clumsy way. Then, suddenly, there is a coincidence, and we become one. We are one in a point of light. For once, there ceases to be any difference, and this is joy.

When we are one in all points, then that will be the life divine.

This point of coincidence brings knowledge, which may translate itself in one form or another depending upon our current preoccupation, but it is always, essentially, a movement of identity, a meeting: we know because we recognize. Sri Aurobindo used to say that intuition is *a memory of the Truth.*[31] As the intuitive flash occurs, one clearly sees that knowledge is not discovering something unknown—one only discovers oneself! there is nothing else to discover—but a gradual recognition, in time, of that second of Light which we have *all* seen. Who has not seen, if only once? Who does not have that Memory in his life? Whatever our beliefs or unbeliefs, our capacities or incapacities, our lower or higher altitudes, there is always a moment in life that is *our* moment. Some lives last but a second, and all the rest is oblivion.

The language of intuition is concentrated into a concise phrasing, without superfluous words, in contrast to the opulent language of the illumined mind (which, through its very richness, nevertheless conveys a luminous rhythm and a truth, perhaps less precisely connoted, but warmer). When Plotinus packed the entire cycle of human effort into one phrase—"A flight of the Alone to the Alone"—he used a highly intuitive language, as do the Upanishads. But this quality also signals the limits of intuition: no matter how replete with meaning our flashes and phrases, they cannot embrace the whole truth; a fuller, more encompassing warmth would be needed, like that of the illumined mind but with a higher transparency. For *the Intuition . . . sees things by flashes, point by point, not as a whole.*[32] The area unveiled by the flash is striking and irrefutable, but it is only *one space of truth.*[33] Moreover, the mind hastens to seize upon the intuition and, as Sri Aurobindo remarked, it *makes at once too little and too much of it.*[33] Too much, because it unduly generalizes the intuitive message and would extend its discovery to all space; too little, because instead of letting the flash quietly perform its work of illumination and clarification of our substance, it immediately seizes it, coats it with a thinking layer (or a pictorial, poetic, mathematical, or religious one), and no longer understands its flash except through the intellectual, artistic, or religious form it has put over it. It is terribly difficult for the mind to comprehend that a revelation can be all-powerful, even overwhelming, without our understanding anything about it, and that it is especially powerful *as long as* it is not brought down several degrees, diluted, and fragmented in order, supposedly, to be "understood." If we could remain quiet while the intuitive flash occurs, as if suspended in its own light, without pouncing on it to cut it into intellectual pieces, we would notice, after a while, that our *entire* being has shifted to a different altitude, and that we possess a new kind of vision instead of a lifeless little phrase. The very act of explaining causes most of the transformative power to evaporate.

If, instead of rushing to his pen or brush or into a torrent of words to relieve himself of the excess of light received, the seeker strives to preserve his silence and transparency, if he remains patient, he will see the flashes gradually multiply, draw nearer, as it were, and observe another consciousness slowly dawn within him—at once the fulfillment and the source of both the illumined mind and the intuitive mind, and of all human mental forms. This is the overmind.

e) The Overmind

The overmind is the rarely attained summit of human consciousness. It is a cosmic consciousness, but with no loss of the individual. Instead of rejecting everything to soar to celestial heights, the seeker has patiently ascended each step of his being, so that the bottom remains linked to the top without any break. The overmind is the world of the gods, the source of inspiration of the great founders of religions. This is where all the religions we know were born; they all derive from an overmental experience in one of its countless aspects. For a religion or revelation, a spiritual experience, belongs to a certain plane; it does not come from God's thunders or from nowhere; those who incarnate the particular revelation have not conceived it from nothing: the overmind is their source. It is also the source of the highest artistic creations. But we must remember that, although it is the summit, it is still a mental plane.

When consciousness rises to that plane, it no longer sees "point by point," but *calmly, in great masses.*[34] There is no longer the diffused light of the illumined mind or the isolated flashes of the intuitive mind, but, to quote the wonderful Vedic phrase, "an ocean of stable lightnings." The consciousness is no longer limited to the brief present moment or the narrow range of its visual field; it is unsealed, seeing in a single glance *large extensions of space and time.*[34] The essential difference with other planes lies in the evenness, the almost complete uniformity of the light. In a particularly receptive illumined mind one would see, for example, a bluish background with sudden jets of light, intuitive flashes, or moving luminous eruptions, sometimes even great overmental downpours, but it would be a fluctuating play of light, nothing stable. This is the usual condition of the greatest poets we know; they attain a certain level or rhythm, a particular poetic luminousness, and from time to time they touch upon higher regions and return with those rare dazzling lines (or musical phrases) that are repeated generation after generation like an open sesame. The illumined mind is generally the base (an already very high base), and the overmind a divine kingdom one gains access to in moments of grace.

But for a full and permanent overmental consciousness, such as was realized by the Vedic rishis, for instance, there are no more fluctuations. The consciousness is *a mass of stable light.* There results an unbroken universal vision; one knows universal joy, universal beauty, universal love; for all the contradictions of the lower planes came from a deficiency of light, or narrowness of light, which lit up only a limited field; while in this even light the contradictions, which are like small shadowy intervals between two flashes or dark frontiers at the end of our light, melt into a unified visual mass. And since there is light everywhere, there are also, necessarily, joy and harmony and beauty everywhere, because opposites are no longer felt as negations or shadowy gaps between two sparks of consciousness but as elements of varying intensity within a continuous cosmic Harmony. Not that the overmental consciousness fails to see what we call ugliness and evil and suffering, but everything is connected within a comprehensive universal play in which each thing has its place and purpose. This is a unifying consciousness, not a dividing one. The degree of unity gives an exact measure of the overmental perfection. Moreover, with the vision of this unity, which is necessarily divine (the Divine is no longer something hypothetical or theoretical, but seen and touched, something that we have become naturally, just as our consciousness has become materially luminous), the overmental being perceives the same light everywhere, in all things and in all beings, just as he perceives it within his own self. There are no more separating gaps, no more lapses of strangeness; everything is bathed continuously in a single substance. The seeker feels universal love, universal understanding, universal compassion for all those other "selves" who are likewise moving toward their own divinity or, rather, gradually becoming the light that they are.

Therefore, we can attain the overmental consciousness in many different ways: through religious passion, through poetic, intellectual, artistic, or heroic zeal, or through anything that helps man to exceed himself. Sri Aurobindo assigned a special place to art, which he considered one of the major means of spiritual progress. Unfortunately, artists and creators too often have a considerable ego standing in the way, which is their main difficulty. The religious man, who has worked to dissolve his ego, finds it easier, but he rarely attains universality through his individual efforts, leaping instead beyond the individual without bothering to develop all the intermediate rungs of the personal consciousness, and when he reaches the "top" he no longer has a ladder to come down, or he does not want to come down, or there is no individual self left to express what he sees, or else his old individual self tries its best to express his new consciousness, provided he feels the need to express anything at all. The Vedic rishis, who have given us perhaps the only instance of a systematic and continuous spiritual progression from plane to plane, may be among the greatest poets the earth has ever known, as Sri Aurobindo has shown in his *Secret of the Veda*. The Sanskrit word *kavi* had the double meaning of "seer of the Truth" and "poet." One was a poet because one was a seer. This is an obvious and quite forgotten reality. It may be worthwhile, then, to say a few words about art as a means of ascent of the consciousness, and, in particular, about poetry at the overmental level.

Mantric Poetry

The planes of consciousness are characterized not only by different intensities of luminous vibrations, but by different sound-vibrations or rhythms one can hear when one has that "ear of ears" the Veda speaks of. Sounds or images, lights or forces or beings are various aspects of the same Existence manifesting differently and in varying intensities according to the plane. The farther one descends the ladder of consciousness, the more fragmented become the sound-vibrations, as well as the light, the beings, and the forces. On the vital plane, for example, one can hear the discordant and jarring vibrations of life, like certain types of music issuing from this plane or certain types of vital painting or poetry, which all express that broken and highly colored rhythm. The higher one rises, the more harmonious, unified and streamlined the vibrations become, such as certain great notes of Beethoven's string quartets, which seem to draw us upward, breathlessly, to radiant heights of pure light. The force of the music is no longer a matter of volume or muti-hued outbursts, but of a high inner tension. The high frequency of vibration turns the muti-hued rainbow to pure white, to a note so high that it seems motionless, as if captured in eternity, one single sound-light-force which is perhaps akin to the sacred

Indian syllable *OM—[the] Word concealed in the upper fire.*[35] "In the beginning was the Word," the Christian Scriptures also say.

There exists in India a secret knowledge based upon sounds and the differences of vibratory modes found on different planes of consciousness. If we pronounce the sound *OM*, for example, we clearly feel its vibrations enveloping the head centers, while the sound *RAM* affects the navel center. And since each of our centers of consciousness is in direct contact with a plane, we can, by the repetition of certain sounds (*japa*), come into contact with the corresponding plane of consciousness.* This is the basis of an entire spiritual discipline, called "tantric" because it originates from sacred texts known as *Tantra.* The basic or essential sounds that have the power to establish the contact are called *mantras.* The mantras, usually secret and given to the disciple by his Guru,** are of all kinds (there are many levels within each plane of consciousness), and may serve the most contradictory purposes. By combining certain sounds, one can at the lower levels of consciousness—generally at the vital level—come in contact with the corresponding forces and acquire many strange powers: some mantras can cause death (in five minutes, with violent vomiting), some mantras can strike with precision a particular part or organ of the body, some mantras can cure, some mantras can start a fire, protect, or cast spells. This type of magic, or chemistry of vibrations, derives simply from a conscious handling of the lower vibrations. But there is a higher magic, which also derives from handling vibrations, on higher planes of consciousness. This is poetry, music, the spiritual mantras of the Upanishads and the

---

* Looking at the diagram of the centers of consciousness, we notice that each center contains a Sanskrit letter: *Lam, Vam, Ram, Yam, Ham, Om,* in ascending order. These essential sounds represent the particular vibrations that command the forces of each plane. (See A. Avalon, *The Serpent Power.*)

** One may read mantras in a book and repeat them endlessly to no avail. They will have no power or "active force" unless given by a Master or Guru.

Veda, the mantras given by a Guru to his disciple to help him come consciously into direct contact with a special plane of consciousness, a force or a divine being. In this case, the sound holds in itself the power of experience and realization—it is a sound that makes one see.

Similarly, poetry and music, which are but unconscious processes of handling these secret vibrations, can be a powerful means of opening up the consciousness. If we could compose conscious poetry or music through the conscious manipulation of higher vibrations, we would create masterpieces endowed with initiatory powers. Instead of a poetry that is a fantasy of the intellect and a *nautch-girl of the mind*,[36] as Sri Aurobindo put it, we would create a mantric music or poetry *to bring the gods into our life*.[37] For true poetry is action; it opens little inlets in the consciousness—we are so walled in, so barricaded!—through which the Real can enter. It is a *mantra of the Real*,[38] an initiation. This is what the Vedic rishis and the seers of the Upanishads did with their mantras, which have the power of communicating an illumination to one who is ready.* This is what Sri Aurobindo has explained in his *Future Poetry* and what he has accomplished himself in *Savitri*.

Mantras, great poetry, great music, or the sacred Word, all come from the overmind plane. It is the source of all creative or spiritual activity (the two cannot be separated: the categorical divisions of the intellect vanish in this clear space where everything is sacred, even the profane). We might now attempt to describe the particular vibration or rhythm of the overmind. First, as anyone knows who has the capacity to enter more or less consciously in contact with the higher planes—a poet, a writer, or an artist—it is no longer ideas one perceives and tries to translate when one goes beyond a certain level of consciousness: one *hears*. Vibrations, or

---

* Unfortunately, these texts have reached us in translation, such that all the magic of the original sound has vanished. The remarkable thing, however, is that if one hears the original Sanskrit text chanted by someone who has knowledge, one can receive an illumination without understanding a word of what has been chanted.

waves, or rhythms, literally impose themselves and take possession of the seeker, and *subsequently* garb themselves with words and ideas, or music, or colors, during the descent. But the word or idea, the music or color is merely a result, a byproduct: it only gives a body to that first, highly compelling vibration. If the poet, the true one, next corrects and recorrects his draft, it is not to improve the form, as it were, or to find a more adequate expression, but to capture the vibrating life behind more accurately; if the true vibration is absent, all the magic disintegrates, as a Vedic priest mispronouncing the mantra of the sacrifice. When the consciousness is transparent, the sound can be heard distinctly, and it is a *seeing* sound, as it were, a sound-image or a sound-idea, which inseparably links hearing to vision and thought within the same luminous essence. All is there, self-contained, within a single vibration. On all the intermediate planes—higher mind, illumined or intuitive mind—the vibrations are generally broken up as flashes, pulsations, or eruptions, while in the overmind they are vast, continuous, and luminous in themselves, like Beethoven's great notes. They have neither beginning nor end, and they seem to be *born out of the Infinite and disappear into the Infinite*[39]; they do not "begin" anywhere, but rather flow into the consciousness with a kind of halo of eternity, which was vibrating beforehand and continues to vibrate long afterward, like the echo of *another* voyage behind this one:

> *Sunt lacrimae rerum et mentem mortalia tangunt.*

This line by Virgil, which Sri Aurobindo has cited as foremost among inspirations of an overmental origin, owes its overmental quality not to the meaning of the words but to the rhythm that precedes the words and follows them, as if they were inscribed on a backdrop of eternity or, rather, *by* Eternity itself. So, too, this line by Leopardi does not owe its greatness to the meaning but to that something so subtly more than the meaning, which quivers behind it:

Insano indegno mistero delle cose.

Or this line by Wordsworth:

Voyaging through strange seas of thought, alone.

And Sri Aurobindo also cited Rimbaud:

Million d'oiseaux d'or, ô future Vigueur!

Poetry is restored to its true role, which is not to please but to make the world more real by infusing more Reality into it.

If we are religious-minded, perhaps we will see the gods who inhabit this world. Beings, forces, sounds, lights, and rhythms are just so many true forms of the same indefinable, but not unknowable, Essence we call "God"; we have spoken of God, and made temples, laws or poems to try to capture the one little pulsation filling us with sunshine, but it is free as the wind on foam-flecked shores. We may also enter the world of music, which in fact is not different from the others but a special expression of this same, great inexpressible Vibration. If once, only once, even for a few moments in a lifetime, we can hear that Music, that Joy singing above, we will know what Beethoven and Bach heard; we will know what God is because we will have heard God. We will probably not say anything grandiose; we will just know that *That* exists, whereupon all the suffering in the world will seem redeemed.

At the extreme summit of the overmind, there only remain *great waves of multi-hued light,* says the Mother, the play of spiritual forces, which later translate—sometimes much later—into new ideas, social changes, or earthly events, after crossing one by one all the layers of consciousness and suffering a considerable distortion and loss of light in the process. There are some rare and silent sages on this earth who can wield and combine these forces and draw them down onto the earth, the way others combine sounds to write a poem. Perhaps they are the true poets. Their existence is a living mantra precipitating the Real upon earth.

This concludes the description of the ascent Sri Aurobindo underwent alone in his cell at Alipore. We have only presented a few human reflections of these higher regions; we have said nothing about their essence, nothing about these worlds as they exist in their glory, independently of our pale translations: one must *hear* and *see* that for oneself!

> *Calm heavens of imperishable Light,*
> *Illumined continents of violet peace,*
> *Oceans and rivers of the mirth of God*
> *And griefless countries under purple suns.*[40]

On May 5, 1909, after one year of confinement, Sri Aurobindo was acquitted. He owed his life to two unexpected events. One of the prisoners had betrayed him, denouncing him as the leader of the underground movement. His testimony in court would have meant the death penalty for Sri Aurobindo, but mysteriously he was shot in his cell. Then came the day of the trial, and as everyone sat expecting a verdict of capital punishment, Sri Aurobindo's lawyer was seized by a sudden illumination, which spread through the entire courtroom and profoundly shook the jury: "Long after he is dead and gone, his words will be echoed and re-echoed, not only in India, but across distant seas and lands. Therefore I say that a man in his position is standing not only before the bar of this court, but before the bar of the High Court of History." Sri Aurobindo was thirty-seven. His brother Barin, beside him in the cage, was sentenced to the gallows.*

Sri Aurobindo continued to hear the voice: *Remember never to fear, never to hesitate. Remember that it is I who am doing this, not you nor any other. Therefore whatever clouds may come, whatever dangers and sufferings, whatever difficulties, whatever impossibilities, there is nothing impossible, nothing difficult.*

It is I who am doing this.[41]

---

* His penalty was later commuted to life deportation to the Andaman Islands.

CHAPTER 13

Under the Auspices of the Gods

When he came out of the Alipore jail, Sri Aurobindo found the political scene purged by the executions and mass deportations of the British government. He resumed his work, however, starting a Bengali weekly and another in English, the *Karmayogin*, with the Gita's very symbolic motto: "Yoga is skill in works." At the risk of a new imprisonment, Sri Aurobindo affirmed once again the ideal of complete independence from and noncooperation with the British—except that now it was not only India's destiny that preoccupied him, but the world's. He had attained that overmental consciousness from which one sees, in a single glance, "great extensions of space and time," and he wondered about man's future. What could man *do*?

He had reached the limits of human consciousness. Higher up, there seemed to be nothing but a rarefied whiteness, fit for other beings or another mode of existence, but not for the earthlings' lungs. Whether one takes the mystic path or the slower path of the poet, the artist, or all the great creators, ultimately the consciousness seems to vanish at a white frontier, and everything is canceled out. The "someone" who could serve as a bridge disappears, all pulsations die out, all vibrations cease in a frost of light. Sooner or later, the human dissolves into the Nonhuman, as if the goal of this whole evolutionary ascent were only to leave the human smallness and return to the Source, which—logically—we never should have left in the first place. Even assuming there were some unknown gradation of consciousness beyond the overmind, would it not be a more rarefied, more evanescent gradation? One climbs higher and higher, more and more divinely, but farther and farther away from the earth. The individual may be transfigured, but the world remains as it is. What, then, is our earthly future if there is really nothing else but this overmental consciousness?

We all hope the development of consciousness and science combined will bring about a better human world, a more harmonious life. But life is not changed through miracles; it is changed through instruments, and we have only one instrument—the Mind. So if we want to look sensibly at our future, without being carried away by present circumstances and their apparent triumphs—others have triumphed before us, at Thebes, at Athens, at Ujjain—we must look more closely at our instrument, the Mind; for as the Mind is, so will be our future. Indeed, it would appear that the most beautiful ideas, the highest creative schemes, the purest acts of love all become distorted, counterfeited, polluted the minute they reach the level of life. Nothing reaches us in its pure form. Mentally, we have already devised the most ingenious systems, but Life has never accepted them. Barely twenty years after Lenin, to speak only of our present civilization, what remained of pure communism? What remains even of Christ beneath the mass of dogmas and prohibitions? Socrates was poisoned, and Rimbaud fled to the Abyssinian desert; we know the fate of the Fourierists, of nonviolence; the Cathars wound up at the stake. History keeps turning like a Moloch. We may now appear to be a "triumph" after many failures, but of what other greater triumph are we not the failure? Is this a chronology of victories or of defeats? Life seems made of a hopelessly distorting substance; everything gets swallowed up in it as in the sands of Egypt, leveled by some irresistible gravitational pull. *It is clear*, Sri Aurobindo remarked, *that Mind has not been able to change human nature radically. You can go on changing human institutions infinitely*

and yet the imperfection will break through all your institutions. . . .
It must be another power that can not only resist but overcome that
downward pull.[1]

Even if our ideas reached life in their pure form, they would
still be incapable of creating anything other than a military
order—or perhaps a holy, comfortable, religious order, but an
order all the same, because the Mind can only devise systems and
seek to confine everything in them. *The reason of man struggling*
with life becomes either an empiric or a doctrinaire.[2] It seizes upon
a bit of truth, one drop of divine illumination, and makes it a
universal law; it constantly confuses unity with uniformity. Even
when it is capable of understanding the need for diversity, it is
practically incapable of implementing it, because it only knows
how to deal with what is invariable and finite, while the world is
teeming with an infinite variety. *Ideas themselves are partial and*
insufficient: not only have they a very partial triumph, but if their
success were complete, it would still disappoint, because they are not
the whole truth of life and therefore cannot securely govern and perfect
life. Life escapes from the formulas and systems which our reason labors
to impose on it; it proclaims itself too complex, too full of infinite
potentialities to be tyrannized over by the arbitrary intellect of man.
. . . The root of the difficulty is this that at the very basis of all our life
and existence, internal and external, there is something on which the
intellect can never lay a controlling hold, the Absolute, the Infinite.
Behind everything in life there is an Absolute, which that thing is
seeking after in its own way; everything finite is striving to express an
infinite which it feels to be its real truth. Moreover, it is not only each
class, each type, each tendency in Nature that is thus impelled to strive
after its own secret truth in its own way, but each individual brings
in his own variation. Thus there is not only an Absolute, an Infinite
in itself which governs its own expression in many forms and tenden-
cies, but there is also a principle of infinite potentiality and variation
quite baffling to the reasoning intelligence; for the reason deals
successfully only with the settled and the finite. In man this difficulty
reaches its acme. For not only is mankind unlimited in potentiality,

not only is each of its powers and tendencies seeking after its own
absolute in its own way and therefore naturally restless under any rigid
control by the reason; but in each man their degrees, methods,
combinations vary, each man belongs not only to the common human-
ity, but to the Infinite in himself and is therefore unique. It is because
this is the reality of our existence that the intellectual reason and the
intelligent will cannot deal with life as its sovereign, even though they
may be at present our supreme instruments and may have been in our
evolution supremely important and helpful.[3]

But if evolution is, as Sri Aurobindo insists, an evolution of
consciousness, we may assume that humanity will not remain
stuck forever at the present mental level; its mind will become
illumined, more and more intuitive, and will perhaps finally open
to the overmind. One might suppose that a humanity opened to
the overmind would be capable of handling life's intricate diversity. The overmind is a godlike consciousness, indeed the very
consciousness of the greatest prophets the world has ever known,
a mass of stable light, so it would seem that everything should be
harmonized in that all-embracing light. Unfortunately, however,
two facts shatter this hope: the first has to do with the unequal
development of individuals and the other with the very nature of
the overmind itself. To be sure, the overmind seems formidably
powerful compared to our mind, but this is a superiority in degree
within the *same type*; it is not a transcendence of the mental
principle, but only an epitomization of it. The overmind can
broaden the human scope, not change it. It can divinize man, but
it also *colossalises*[4] him, as Sri Aurobindo puts it; for if man attaches
this new power to his ego instead of to his soul, he will become a
Nietzschean superman, not a god. We do not need a supercon-
sciousness; what we need is *another* consciousness. Even if man
accepted to obey his soul and not his ego, the overmind would
still not transform life, for the very reasons that prevented Christ
and all the great prophets from transforming life: because the
overmind is not a *new* principle of consciousness, but the very one
that has presided over our evolution since the appearance of man;

from the overmind have come all the higher ideas and creative forces, and we have lived under the auspices of the gods for thousands of years—sometimes through the voices of our prophets and religions, sometimes through the voices of our poets and great creators. It is plain enough, however, that none of them have transformed the world, though they may have ameliorated it. Can we even say that our present life is more livable than that of the Athenians?

The deficiencies of the overmind are retraceable to several causes. First of all, it embodies a principle of division. Yet, we had said earlier that the overmental consciousness is a mass of stable light, that it possessed the vision of a cosmic harmony and a cosmic unity, since it sees light everywhere as in itself. As such, it is not a principle of division within division (as is the ordinary mind), but a principle of division within unity. The overmind sees that all is one, but by the very structure of its consciousness it cannot, in practice, help dividing the unity: *It sees all but sees all from its own viewpoint.*[5] We need only remember the seemingly contradictory voices of our prophets to realize that each one saw the unity, but saw it *from his own viewpoint;* their consciousness were like floodlights sweeping across the world and capable of embracing anything in their beams without casting any shadows, but they were still beams ending in particular points. Hence, the series of apparently irreconcilable divine experiences or visions invariably confronting us: some see the cosmic Divine everywhere, others the Transcendent beyond the cosmos everywhere, and others the immanent Divine everywhere; or there is affirmed the truth of the personal God, the truth of the impersonal God, the truth of Nirvana, the truth of Love, the truth of Force, of Beauty, of Intellect—all the truths of the countless sages, sects, churches, and visionaries that have imparted the Word to us. All are divine truths, all are true and genuine experiences within themselves, but each one is still only a single ray of the total Light. Naturally, these great prophets were wise enough to recognize the truth in other divine expressions—they were wiser than their churches or their followers!—yet they still remained bound by an essential impairment of consciousness, which could not help dividing, as a prism divides light. Whether mental or overmental, the consciousness can experience only one truth at a time. This is what all the past and present mythologies express: each god is the incarnation of a *single* cosmic power—love, wisdom, destruction, preservation, etc. Buddha expresses the transcendent Nought that sees only Nought; Christ expresses loving Charity and sees only Charity, and so on; but no matter how high each of these truths may be, it is still only *one* truth. The farther the overmental truth (which is already fragmented) descends from plane to plane in order to express itself in life, the more fragmented it becomes; beginning in division, it inevitably ends in a superdivision. From the Buddha to the "vehicles," and from Christ to all the Christian sects, the process is visible. This applies not only to the spiritual or religious spheres but to all spheres of life, since the very function of the overmind is to bring into play *one* possibility and one only: *It gives to each* [possibility] *its full separate development and satisfaction. . . . It can give to intellect its austerest intellectuality and to logic its most sheer unsparing logicality. It can give to beauty its most splendid passion of luminous form and the consciousness that receives it a supreme height and depth of ecstasy.*[6] This is how millions of idea-forces have divided our world: communism, individualism; nonviolence, warmongering; epicureanism, asceticism, etc. Each is one part of the divine Truth, each a single ray of God. There is no such thing as absolute error, but only divisions of the one Truth. Of course, we can see the Unity, the truth in others, and attempt to form a synthesis, but even our synthesis will not bring about unity, because it will still be a mental synthesis, *a potpourri, not unity,* as the Mother says. It will be the prism pretending that all the colors do come from a single Light, but meanwhile, *in practice,* all the colors are divided in the world, and all the forces emanating from the overmental plane result from its own original division. Again, let us emphasize that this is not a matter of intellectual speculation, a philosophical dilemma to be resolved, but a cosmic fact, an organic reality like the needles on the porcupine's back. For division to cease, the prism has to go. The world is divided and will remain so inevitably as long as the mental principle of consciousness, whether high or low, ordinary or extraordinary, remains in control of the world.

It is nevertheless conceivable, in a nearer or farther evolutionary future, that one perfect overmental consciousness, or even several simultaneously, could incarnate on the earth. The less evolved human fraction rallying around these luminous centers would then be able to know a harmonious life and, to that extent, life would be changed; there would be a sort of unity. But it would be unity within a single luminous beam. Some would bask in the beam of pure Beauty, say, while others would be in the beam of integral Communism based on fraternal love (given the current evolutionary trend, however, these beams would more than likely be made of a hard light, centered around some economic or titanic ideology). Yet even if such divine centers were to appear on the earth, not only would their brand of unity go against life's diversity, but they would also be constantly threatened by the surrounding darkness; humans are at unequal stages of development—a fact we always tend to forget. This is the eternal weakness in all our grand schemes. Our centers of grace would be like *islands of light*[7] amid a less evolved humanity, which would naturally tend to overrun, obscure, or even extinguish the privileged light. We all know the fate of ancient Greece and Rome in the midst of a barbarian world. It appears that the world moves according to a wiser evolutionary law, whereby nothing can be saved unless everything is saved. Excommunications and hells are the infantile products of Ignorance, our brainchildren on the earth or above; there can be no paradise so long as a single man is in hell! Because there is only one Man. In addition, assuming that one of these islands of light could, through the Power of its center, prevent incursions from outside, nothing guarantees that this protection would outlast that Power. The history of all the religious, occult, initiatory, or chivalrous movements throughout the world testifies to the fact that, after the death of the Master and his immediate disciples, everything becomes scattered, vulgarized, degraded, distorted, or simply dies. Until now the law of the "downward pull" has seemed insurmountable. If evolution is to triumph, then life must be transformed in its entirety—not just a fragment of life, not just a privileged beam or a blessed island. For this, another type of Power is required, a Power capable of resisting the downward pull, another undivided or global principle of consciousness capable of containing the innumerable diversity of life without mutilating it.

If we look at the evolutionary future from an individual standpoint instead of a collective one, the overmind does not bring us, either, the living fulfillment to which we aspire. If the goal of evolution is merely to produce more Beethovens and Shelleys, and perhaps even a few super Platos, one cannot help thinking that this is really a paltry culmination for so many millions of years and so many billions of individuals expended along the way. Beethoven or Shelley, or even St. John, cannot be evolutionary goals, or else life has no true meaning—for who could fail to see that their works are admirable precisely because of their lack of contact with life? They all tell us that it is so much more beautiful up there—complete with millions of golden birds and divine music—than down here. Everything happens above, but what is happening here? Here, life goes on as usual. Some may say that these lofty thoughts, these poems and quartets and divine visionary moments are worth far more than all the hours of our life put together, and they are right . . . which is just the point! This in itself is the acknowledgment that life is woefully lacking, that life's very goal is not *in* life. We need a truth of body and of the earth, not just a truth above our heads. We do not seek recreation but a re-creation.

Until now, it is as if the individual's progress in evolution has been to discover higher planes of consciousness, and once there, to build his own private nest apart from the rest of creation, an island of light in the midst of economic philistinism: this one with music, that one with poetry, another with mathematics or religion, and yet another on a sailboat or in a monk's cell, as if the sole purpose of life in a body were to escape from both life and the body. Indeed, we need only look at our own life; we are never in it! We are before or after, engrossed in memories or in hopes; but the here-and-now is so miserable and dull . . . we do not even know if it exists, except in those moments that no longer belong to life as such. We cannot blame the churches, because we all live in the beyond, all the time; they merely preach a larger beyond. Even Rimbaud said it: "True life is elsewhere."

Sri Aurobindo was searching for a true life here. *Life, not a remote silent or high-uplifted ecstatic Beyond—Life alone, is the field of our Yoga.*[8] He was realizing that the summits of consciousness are not sufficient to turn life into a true life. We may have attained the overmind, found joy, a singing immensity, but not that of life, which continues to grate. *When you are high up in the consciousness,* the Mother remarked, *you see things, you know, but when you come back down in Matter, it is like water entering sand.* We have sent our rockets high into the spiritual heavens, have sung what is best in man without bothering with the lower levels, content if the brute in us was asleep enough not to upset our divine dreams; but this is precisely why life does remain brute, like ourselves: *To hope for a true change of human life without a change of human nature is an irrational and unspiritual proposition; it is to ask for something unnatural and unreal, an impossible miracle.*[9] This is also why our islands of light are periodically overrun by our own inner barbarity, or some insidious cancers, as were those islands called Athens and Thebes. This is why they die and die again, as if the Lord of Evolution were rubbing our noses in the earth each time to remind us that we have not found all the light when we have found it exclusively above. Life does not die because of exhaustion, but because it has not found itself. For centuries we have trod the upward path, conquered island after island, but we have found only half of the Secret, and we have been ruined each time; yet this may not be because history is hopeless, to punish us for our "sins," or to expiate some improbable Fault, but in order for us to find here, in Matter, the other half of the Secret. Pursued by Death and Unconsciousness, harassed by suffering and evil, the only solution left to us is not to escape but to find in the depths of Death and Unconsciousness, in the very heart of Evil, the key to divine life. It is to transform the barbarity and darkness down here, not to banish it from our islands. After the ascent of consciousness, the descent. After the illuminations above, the joy here and the transformation of Matter. *One can say that it is when the circle is truly completed and the two opposites are joined, when the highest manifests in the most physical—the supreme Reality in the heart of the atom—that the experience will reach its true conclusion. It seems,* said the Mother, *that one never really understands unless one understands with one's body.*

The Secret, what Sri Aurobindo called the Supramental, is not a further gradation above the overmind, not a super-mind or a super-ascent, but a new Auspice, unconnected to the gods and the religions, on which the very future of our evolution depends.

One evening in February 1910, less than a year after his release from Alipore, someone came to the office of the *Karmayogin* to warn Sri Aurobindo that he was to be arrested again and deported to the Andaman Islands. Suddenly, he heard the Voice speak three distinct words: Go to Chandernagore. Ten minutes later, Sri Aurobindo was aboard the first boat going down the Ganges. It was the end of his political life, the end of the integral yoga, and the beginning of the supramental yoga.

CHAPTER 14

The Secret

We can try to say something of this Secret, though keeping in mind that the experience is in progress. Sri Aurobindo began; he found the Secret in Chandernagore in 1910 and worked on it for forty years; he gave up his life to it. And so did Mother.

Sri Aurobindo has never told us the circumstances of his discovery. He was always extraordinarily silent about himself, not out of reserve but simply because the "I" did not exist. "One felt," his Chandernagore host reports with naive surprise, "one felt when he spoke as if somebody else were speaking through him. I placed the plate of food before him,—he simply gazed at it, then ate a little, just mechanically! He appeared to be inwardly absorbed even when he was eating; he used to meditate with open eyes."[1] It was only later, from his writings and some fragments of conversations, that his experience could be pieced together. The first clue came from a chance remark made to one of his disciples. It shows that from Alipore onward he was on the trail: *I was mentally subjected to all sorts of torture for fifteen days. I had to look upon pictures of all sorts of suffering.*[2] We must remember that in those worlds, seeing is synonymous with experiencing. Thus, as Sri Aurobindo ascended toward the overmind, his consciousness was descending into what we are used to calling hell.

This is also one of the first phenomena the seeker experiences, in varying degrees. *This is not a yoga for the weak,* as the Mother says, and it is true. For if the first tangible result of Sri Aurobindo's yoga is to bring out new poetic and artistic faculties, the second, perhaps even the immediate *consequence,* is to shine a merciless spotlight on all the undersides of the consciousness, first individual, then universal. This close, and puzzling, linkage between superconscient and subconscient was certainly the starting point of Sri Aurobindo's breakthrough.

The Gradations of the Subconscient

The "subconscious" of modern psychology is only the outer fringe of a world almost as vast as the Superconscient, with many levels, forces, beings (or being-forces, if we prefer). It is our immediate as well as distant evolutionary past, with all the impressions of our present life and all those of our past lives, just as the Superconscient is our evolutionary future. All the residues and forces that have presided over our evolutionary ascent from inanimate matter to animal to man are not only stored there, but continue to live and to influence us. If indeed we are more divine than we think by virtue of the superconscious future that is drawing us ahead, we are also more beast-like than we imagine thanks to the subconscious and unconscious past we drag behind us. This double mystery holds the key to the total Secret. *None can reach heaven who has not passed through hell.*[3]

True, one can reach spiritual heavens without even knowing these squalid places, except by accident. But there are different kinds of heavens, just as there are different kinds of hells (each level of our being has its own "heaven" and "hell"). Generally, the religious man leaves behind the individual self, thereby leaving behind the subconscient. He merely has to pass through one gate, with "guardians" unpleasant enough to account for all the "nights" and "temptations" mentioned in the lives of saints. But there is only *one* gate to pass through. Similarly, the heaven he aspires to means leaving the outer existence and plunging into ecstasy. As we have said, though, the goal of this yoga is not to lose consciousness, any more below than above, and in particular not to close our eyes to the conditions below. The integral seeker is meant neither for total darkness nor for blinding light. Everywhere he goes, he must see. This is the foremost condition of mastery. Indeed, we do not seek to move on to a better existence but to transform this one.

Just as there are several gradations in the superconscient, there are also several layers or worlds in the subconscient, several "dark caves," as the Rig Veda calls them. In fact, there is a subconscient behind each level of our being—a mental subconscient, a vital subconscient, and a physical subconscient, opening onto the material Inconscient.* There we will find, respectively, all the elementary and crude mental forms or forces that first appeared in the world of Matter and Life; all the aggressive impulses of the beginnings of Life, its reflexes of fear and suffering; and finally the forces of illness and disintegration, and Death, which subconsciously preside over our physical life. It becomes obvious, therefore, that no real life on earth is possible so long as all these worlds remain in control of our physical destiny. We are ourselves the

---

* For Sri Aurobindo, human psychological divisions follow our evolutionary ascent, which seems logical since it is in Matter, and beginning with it, that increasingly higher forms of consciousness have manifested. The Inconscient then represents our material, bodily base (Sri Aurobindo prefers to call it "Nescience," since this Inconscient is not really unconscious), while the Subconscient encompasses our earthly past and the Superconscient our future. Within these three zones rise the various universal planes of consciousness (which Sri Aurobindo sometimes calls "subliminal" in order to distinguish them from the subconscient, whose consciousness is very limited or very dim, *sub*-conscious, whereas the subliminal planes are full of highly conscious forces). The "personal" portion of these various zones is but a thin layer: our own body, plus whatever we have been able to individualize or colonize in this life and in previous lives.

battlefield: all these worlds, from the highest to the lowest, meet within us. So we must not run away, holding our noses or crossing ourselves, but squarely enter the battlefield and conquer:

> *He too must carry the yoke he came to unloose;*
> *He too must bear the pang that he would heal. . .* [4]

The Limits of Psychoanalysis

Contemporary psychology, too, has become aware of the importance of the subconscient and of the need to cleanse it. But psychologists have seen only half of the picture—the subconscient without the superconscient—presuming, moreover, that their small mental glimmers would be able to illuminate that den of thieves. They might as well try to find their way through the darkest jungle armed with a flashlight! In fact, in most cases they see the subconscient only as the underside of the small frontal personality, for there is a fundamental psychological law none can escape: descent is commensurate with ascent. One cannot descend farther than one has ascended, because the force necessary for descent is the very same force needed for ascent. If, by accident, someone descended lower than his capacity for ascent, this would immediately result in some serious accident, possession or madness, because the corresponding power would be missing. The closer we draw to a beginning of Truth down here, the more we uncover an unfathomable wisdom. Mr. Smith's obscure inhibitions are merely a few inches below the surface, we might say, just as his conscious life is merely a few inches above. So unless our psychologists are particularly enlightened, they cannot really go down into the subconscient, and therefore cannot really heal anything, except for a few superficial anomalies (and even then, there is constant risk of seeing these disorders resurface elsewhere, in some other form). One cannot heal unless one has gone all the way to the base, and one cannot go all the way to the base unless one has risen to the heights. The farther one descends, the more powerful the light needed, otherwise one is simply eaten alive.

If psychoanalysis were content to remain within its narrow limits, there would be nothing to fear; it would eventually realize its own limitations, while fulfilling in the meantime a useful social function by treating minor scratches. Unfortunately, psychoanalysis has become for many a kind of new gospel. By its insistent focus on all our murky possibilities rather than on our divine ones, it has become a powerful instrument of mental corruption. No doubt, in the course of evolution, our "blunders" eventually find their place and purpose; our moral, middle-class self-righteousness certainly had to be shaken, but the method chosen is a dangerous one because it calls up the disease without having the corresponding power to cure it. *It tends,* says Sri Aurobindo, *to make the mind and vital more and not less fundamentally impure than before.*[5] . . . *Modern psychology is an infant science, at once rash, fumbling and crude. As in all infant sciences, the universal habit of the human mind—to take a partial or local truth, generalize it unduly and try to explain a whole field of Nature in its narrow terms—runs riot here. . . . The psychoanalysis [especially] of Freud . . . takes up a certain part, the darkest, the most perilous, the unhealthiest part of the nature, the lower vital subconscious layer,* isolates some of its most morbid phenomena and attributes to it and them an action out of all proportion to its true role in the nature. . . . To raise it up prematurely or improperly for experience is to risk suffusing the conscious parts also with its dark and dirty stuff and thus poisoning the whole vital and even the mental nature. Always therefore one should begin by a positive, not a negative experience, by bringing down something of the*

---

* As we have said, there are numerous gradations and sub-gradations within the subconscient. We deliberately did not dwell on the description of these lower worlds; the seeker will experience them himself when the time comes. To give a specific mental form to these lower forces does not help to exorcise them, as some might imagine, but gives them an even greater hold on our consciousness. The mind is simply incapable of healing anything.

divine nature, calm, light, equanimity, purity, divine strength into the parts of the conscious being that have to be changed; only when that has been sufficiently done and there is a firm positive basis, is it safe to raise up the concealed subconscious adverse elements in order to destroy and eliminate them by the strength of the divine calm, light, force and knowledge.[6]

There is another drawback to psychoanalysis, a more serious one. If by chance psychoanalysts had the power to descend into the subconscient, not only would they not heal anything, not only would they risk setting in motion forces which, like the sorcerer's apprentice, they could not control, but even if they did have the power to master and to destroy these forces, they would very probably destroy the good along with the evil, thus irreparably mutilating our nature. For they do not possess knowledge. From their mental poise, they cannot see far enough into the future to discern the good that a certain evil may be preparing and the dynamic Force concealed behind the play of opposites. Another kind of power is needed in order to sort out this bizarre amalgam, and above all another vision: *You must know the whole before you can know the part and the highest before you can truly understand the lowest. That is the promise of the greater psychology awaiting its hour before which these poor gropings will disappear and come to nothing.*[6]

Here we touch upon the fundamental error of our modern psychology: it fails to understand anything because it searches below, in our evolutionary past. True, half the Secret may be there, but we still need the force above to open the door below. We were never meant to look behind, but ahead and above in the super-conscious light, because it is our future, and only the future can explain and heal the past: *I find it difficult,* Sri Aurobindo wrote to a disciple, *to take these psychoanalysts at all seriously—yet perhaps one ought to, for half-knowledge is a powerful thing and can be a great obstacle to the coming in front of the true Truth. . . . They look from down up and explain the higher lights by the lower obscurities; but the foundation of these things is above and not below. The supercon-*

scient, not the subconscient, is the true foundation of things. The significance of the lotus is not to be found by analyzing the secrets of the mud from which it grows here; its secret is to be found in the heavenly archetype of the lotus that blooms for ever in the Light above.[6]

We appear to progress from below upward, from past to future, from night to conscious light, but this is just our small momentary understanding that obscures the whole, for otherwise we would see that it is not the past that impels us, but the future that draws us and the light above that gradually pervades our darkness—for how could darkness ever have created all that light? If we had been born out of darkness, we would end up only in darkness. "This is the eternal Tree with its roots above and its branches downward," says the Katha Upanishad. (VI.I) We feel we are making great efforts to progress toward more understanding and greater knowledge; we have a sense of tension toward the future. But this is still our limited perspective. If we had a different perspective, we might see the superconscious Future trying to enter our present. And we would realize that our sense of effort is just the resistance put up by our denseness and darkness. The future does not move only from below upward, otherwise there would be no hope for the earth, as it would end up exploding in the sky from a supreme psychic tension, or falling back into its darkness. The future moves also from above downward; it penetrates deeper and deeper into our mental fog, into our vital confusion, into the subconscious and unconscious night, until it illuminates everything, reveals everything, heals everything—and ultimately fulfills everything. Yet the deeper it goes, the greater the resistance—for this is the Iron Age, the time of the great Revolt and Peril—but also the time of Hope. At the supreme point where this Future touches the rock-bottom past, where this Light bursts into night's nethermost level, God willing, we will find the secret of Death and of immortal Life. But if we look below and only below, we will find mud and only mud.

The Dark Half of the Truth

Now we are drawing nearer. The seeker began his journey with a positive experience. He set out on the way because he needed something else. He strove for mental silence and found that his very effort produced an Answer. He felt a descending Force, a new vibration within him, which made life clearer, more alive. Perhaps he even experienced a sudden tearing of the limits and emerged at another altitude. The signs might have come in a thousand ways to indicate that a new rhythm was setting in. But then, after this hopeful start, everything became veiled, as if he had been dreaming or had become carried away by some childish enthusiasm: something within him is now busy taking its revenge through a spell of skepticism, disgust, or revolt. This will be the second sign, perhaps the *true* sign, that he is progressing and has come to grips with the realities of his nature or, rather, that the descending Force has begun its churning work. Ultimately, progress is not so much a matter of ascending as of clearing up the prevailing obstructions—for when we are clear, everything is right there. Thus the seeker begins to discover his many obstructions. On the path of integral yoga, the feeling is often of finding the worst when we had wished for the best, of waging war when we had sought peace and light. Actually, let us face it, it *is* a battle. As long as we are swimming with the current, we can believe ourselves to be very nice, proper and well-intentioned individuals, but the instant we take another direction, everything begins to resist. We begin tangibly to appreciate the colossal forces that weigh upon human beings and stupefy them; yet it is only by trying to get out of their clutches that we can realize this. Once the seeker has had a first decisive opening above, once he has seen the Light, then almost simultaneously he feels a kick in the shins, as if something in him were in pain. Now he knows what Sri Aurobindo meant by *the wounded gloom complaining against light.*[7] And he will have learned his first lesson: each step upward is necessarily followed by a step downward.

Instead of taking these sharp jolts as a kind of fatality, the seeker will make them the basis of his work. Indeed, this dual movement of ascent and descent is the fundamental process of the integral yoga: *On each height we conquer we have to turn to bring down its power and its illumination into the lower mortal movement.*[8] Such is the price for transforming life, otherwise we merely poeticize and spiritualize on the peaks, while below the old life keeps bumping along. In practice, the downward movement is never created by an arbitrary mental decision; the less the mind interferes in this, the better. Besides, one wonders how the Mind could ever "descend," comfortably seated, as it is, behind its little desk. It is the awakened and individualized consciousness-force in us that does all the work, automatically. The moment we have attained a certain intensity of consciousness and light, it automatically exerts a pressure on the rest of our nature, which results in corresponding reactions of obscurity or resistance. It is as if an overdose of oxygen were abruptly pumped into the ocean's underworld: the deep-sea creatures would struggle frantically, or even explode. This reversal of consciousness is strange indeed, as if going from a well-lighted room to the *same* room filled with darkness, or from a joyous room to the *same* room riddled with pain: everything is the same, and yet everything is changed. As if it were the same force, the same vibratory intensity—perhaps even the same vibration—but with a minus sign in front of it instead of a plus sign. One can then observe, almost step by step, how love changes into hate, for example, or how the pure becomes impure; everything is the same, only reversed. Yet, as long as our psychological states are merely the reverse of one another, and our good the back side (perhaps we should say the front side?) of evil, life will never change. Something radically different is needed—another type of consciousness. All the poets and creative geniuses have known these swings of consciousness. Even as he experienced his *Illuminations,* Rimbaud visited strange realms that struck him with "terror"; he, too, went through the law of dark inversion. But instead of being unconsciously tossed from one extreme to another, of ascending without knowing how and descending against his will, the integral seeker works methodically, consciously, without ever losing his balance, and, above all, with a growing confidence in the Consciousness-Force, which *never* initiates more resistance than he can meet, and never unveils more light than he can bear. After living long enough from one crisis to the next, we will ultimately discern a pattern in the action of the Force, and will notice that each time we seem to leave the ascending curve or even lose something we had achieved, we ultimately retrieve the same realization, but on a higher, more expanded level, made richer by the part that our "fall" has added; had we not "fallen," this lower part would never have become integrated into our higher ones. Perhaps it was the same collective process that brought about Athens' fall, so that some old barbarians, too, might be exposed to Plato. The integral yoga does not follow a straight line rising higher and higher out of sight, toward a smaller and smaller point, but, according to Sri Aurobindo, a *spiral* that slowly and methodically annexes all the parts of our being in an ever vaster opening based upon an ever *deeper* foundation. Not only will we observe a pattern behind this Force, or rather this Consciousness-Force, but also regular cycles and a rhythm as certain as that of the tides and the moons. The more we progress, the wider the cycles, and the closer their relationship with the cosmic movement itself—until the day when we can perceive in our own descents the periodical descents of consciousness on earth, and in our own difficulties all the turmoil, resistance and revolt of the earth. Eventually, everything will become so intimately interconnected that we will be able to read in the tiniest things, the most insignificant events of daily life or the objects nearby, the signs of vaster depressions that will sweep over all men and compel their ascent or descent within the same evolutionary wave. Then we will understand that we are unfailingly being guided toward a Goal, that everything has a meaning, even the slightest thing—nothing moves without moving everything—and that we are on our way to a far greater adventure than we had ever imagined.

Soon, a second paradox will strike us, which is perhaps the very same one. Not only is there a law of ascent and descent, but there is also, it seems, a kind of central contradiction. We all have a goal in this life and through all our lives, something unique to express, since every human being is unique; this is our central truth, our own special evolutionary struggle. This goal appears only gradually, after numerous experiences and successive awakenings, as we begin to be a person with an inner development; we then realize that a kind of thread runs through our life, as well as through all our lives (if we have become conscious of them), indicating a particular orientation, as if everything always propelled us in the same direction—a direction that becomes increasingly poignant and precise as we advance. Yet as we become conscious of this goal, we also uncover a particular difficulty that seems to represent the very opposite or contradiction of our goal. It is a strange situation, as if we carried within us the exact shadow of our light—a shadow or difficulty or problem that confronts us again and again with a baffling insistence, always the same beneath different masks and in the most diverse circumstances, returning with increasing strength after every battle won and in exact proportion to our new intensity of consciousness—as if we had to fight the same battle over and over again on each newly conquered plane of consciousness. The clearer the goal becomes, the stronger the shadow. Now we have met the Foe:

> *This hidden foe lodged in the human breast*
> *Man must overcome or miss his higher fate.*
> *This is the inner war without escape.*[9]

Sri Aurobindo also calls it the Evil Persona. Sometimes, we can even negatively guess what our goal must be, before understanding it positively, through the sheer repetition of the same difficult circumstances or the same failures that seem to point to a single direction, as if we were forever revolving in an oppressive circle, drawing nearer and nearer to a central point that is both the goal and the opposite of the goal. *A person greatly endowed for the work,*

Sri Aurobindo wrote, *has always or almost always, perhaps one ought not to make a too rigid universal rule about these things—a being attached to him, sometimes appearing like a part of him, which is just the contradiction of the thing he centrally represents in the work to be done. Or if it is not there at first, not bound to his personality, a force of this kind enters into his environment as soon as he begins his movement to realize. Its business seems to be to oppose, to create stumblings and wrong conditions, in a word, to set before him the whole problem of the work he has started to do. It would seem that the problem could not, in the occult economy of things, be solved otherwise than by the predestined instrument making the difficulty his own. That would explain many things that seem very disconcerting on the surface.*[10] In her talks to the disciples, Mother stressed the same phenomenon: *If you represent a possibility of victory, you always have in you the opposite of this victory, which is your constant torment. When you see a very black shadow somewhere in you, something truly painful, you can be sure that you also have the corresponding possibility of light.* And she added: *You have a special goal, a special mission, your own particular realization, and you carry within yourself all the obstacles needed to make this realization perfect. Always you will find that shadow and light go together in you: you have a capacity, you have also the negation of that capacity. And if you discover a very dense and deep-rooted shadow in you, you can be certain there is also a great light somewhere. It is up to you to use the one in order to realize the other.*

Life's secret may have eluded us simply because of our imperfect grasp of this dual law of light and darkness and of the enigma of our double nature—animal and divine. Trained in a Manichaean conception of existence, we have seen in it, as our ethics and religions have taught us, a relentless struggle between Good and Evil, Truth and Falsehood, in which it was important to be on the good side, on the right hand of the Lord. We have cut everything in two: God's kingdom and the Devil's, the lower life in this world and the true life in heaven. We have tried to do away with the opposite of the goal, but have at the same time done away with the goal itself. For the goal is not to be amputated, either from the bottom or from the top. As long as we reject one for the other, we will fail miserably and miss the goal of existence. Everything is one: if we remove anything, everything falls apart. How could we possibly remove "evil" without blowing up the whole world? If a single man were to free himself from "evil," then the world would utterly disintegrate, because all is *one*. There is one single substance in the world, not two, not a good one and an evil one. One can neither remove nor add anything. This is why, also, no miracle can save the world. The miracle is *already* in the world, all possible lights are *already* in the world, all imaginable heavens are *already* here; any foreign element would upset the whole. All is right here. We are right in the middle of the miracle, only we are missing the key to it. Perhaps there is nothing for us to remove or to add, not even "something else" to discover, but *the same thing*, only perceived differently.

If we want to find the Goal, we must set aside our Manichaeism and come to a realistic appreciation of what Sri Aurobindo called "the dark half of truth." [11] *Human knowledge*, he wrote, *throws a shadow that conceals half the globe of truth from its own sunlight. . . . The rejection of falsehood by the mind seeking utter truth is one of the chief causes why mind cannot attain to the settled, rounded and perfect truth.* [12] If we eliminate everything that is wrong—and God knows this world is full of mistakes and impurities—we may well arrive at some truth, but it will be an empty truth. The practical approach to the Secret is, first of all, to realize, and then to *see* that each thing in this world, *even the most grotesque or far-wandering error,* [13] contains a spark of truth beneath its mask, because everything here is God advancing toward Himself; there is nothing outside Him. *For error is really a half truth that stumbles because of its limitations; often it is Truth that wears a disguise in order to arrive unobserved near to its goal.* [13] If a single thing in this world were totally wrong, the whole world would be totally wrong. Thus, if the seeker sets out with this premise—a positive premise—and ascends step by step, each time accepting to take the corresponding step downward in order to free the *same light*[14] hidden under every mask, in every element, even in the darkest mud, the most grotesque mistake or sordid evil, he will gradually see everything becoming clearer before his eyes, not only in theory but tangibly, and he will discover not only summits but *abysses of Truth*.[15] He will realize that his Foe was a most diligent helper, most concerned with ensuring the perfect effectiveness of his realization, first, because each battle has increased his strength, and then because each fall has compelled him to free the truth below instead of escaping alone to empty summits. Ultimately, he will understand that his particular burden was the very burden of our Mother the Earth, also striving toward her share of light. The Princes of Darkness are already saved! They are at work, the scrupulous exactors of an all-inclusive Truth, rather than a truth that excludes everything:

> *Not only is there hope for godheads pure;*
> *The violent and darkened deities*
> *Leaped down from the one breast in rage to find*
> *What the white gods had missed; they too are safe.*[16]

Now the seeker will realize that each thing has its own inevitable place in the whole. Not only can nothing be left out, but *nothing is more important or less important*, as if the total problem were represented in the smallest incident or the slightest everyday gesture, as much as in cosmic upheavals; perhaps, too, the total Light and Joy are contained as much in the most infinitesimal atom as in the superconscious infinities. Now the dark half of the truth has become illuminated. Every stumbling or error kindles a flame of pain and seems to produce a breach of light below; every weakness summons up a corresponding force, as if the energy of the fall were the very energy of the ascent; every imperfection is a step toward a greater fulfillment. There are no sins, no errors, but only countless mishaps that compel us to attend to the full extent of our kingdom and to embrace everything in order to heal and fulfill everything. Through a tiny crack in our armor, a love and compassion for the world have entered in, which none of the radiant purities can ever understand; purity is impregnable, self-contained, sealed off like a fortress; some fissure is needed for the Truth to come in!

[He] made error a door by which Truth could enter in.[17]

There is a truth of Love behind evil. The nearer one draws to the infernal circles, the more one uncovers the great *need* in the depths of Evil and begins to understand that nothing can be healed without a corresponding intensity: a flame is kindled within, more and more powerful and warm beneath the suffocating pressure—there is just Her, nothing but Her—as if Love alone could confront the Night and persuade it of its luminous half. As if all that Shadow had been necessary so that Love might be born. In truth, the heart of every shadow, of every evil harbors the inverse mystery. And as each of us bears or harbors a special difficulty, at once the contradiction and the sign of our destiny, it may be that, similarly, the immense "faults" of the earth—her sins and sufferings and the thousand gaping wounds of a pauper—are the very sign of her destiny, and that someday she will incarnate perfect Love and Joy because she will have suffered all and understood all.

As we progress, the superconscious line recedes upward and the subconscious line downward. Everything widens, everything is illuminated, but everything also closes in and converges around a sharp point of darkness, increasingly acute, crucial and pressing, as if we had turned for years and years—for lifetimes—around the same Problem without ever having truly touched it. Then, suddenly, it is right there, at the bottom of the hole, wriggling beneath the Light—all the evil of the world within one point. The time of the Secret is drawing near. For the law of descent is not a law of oppression, sin, or fall, any more than it is a law of repentance or heavenward escape, but truly a Golden Law, an unfathomable Premeditation that draws us simultaneously upward and downward into the depths of the subconscient and inconscient, to that *central point,*[18] that knot of life and death, shadow and light, where the Secret awaits us. The nearer we draw to the Summit, the more we touch the Depths.

The Great Passage

The last steps of the descent take place beyond the subconscient, in our evolutionary past, in our former, prehistorical consciousness, at the level where, for the first time in the world, life emerged from what seemed to be death; that is, at the border between the material inconscient and the physical consciousness—the witness and residue of that original birth—in our body. The organs and cells of our body have their own type of highly organized, efficient consciousness, which knows how to choose, to receive or to reject, and which can be manipulated once we have reached a sufficient yogic development. If it were merely a question of improving life's present conditions, the ordinary yogic consciousness would be enough: extension of life at will, immunity against diseases, and even a lasting youth are but some of the frequent results of that discipline. But, as we have said, we seek to change life, not just to improve its facade. Beneath our present physical consciousness lies a physical subconscient, the product of life's evolution in Matter, which keeps a record of all the old habits of life, of which the worst is the habit of dying—its reflexes, its fears, its contractions, and above all its habits of closure, as if it had retained the memory of the many protective shells it had to build around itself in order to protect its growth. In the very depths of this physical subconscient, where every form of consciousness or memory seems to die out, one reaches the bedrock, the initial Shell, the underlying Death from which life wrenched itself free. It is something very hard and very vast, so vast and so hard that the Vedic rishis called it "the infinite rock." This is the Inconscient. It is a wall—or perhaps a door. It is the bottom, or perhaps merely a crust. Moreover, it may not be completely dead or unconscious, for it does not feel like something negatively inert, but like something positively negative, as it were, something that refuses, that says *No* to life:

> *The stubborn mute rejection in Life's depths,*
> *The ignorant No in the origin of things.*[19]

If the very depths were total Nothingness, there would be no hope, and, in fact, nothing could have grown from nothing, whereas this bedrock bottom *is* something. If there is a *No*, there must be a *Yes* inside; if there is Death, there must be Life inside. And finally, if there is an end, there must be a beginning on the other side. Every negative is necessarily the other half of a positive. Every bottom is a surface covering something else. The very meaning of Sri Aurobindo's yoga is to uncover the positive of all these negatives, in every element and at every level of consciousness and, God willing, to uncover the supreme Positive (neither positive nor negative, it just *is*), which will unravel our dualities once and for all, those of the bottom as well as the duality of a life that dies or of a Death that lives.

At Chandernagore, Sri Aurobindo had reached the last levels of the physical subconscient. He was before a wall: *No, it is not with the Empyrean that I am busy, I wish it were. It is rather with the opposite end of things.*[20] Knowing the kind of resistance and violent reactions one meets when barely touching the mental and vital subconscient, the snakepit, one can imagine the difficulty of that descent. The farther one descends, the higher the consciousness required, the stronger the light, since one can only descend as low as one has ascended. And if one understands that consciousness is a force, as tangible as an electric current, one can imagine the traumas and ordeals the overmental power and light can cause as they pour like a cataract into the quagmire of the physical subconscient—*an assault of ether and of fire.*[21] There are tremendous difficulties, and even dangers, in this to which we will return when discussing the transformation. As long as we are merely involved with mental or vital resistances, our moral lies, we need only to cultivate willpower and patience, but when we descend lower we must face *the lies of the body*, as the Mother says, namely, diseases and death. This is why Sri Aurobindo and Mother insisted upon a sound physical base for their disciples: *Work from both ends; do not neglect one for the other.*

As he reached the extreme overmental frontiers, where "great colored waves" fade into white confines, Sri Aurobindo simultaneously touched the black rock at the bottom:

> *I have been digging deep and long*
> *Mid a horror of filth and mire. . . .*
> *A voice cried, "Go where none have gone!*
> *Dig deeper, deeper yet*
> *Till thou reach the grim foundation stone*
> *And knock at the keyless gate."* [22]

Then, one day in 1910, at Chandernagore, a strange thing happened. . . . But before describing the experience that would change the course of our evolution, let us stop to take stock and briefly review the present human condition. It is really quite simple: we are stuck in Matter, imprisoned in the Black Egg that constrains us on all sides every second of the day. There are not a hundred ways of getting out of it, but only two: one is to fall asleep (to dream, to fly into ecstasy, or to meditate, but all are more or less lofty, conscious or divine gradations of sleep), and the other is to die. Sri Aurobindo's experience, however, provides a third possibility, allowing us to get out without flying into ecstasy or dying— that is, to get out without actually getting out—thereby reversing the course of man's spiritual evolution, since the goal is no longer only above or outside, but inside; and, in addition, opening the door of waking life to all the dreams, all the ecstasies, and especially to all the powers that can help us incarnate our dreams and transform the Black Egg into an open, clear and livable place. That day of 1910, in Chandernagore, Sri Aurobindo had reached the very depths, had broken through all the squalid layers upon which Life has grown like an inexplicable flower. There was only that Light above shining more and more intensely as he went down, bringing out all the impurities one after another under its keen ray, as if all that night were drawing in an ever greater amount of Light, as if the subconscious boundaries were receding farther and farther downward in an ever greater concentration—the mirror image of the concentration above—and leaving just that one wall of Shadow beneath that one Light. Then, suddenly, without warning, in the depths of this "unconscious" Matter and in the very cells of this body, Sri Aurobindo was thrust into the supreme Light, without trance, without loss of individuality, without cosmic dissolution, and with his eyes wide open:

He broke into another Space and Time.[23]

Night, Evil, Death are masks. The supreme Opposition awakens the supreme Intensity, and the analogous becomes Itself—there is only One, *tad ekam*. The Solar World, the supreme, supramental, divine consciousness, of which all the other worlds are separate rays, was present in the very heart of Matter. The step above the overmind is not "above"; it is here within all things. The door below opens the door above and everywhere:

A fathomless sealed astonishment of Light.[24]
A grand reversal of the Night and Day
All the world's values changed. . . .[25]
The high meets the low, all is a single plan.[26]

The most remote Past touches the heart of the Future that conceived it, God-Spirit meets God-Matter, and there is a divine life in a body. *Sat-Chit-Ananda* above is *Sat-Chit-Ananda* below, Existence-Consciousness-Power-Joy. Evolution does not abort into a white or black sleep; nothing is swallowed up into Darkness; nothing is annihilated heavenward; everything connects at last in a perfect circle. Joy above is Joy below:

An exultation in the depths of sleep,
A heart of bliss within a world of pain.[27]

An active joy, a powerful illumination within our very veins, instead of a sterile bliss above our heads:

Almighty powers are shut in Nature's cells.[28]

For the Supramental is not a more ethereal consciousness, but a denser one. It is the very Vibration that creates and endlessly recreates Matter and the worlds. It is what can transform the Earth:

> *In the very depths of the hardest, most rigid,*
> *narrowest and most asphyxiating unconsciousness,*
> wrote the Mother, *I struck upon an Almighty Spring*
> *that cast me up forthwith into a formless,*
> *limitless Vast vibrating with the seeds of a New World.*

Such is the key to the Transformation, the key to overcoming the laws of Matter by using the Consciousness within Matter—Consciousness above is Consciousness below. It is the door to the future world and the new earth announced by the Scriptures two thousand years ago: "A new earth wherein the Truth shall dwell." (2 Peter 3. 13) For, actually, the earth is our salvation, the ultimate place of Victory and of perfect accomplishment. There is no need to escape to heaven. All is here, totally, in the body—Joy, Consciousness, supreme Powers—if we have the courage to unseal our eyes and to descend, to dream a living dream instead of a sleeping one:

> *They must enter into the last finite if they want*
> *to reach the last infinite.*[29]

At the same time, Sri Aurobindo was retrieving the lost Secret, that of the Veda and of all the more or less distorted traditions from Persia to Central America and the Rhine Valley, from Eleusis to the Cathars and from the Round Table to the Alchemists—the ancient Secret of all the seekers of perfection. This is the quest for the Treasure in the depths of the cave; the battle against the subconscious forces (ogres, dwarves, or serpents); the legend of

Apollo and the Python, Indra and the Serpent Vritra, Thor and the giants, Sigurd and Fafner; the solar myth of the Mayas, the Descent of Orpheus, the Transmutation. It is the serpent biting its own tail. And above all, it is the secret of the Vedic rishis, who were probably the first to discover what they called "the great passage," *mahas pathah*, (II.24.6) the world of "the unbroken Light," *Swar*, within the rock of the Inconscient: "Our fathers by their words broke the strong and stubborn places, the Angiras seers* shattered the mountain rock with their cry; they made in us a path to the Great Heaven, they discovered the Day and the sun-world," (*Rig Veda* I.71.2) they discovered "the Sun dwelling in the darkness." (III.39.5) They found "the treasure of heaven hidden in the secret cavern like the young of the Bird, within the infinite rock." (I.130.3)

Shadow and Light, Good and Evil have all prepared a divine birth in Matter: "Day and Night both suckle the divine Child."[30] Nothing is accursed, nothing is in vain. Night and Day are "two sisters, immortal, with a common Lover (the Sun) . . . common they, though different their forms." (I.113.2.3) At the end of the "pilgrimage" of ascent and descent, the seeker is "a son of the two Mothers" (III.55.7): the son of *Aditi*, the white Mother** of the superconscious infinite, and the son of *Diti*, the earthly Mother of "the dark infinite." He possesses "the two births," human and divine, "eternal and in one nest . . . as the Enjoyer of his two wives" (I.62.7): "The contents of the pregnant hill† (came forth) for the supreme birth . . . a god opened the human doors." (V.45) "Then, indeed, they awoke and saw all behind and wide around them, then, indeed, they held the ecstasy that is enjoyed in heaven. In all gated houses‡ were all the gods." (*Rig Veda* IV.1.18)

---

* The first rishis.

** This ancient tradition, known also to the Hebrews, seems to have been revived, quite literally, by Christianity and the immaculate conception of the Virgin Mary.

† The material Inconscient.

‡ On all the planes of our being or in all the centers of consciousness.

Man's hope is fulfilled as well as the rishi's prayer: "May Heaven and Earth be equal and one."[31] The great Balance is at last restored.

> *Heaven in its rapture dreams of perfect earth,*
> *Earth in its sorrow dreams of perfect heaven. . .*
> *They are kept from their oneness by enchanted fears.*[32]

And finally, there is joy—*Ananda*. It is at the beginning of things and at the end and everywhere, if we dig deep enough. It is "the well of honey covered by the rock." (*Rig Veda* II.24.4)

CHAPTER 15

The Supramental Consciousness

It is quite difficult to define the supramental consciousness in mental terms, for it is nonmental by definition, and it defies all our three-dimensional laws and perspectives. The word itself may mislead us, because it is not an epitome of human consciousness, but another type of consciousness. We might try to approach it by distinguishing two aspects, one of consciousness or vision, and one of power. But this means becoming caught in the mental trap again, because these two aspects are inseparable; this consciousness *is* power, an *active* vision. Often, when Sri Aurobindo and Mother tried to describe their experience, their remarks would echo one another in English and in French: Another language would be needed, *une autre langue*.

The Supramental Vision

The supramental vision is a global vision. The mind dissects little fragments and opposes them to one another. The overmind connects everything within a single beam, but its beam terminates in a single point, and it sees everything from its own particular point of view; it is unitary and universal either by way of excluding all other perspectives or else by annexing them. The Supramental, or Supermind, sees not only the whole of things and beings within a single vision, connecting all the beams together without opposing anything, but it also sees the point of view of each separate thing, each being, each force; it is an all-encompassing view that does not terminate in a single, central point but in myriads of points:

a single innumerable look. . .[1]

The supramental being sees things not as one on the levels surrounded by a jungle of present facts and phenomena but from above, not from outside and judged by their surfaces, but from within and viewed from the truth of their centre.[2] Therefore, we cannot understand anything about the Supramental if we do not constantly refer it to another dimension. But we can understand that it is the very vision of Wisdom, because each thing, each being, each force on this earth moves toward a special absolute, expressing it more or less accurately and often perversely, but despite all the flaws and perversions it obeys an intimate law that impels it towards the *one* truth of its being—even the leaves on the same tree are all unique. If it were not for that absolute and unique truth at the center of each one of us, we would crumble. This is also why we are so attached to our own smallness and stumblings, because we do sense the truth that is behind them, growing behind them, as if *protected,*[3] Sri Aurobindo said, by that very smallness and all those stumblings. If we got hold of the whole truth at once, we would turn it into some gnome in our own present image! Truth has nothing to do with thought or good deeds, though these may be steps on the way; it has to do with a vastness of being. And the growth process is slow and difficult. *Errors, falsehoods, stumblings! they cry. How bright and beautiful are Thy errors, O Lord! Thy falsehoods save Truth alive; by Thy stumblings the world is perfected.*[4] But the mind, which sees only the present surface of things, seeks to trim off all the rough edges, purify by exclusion, and reduce its world to a uniform, righteous and equitable truth. It decrees, "This is good, that is bad; this is friendly, that is hostile." It might want to eliminate all the Nazis from the world or all the Chinese, for instance, thinking they are quite unnecessary calamities. And the mind is right, by definition, since it is designed to be reasonable and since it, too, expresses a mental or moral absolute that has its place and purpose. But this is not the whole truth; it is only *one* point of view.* Finally, this is why we lack power, for if we possessed power, we would, with the best of intentions, precipitate a catastrophe through ignorance or shortsightedness. Our shortcomings are necessary shortcomings. Not only does the supramental consciousness capture all the points of view, but also the deeper forces at work behind each thing as well as the truth within each thing: it is a *Truth-Consciousness*—and because it *sees* all, it automatically possesses Power. We are powerless because we do not see. To see, and to see totally, necessarily means to have power. But the supramental power does not obey our logic or morality; it sees far into space and time, and it does not try to do away with evil in order to save the good, nor does it work through miracles; it frees the good that is within the evil, applying its force and light on the dark half so it consents to its luminous counterpart. Wherever it is applied, the immediate effect is to touch off a crisis; that is, to place the shadow in front of its own light. It is a stupendous evolutionary ferment.

Sri Aurobindo's written work, although a mental expression of a supramental fact, is a practical example of this global vision. It is bewildering to many because it lacks all the angles that make a thought readily understandable; it is so easy to be doctrinaire. Sri Aurobindo literally surveys all points of view in order to draw the deeper truth from each one of them, but he never imposes his own point of view (perhaps because he has none, or has them all!),

---

* Some will say that our partiality, our mind, our morals are necessary instruments for living in the world as it is now, and this is true. We do need to be partial. But this is also why the world is not whole. We should never lose sight of the fact that these are *transitory* instruments, and that we must aim at replacing these *stopgaps*,[5] as Sri Aurobindo called them, with a consciousness that is vision and power.

merely indicating how each truth is incomplete in itself and in what direction it may be widened. The Supermind does not set *truth against truth to see which will stand and survive, but completes truth by truth in the light of the one Truth of which all are the aspects. . . .* [6] And he spoke of *the light of the Thought that carries in it its own opposites.* [7] This is what the Mother calls *thinking spherically.* One always feels terribly dogmatic and mental when speaking of Sri Aurobindo, probably because of the inadequacy of our language, which focuses on one point rather than another and hence casts shadows, whereas Sri Aurobindo embraces everything, not out of "tolerance," which is a mental substitute for Oneness, but through an undivided vision that is truly *one* with each thing, in the heart of each thing. Perhaps this is the very vision of Love?

This undivided vision is so real that even the world's physical appearance is changed for the supramental consciousness, or, rather, the physical world appears as it really is; the separatist optical illusion we usually live in dissipates; the stick is no longer broken, and everything is related to everything else. The world is not as we see it: *Nothing to the supramental sense is really finite: it is founded on a feeling of all in each and of each in all: its sense definition . . . creates no walls of limitation; it is an oceanic and ethereal sense in which all particular sense knowledge and sensation is a wave or movement or spray or drop that is yet a concentration of the whole ocean and inseparable from the ocean. . . . It is as if the eye of the poet and artist had replaced the vague or trivial unseeing normal vision, but singularly spiritualised and glorified,—as if indeed it were the sight of the supreme divine Poet and Artist in which we were participating and there were given to us the full seeing of his truth and intention in his design of the universe and of each thing in the universe. There is an unlimited intensity which makes all that is seen a revelation of the glory of quality and idea and form and colour. The physical eye seems then to carry in itself a spirit and a consciousness which sees not only the physical aspect of the object but the soul of quality in it, the vibration of energy, the light and force and spiritual substance of which it is made. . . . There is at the same time a subtle change which makes the sight see in a sort of fourth dimension, the character of which is a certain internality, the seeing not only of the superficies and the outward form but of that which informs it and subtly extends around it. The material object becomes to this sight something different from what we now see, not a separate object on the background or in the environment of the rest of Nature but an indivisible part and even in a subtle way an expression of the unity of all that we see. And this unity . . . is that of the identity of the eternal, the unity of the Spirit. For to the supramentalised seeing the material world and space and material objects cease to be material in the sense in which we now on the strength of the sole evidence of our limited physical organs . . . receive [them]; . . . they appear and are seen as Spirit itself in a form of itself and a conscious extension.*[8]

Global vision, undivided vision, and also eternal vision. Time is conquered. While the overmental consciousness saw "large extensions of space and time," the supramental consciousness completely embraces all three tenses: [it] *links past, present and future in their indivisible connections, in a single continuous map of knowledge, side by side.*[9]*

All time is one body, Space a single book.[10]

Consciousness is no longer the narrow shutter that needed to be kept narrow lest it explode; it is a great, tranquil Gaze: "Like an eye extended in heaven," says the Rig Veda (I.17.21). *The ordinary individual consciousness is like an axis,* says the Mother, *and everything revolves about that axis. If it moves we feel lost. There is this tall axis (more or less tall; it may also be very small) fixed in time, and everything revolves about it. The consciousness may extend more or*

---

* It may be interesting here to draw a parallel with Einstein's theory of relativity. According to Einstein, the closer one approaches the speed of light, the more time slows down and distances shorten. At the speed of light, our clocks would stop, and our measuring tapes would be reduced to nothing. The supramental consciousness, which is Light itself, is also the conquest of time and distance. There is perhaps less difference than we might imagine between the physicist's light and the seer's.

less far, be more or less high, more or less strong, but it still revolves
about that axis. Yet for me, there is no longer any axis—it's gone,
disappeared! So it can move to the north, to the south, the east, or the
west—forward, backward, or anywhere at all. There is no more axis.

It is hard for us to imagine what the vision of such a universal
being could be. With our mental outlook, we might be tempted
to think that total knowledge of the three tenses immediately
removes all the unpredictability of existence. But this is applying
to the supramental consciousness characteristics and reactions that
belong uniquely to the mind. The way of perceiving and *experi-*
encing the world is different. The supramental consciousness is not
anxiously turned toward the future as we habitually are. Everything is exposed before its eyes, but it lives time divinely: *every*
second of time is an absolute, as filled with plenitude as all the
millennia combined. It is the utter perfection of time. In ordinary
life, we never live in the present; we are either thrust ahead by our
hopes or pulled backward by our regrets, because the present
moment never quite meets our expectations; it is always lacking
something, always terribly empty. For the supramental consciousness, each thing is at each instant fully what it should be and as it
should be. There is a constant, unalterable bliss. Each portion,
each image of the great cosmic Film is full of all the preceding
images and all those that follow; it lacks neither future perspectives
nor past memories. "That bliss which is most large and full and
without a gap," says the Rig Veda (V.62.9); that *unwounded*
Delight,[11] says Sri Aurobindo. It is also the utter perfection of
space. We are forever seeking new things or new objects because
each thing lacks all the other things that are not present in it; our
objects are as empty as our minutes. While for the supramental
consciousness, each object, each thing it touches feels as full and
infinite as a vision of the immensities or the sum of all possible
objects: *The Absolute is everywhere . . . every finite is an infinite.*[12]
And there is a sense of ever-renewed wonder arising not from
surprise but from the constant rediscovery of that eternal infinity,
that timeless Absolute in each space-bound object and each second

of time. There is an utter plenitude of life. Indeed, our finite, temporal life is not full at all; it is terribly wanting: we have either to turn our backs on the temporal to find timelessness, or to renounce our need for infinity in order to experience the finite— while the supramental plenitude finds infinity in the finite and timelessness in the temporal. It lives spontaneously every second, every object, as well as the immensity that contains all seconds and all objects; and these are two *simultaneous* ways of experiencing and perceiving the same thing.

Not only does the supramental consciousness have a cosmic status, but it also possesses a transcendent one, and the two do not contradict each other. And not only are they not contradictory, but their simultaneity is the key to true life. Life is deficient not only because its objects are empty and its time fragmented, but also because of its lack of foundation and solidity. All religions and spiritualities have sprung from this fundamental need in man: To find a permanent Base, a refuge of peace outside the chaos, uncertainty and suffering of the world—something utterly un- touched and protected. Then, in the course of our quest, we suddenly emerged in a stupendous Silence, a Vastness outside the world, which we called God, the Absolute, or Nirvana (the words are unimportant): we secured the great Release. This is the funda- mental experience. Whenever we approach that great Silence, everything changes; we feel Certainty, Peace, like a shipwrecked man who has found a rock. Nothing in life is secure; only that Rock never fails us. That is why it is said that God's kingdom is not of this world. Sri Aurobindo's experience, too, had begun with Nirvana, but it ended with the plenitude of the world. This apparent contradiction is central to our understanding of the practical secret of true life.

The mind, even the overmind of our prophets, is irreversibly bound to dualities (dualities within Unity): if God is above, He cannot be below; if this is white, it is not black. For the supramen- tal experience, however, everything is embraced; *it is always yes and no at the same time*, the Mother remarked. The two poles of each thing are constantly integrated within another "dimension" ("the secret inner spaces," as the Vedic rishis called them, II.4.9). Thus, the Transcendent is not elsewhere, outside the world; it is every-where here, at once fully within and fully without. The supramen-tal consciousness, likewise, is fully in the world and fully outside the world; it is in the eternal Silence as well as in the midst of all turmoil; it is seated on the unshakable Rock *and* in the middle of the current. This is why it can truly enjoy life and be in control of life; for if we are exclusively in the current we find neither peace nor control; we are merely carried away like a straw. We might be able to guess what the supramental experience is by going back to the first experiences of the beginning of yoga. Indeed, we had noticed that by stepping back in our consciousness, by a slight movement of withdrawal, we entered an expanse of silence be-hind, as if a portion of our being were forever gazing upon a great white North. Turmoil, suffering, problems are outside, yet we make a slight movement inward, as if crossing a threshold, and we are suddenly outside (or inside?) everything, a thousand miles away, free of any concern, reposing on velvet snow. The experience eventually becomes so natural that in the midst of the most absorbing activities (on the street, while talking, while working), we can plunge within (or without?), and nothing exists any longer except for a smile; it takes merely a second. Then we begin to know Peace; we have an impregnable Refuge everywhere we go, in any circumstance. And we begin to perceive more and more concretely that this Silence is not only within, inside ourselves, but every-where, as if it were the very substance of the universe, as if each thing stood out against that backdrop, proceeded from it and returned to it. It is like a well of sweetness in the heart of things, a velvet cloak enveloping everything. And this Silence is not empty; it is an absolute Plenitude, but a Plenitude with nothing in it, or a Plenitude that contains the essence of all that can be, as it were, a mere second before things come into existence; they are not there, and yet they are all there, like a song as yet unsung. One feels extraordinarily safe and at home in this Silence (or outside it?). It is a first reflection of the Transcendent. One more step, and one would simply slide into Nirvana. Nothing exists except this Silence. But in the Supermind there is no more "threshold" to cross, no more going from one state to another, from Silence to turmoil, inside to outside, Divine to undivine; both states are fused together in a single experience: the Silence that is outside everything and the Becoming that flows everywhere. One does not cancel out the other; one cannot even *be* without the other. For if the supreme Silence could not contain the opposite of Silence, it would not be infinite. If the Silence could not be totally free and outside that which seems its opposite, then it would be the prisoner of its opposite. God's kingdom is of this world, and it is not of this world. The whole secret is to join the two experiences into one, the infinite into the finite, the timeless into the temporal and the transcendent into the immanent. Then one knows Peace in action and Joy in every way.

> *A still deep sea, he laughs in rolling waves:*
> *Universal, he is all,—transcendent, none.*[13]

The supramental consciousness reproduces the mystery of a great, quiet Light that "one day," outside time, decided to look at itself temporally, sequentially, from a myriad points of view, and yet never ceased to be one and whole, totally self-contained in an eternal instant. The goal of evolution is none other than to recover in the very depths the totality from above, and to discover here on earth, in the very midst of dualities and the most poignant contradictions, the supreme Oneness, the supreme Infinitude, the supreme Joy—*Ananda*. It is in order to find this secret that we have been drawn downward each time we took a step upward.

The Supramental Power

The spiritualists dismiss power as a weapon unworthy of the seeker of truth, but this is not Sri Aurobindo's view. On the contrary, the concept of Power, *Shakti,* is one of the keys to his yoga, because without power nothing can be transformed. *I cherish God the Fire, not God the Dream!* exclaims Savitri.[14]

> *A fire to call eternity into Time,*
> *Make body's joy as vivid as the soul's.*[15]

It is a mistake of the ethical or religious mind to condemn Power as in itself a thing not to be accepted or sought after because naturally corrupting and evil; in spite of its apparent justification by a majority of instances, this is at its core a blind and irrational prejudice. However corrupted and misused, as Love and Knowledge too are corrupted and misused, Power is divine and put here for a divine use. Shakti, *will, Power is the driver of the worlds and whether it be Knowledge-Force or Love-Force or Life-Force or Action-Force or Body-Force, is always spiritual in its origin and divine in its character. It is the use made of it in the Ignorance by brute, man or Titan that has to be cast aside and replaced by its greater natural—even if to us supernormal—action led by an inner consciousness which is in tune with the Infinite and the Eternal. The integral Yoga cannot reject the works of Life and be satisfied with an inward experience only; it has to go inward in order to change the outward.*[16] This aspect of "force" or "power" of consciousness is represented in India by the eternal Mother. Without Consciousness there is no Force, and without Force there is no creation—He and She, two in one, inseparable. *This whole wide world is only he and she.*[17] Evolution is the story of Her rediscovering Him and striving to materialize Him everywhere. We cannot dismiss one for the other—without Him we are prisoners of a blind Force, without Her we are prisoners of a dazzling Void—we must integrate both within a fulfilled world. "Into a blind darkness they enter who follow after the Ignorance, they as if into a greater darkness who devote themselves to the Knowledge alone," says the Isha Upanishad (9).

The Supramental is, above all, a power—a stupendous power. It is the direct power of the Spirit in Matter. All consciousness is power, and the higher we ascend, the greater the power, but also the farther away we are from the earth. Thus if we wish to apply our overmental power, say, to the affairs of this world, it must be brought down from one level to another and overcome the determinisms of all the intermediary levels before it can reach the depths, Matter. Finally, there remains only a dulled and weakened overmental reflection, which must then fight against more and more heavy and rebellious determinisms. This is why the spiritualists have never been able to transform life. The Supramental is the supreme Consciousness-Force in the very heart of Matter, without any intermediary. It is the "sun in the darkness" of the Veda, the meeting place of the highest Heights and the deepest Depths. Therefore it can change everything. As the Mother has said, "The true change of consciousness is one that will change the physical conditions in the world and make it into an entirely new creation."

Let us say immediately that the supramental power does not work either through miracles or violence—the very notion of miracle is absurd, as Sri Aurobindo has often repeated: *There is really no such thing as miracle*,[18] there are only phenomena whose processes we do not understand. For one who sees, there is only an intervention by the determinism of a higher plane in the determinism of a lower plane. Perhaps the mind appears to be a miracle to the determinism of a caterpillar, yet we all know that our mental miracles do follow a certain process. The same applies to the Supermind: it does not upset any existing laws, but simply leaps over them (or within them?), to a dimension where they no longer exist, much as the caterpillar's laws no longer exist for man. Let us be more specific: the habitual repetition of certain vibrations that have coagulated, so to speak, around a person result in imparting to him an apparently stable structure; that person then claims to obey the "law" of his nature. But this so-called law is no more inevitable than choosing a certain route to go home rather than another; it is merely a question of habits. The same holds true for the entire cosmos: all our supposedly absolute physical laws are also coagulated habits, with nothing absolute about them whatsoever, and they can all be undone provided one is willing to take another route, that is, change to a different consciousness. *An ordinary law*, Sri Aurobindo wrote, *merely means an equilibrium established by Nature; it means a balance of forces. It is merely a groove in which Nature is accustomed to work in order to produce certain results. But if you change the consciousness, then the groove also is bound to change.*[19] There have been a number of "changes of grooves" in the course of our evolution, beginning with the introduction of Life into Matter, which changed the material groove, then the introduction of Mind into Life, which changed the vital and material grooves. The Supermind represents a third change of groove, which will change Mind, Life, and Matter. This change has already begun; the experience is in progress. Essentially, the supramental process works to free the consciousness contained in each element. It does not upset the universal order, nor does it violate anything; it only applies its power to cleave through the darkness so that it may radiate its own light. "He has cloven wide away the darkness, as one that cleaves away a skin, that he may spread out our earth* under his illumining sun," says the Rig Veda (V.85.1). Because the same divine solar consciousness is everywhere, the world and every atom in the world are divine; the Lord of all the universe is also "the One conscious in unconscious things" of the Rig Veda. Matter is not a crude substance incapable of change except through the assault of our hands or our heads (which have scarcely produced anything but monsters); it is a divine substance that can respond instead of resisting, and change instead of enslaving us in its old habit of gravitation and decay. But Matter is a clouded or sleeping Divinity, a "somnambulist," as Sri Aurobindo calls it, a "lost, buried sun," says the Veda. *The Inconscient is the Superconscient's sleep.*[20] . . . *The apparent Inconscience of the material universe holds in itself darkly all that is eternally self-revealed in the luminous Superconscient.*[21] The Supra-

---

*   The "earth" in the Veda is also the symbol of our own flesh.

mental, then, will use its own light to awaken the corresponding light—the *same* light—in Matter:

The truth above shall wake a nether truth [22]

For the law is eternally the same: only like can act upon like. Only the highest power can free the nethermost power.

What, then, is this Power? Any concentration releases a subtle heat; this is well known to those who have practiced yogic disciplines (*tapasya,* or yogic discipline, means literally "that which produces heat"). The supramental power is a heat of this kind, only infinitely more intense, within the cells of the body. It is the heat released by the awakening of the Consciousness-Force in Matter: *It's as if our spiritual life were made of silver,* explains the Mother, *while the supramental life is made of gold; as if the whole spiritual life here were a silvery vibration—not cold, but just a light, a light that goes to the top, a light altogether pure, pure and intense; but the other, the supramental one, has a fullness, a power, a warmth that makes all the difference.* This "warmth" is the basis of all supramental transmutations. In fact, the heat released by combustion or other chemical reactions, not to mention the far greater heat released by nuclear fusion or fission, is only the physical translation of a fundamental spiritual phenomenon, which the Vedic rishis knew well and called *Agni,* the spiritual Fire in Matter: "Other flames are only branches of thy stock, O Fire. . . . O Agni, O universal Godhead, thou art the navel-knot of the earths and their inhabitants; all men born thou controllest and supportest like a pillar. . . . Thou art the head of heaven and the navel of the earth. . . . Thou art the power that moves at work in the two worlds." (*Rig Veda* I.59) "That splendour of thee, O Fire, which is in heaven and in the earth and in the plants and in the waters and by which thou hast spread out the wide midair, is a vivid ocean of light which sees with a divine seeing." [23]

"Agni has entered earth and heaven as if they were one." (*Rig Veda* III.7.4) It is this supreme Agni that Sri Aurobindo and Mother have discovered in Matter and in the cells of the body; it is the key to transforming the body and to changing the physical world. Henceforth, instead of being acted upon through the distorted and dulled agency of all the intermediary mental and vital determinisms, Matter itself, aware of its own force, carries out its own transmutation. Instead of an evolution forever torn between two poles—consciousness devoid of force, leading to a blissful ecstasy, and force without consciousness, leading to the crude joy of the atom—the Supermind restores the Equilibrium within a total being: the highest consciousness in the most powerful force, the fire of the Spirit in Matter. "O Flame with the hundred treasures," exclaims the Rig Veda (I.59).

It may be worth remembering that Sri Aurobindo made his spiritual discovery in 1910, even before reading the Veda, and at a time when nuclear physics was still in a theoretical phase. Our science is ahead of our consciousness, hence the haphazard course of our destiny.

The parallel with nuclear physics is even more striking if we describe the supramental power as it appears to one who inwardly sees. We have said that the higher we rise in consciousness, the more stable and unbroken the light: from the intuitive sparks to the "stable flashes" of the overmind, the light becomes more and more homogeneous. One might imagine, then, that the supramental light is a kind of luminous totality, utterly still and compact, without the tiniest interstice. But, remarkably, the quality of the supramental light is very different from that of other levels of consciousness: it combines both complete stillness and the most rapid movement; here, too, the two opposite poles have become integrated. We can only state the fact without being able to explain it. This is how the Mother describes her first experience with the supramental light: *There was an overwhelming impression of power, warmth, gold: it wasn't fluid; it was like a powdering. And each of these things (one can't call them particles or fragments, or even dots, unless "dot" is used in the mathematical sense of a point that takes up no space) was like living gold—a warm gold dust. It wasn't bright, it wasn't dark; nor was it a light as we understand it: a multitude of tiny golden points, nothing but that. It was as if they were touching my eyes, my face. And with a sense of tremendous power! At the same time, there was a feeling of such plenitude—the peace of omnipotence. It was rich, full. It was movement at its utmost, infinitely faster than anything we can conceive of, yet at the same time, there was absolute peace and a perfect stillness.** Years later, when the experience had become quite familiar to her, the Mother spoke of it in these terms: *It is a movement that is like an eternal Vibration, with neither beginning nor end. Something that exists from all eternity, for all eternity, and that has no divisions in time; only when it is projected upon a screen does it begin assuming time-divisions; it isn't possible to say one second, or one instant . . . it's very difficult to explain. Scarcely has it been perceived, and it's already gone—something without limits, without beginning or end, a Movement so total—total and constant, constant—that to any perception, it gives an impression of total, utter stillness. It is absolutely indescribable, yet it is the Origin and Support of all earthly evolution. . . . I have noticed that, in this state of consciousness, the Movement is greater than the force or power holding the cells in an individual form.* The day we learn to apply this Vibration or this "Movement" to our own matter, we will have seized upon the practical secret of the transition from crude Matter to a more subtle Matter, and we will likewise have begun to realize the first supramental or glorious body on the earth.

This immobility within movement is the basis of all the supramental being's activities. It is the practical premise of any discipline leading to the Supermind, perhaps even the premise of any effective action in this world. We have already said that immobility—an inner immobility, that is—has the power to dissolve vibrations, and that if we are able to remain perfectly still inside, without the slightest reaction, we can even stop attacks by animals or by men. This power of immobility can only be attained after we have begun to come into contact with the great Silence behind,

---

* At the speed of light, too, we find a combination of total immobility in extreme movement—immobility when observing the phenomenon from within, movement when looking at it from without.

when we can, at will, step back and withdraw far, far away, thousands of miles away from all immediate circumstances. We must be able to be utterly outside life in order to control the inner substance of life. What is remarkable, yet quite natural after all, is that this supramental Power cannot be attained unless one is completely outside, completely seated upon that eternal Foundation, outside time and outside space, as if supreme Dynamism could come only from the supreme Immobility. However paradoxical this fact may seem, it still makes sense practically. One can understand that if the ordinary consciousness, which is upset by the slightest breeze, were to come in contact with this "warm gold dust," it would fall to pieces and disintegrate instantly. Only complete Immobility can bear this Movement. This is what was so striking to those who saw Sri Aurobindo: it was not only the light in his eyes (as is also the case with the Mother), but that kind of immobile immensity one felt near him, so compact, so tangible, as if one had entered a physical infinity. One then understood spontaneously, without needing further practical proof, why a cyclone could not enter his room. Whereupon this little phrase of his suddenly made perfect sense: . . . *the strong immobility of an immortal spirit.* [24] It is through the power of this immobility that he worked for forty years, was able to write twelve hours a night, walk eight hours a day ("to bring down light into Matter," as he said), and fight the most strenuous battles in the Inconscient without ever feeling tired. *If when thou art doing great actions and moving giant results, thou canst perceive that thou art doing nothing, then know that God has removed the seal on thy eyelids. . . . If when thou sittest alone, still and voiceless on the mountain-top, thou canst perceive the revolutions thou art conducting, then hast thou the divine vision and art freed from appearances.*[25]

Immobility is the basis of the supramental power, but silence is the condition for its perfect operation. The supramental consciousness does not follow mental or moral criteria to determine its actions. There are no more "dilemmas"; its actions arise naturally and spontaneously. Spontaneity is the particular mark of the

Supermind: spontaneity of life, spontaneity of knowledge, spontaneity of power. In ordinary life, we try to know what is good or right, and once we think we have found it, we somehow try to implement our thought. The supramental consciousness, on the contrary, does not try to know or to decipher what it must do or not do; it is perfectly silent and still, living each second of time spontaneously, unconcerned by the future; then at each second, the exact required knowledge falls like a droplet of light in the silence of the consciousness: "This has to be done, that has to be said, or seen, or understood." *Supramental Thought is an arrow from the Light, not a bridge to reach it.*[26] "In the level wideness they meet together and know perfectly," says the Rig Veda (VII.76.5). And every time a thought or a vision flashes by the consciousness, it is no speculation about the future, but an instant action:

There every thought and feeling is an act.[27]

Knowledge is automatically gifted with power, because it is a true knowledge, which embraces everything, and true knowledge is powerful knowledge. We do not have power because we do not see the whole, while that total vision goes well beyond our momentary reasoning, since it perceives the extension of each thing in time; neither is it an arbitrary fiat going against the normal course of things, but a luminous pressure that *accelerates* the movement and strives to put each thing, each force, each event, each being in direct contact with its own luminous essence, its own divine potential, and the very Goal that first set it in motion. As we have said, it is a stupendous evolutionary ferment. Perhaps something should be mentioned about how this power manifests practically, in the lives and actions of those who embody it—so far, Sri Aurobindo and the Mother. But because no explanation is ever truly satisfying unless one experiences it for oneself, and because the experience will only begin to be convincing when it takes place on a more collective scale, it is perhaps wiser to remain silent. As a matter of fact, their actions often eluded even those who benefited from them directly, for the simple reason that we can only relate to a thing if we have reached the same plane. We usually see only the present moment, not the future miracle prepared by a simple gaze, the second of light that will mature for twenty years or three centuries beneath our unconscious layers before becoming "natural." *Neither you nor anyone else knows anything at all of my life,* Sri Aurobindo wrote to one of his biographers, *it has not been on the surface for men to see.*[28] What makes it difficult to speak of this power is that we have a wrong notion of power. When we speak of "power," we immediately imagine something marvelous, but that is not what true Power is; neither is it the true marvel of the universe. The supramental action does not work wonders with flashes of lightning; it is as quiet as eternity, impelling the world and each thing in the world toward its own perfection through all the masks of imperfection. The true miracle is to do no violence to things, to impel them secretly, almost surreptitiously, toward their own center, so that deep within they may recognize the Face as their own face. There is but one miracle: the instant of recognition that nothing, any longer, is "other."

The individual is the key to the supramental power. The supramental being has not only a transcendent and cosmic status but also an individual one: the triple hiatus of experience that divided the monist, the pantheist, and the individualist is healed. His transcendent status does not abolish the world or the individual, no more than his cosmic status deprives him of the Transcendent or of his individuality, or no more than his individual status severs him from the Transcendent or the universe. He has not kicked off the ladder to reach the top, but consciously traveled all the evolutionary rungs, from top to bottom—there is no gap anywhere, no missing link; and because he has kept his individuality instead of exploding in a luminous no-man's-land, he can both ascend and descend the great Ladder of existence and use his individual being as a material bridge between the very top and the very bottom. His work on the earth is to establish a direct connection between the supreme Force and the individual, between the supreme Consciousness and Matter—*to join the two Ends*, as the Mother says. He is a precipitator of the Real upon earth. This is why there is hope that all the blind determinisms that presently rule the world—Death, Suffering, War—can be transformed by that supreme Determinism and yield to a new, luminous evolution: *It is a spiritual revolution we foresee and the material revolution is only its shadow and reflex.*[29]

After two months at Chandernagore, Sri Aurobindo heard the Voice again: *Go to Pondicherry.* A few days later, he was sailing secretly on board the *Dupleix*, outwitting the British police and leaving Northern India for good. *I had accepted the rule of . . . moving only as I was moved by the Divine.*[30] The last forty years of his life, with the Mother, would be devoted to making that individual realization into an earthly one: *We want to bring down the supermind as a new faculty. Just as the mind is now a permanent state of consciousness in humanity, so also we want to create a race in which the supermind will be a permanent state of consciousness.*[31] So that his intentions might not be misinterpreted, Sri Aurobindo repeatedly stressed the following: *It is far from my purpose to propagate any religion, new or old, for humanity in the future. A way to be opened that is still blocked, not a religion to be founded, is my conception of the matter.*[32] We cannot say whether the supramental adventure will succeed. The Vedic rishis were unable to "unblock the way"; they could not open "the great passage" for everyone and transform their personal realization into a permanent and collective one. There must have been a reason. What remains to be seen is whether that reason still holds true today.

CHAPTER 16

Man, A Transitional Being

Sri Aurobindo lived in great poverty during his first years in Pondicherry. He was on the police blacklist, far away from those who could have helped him, his mail censored, his every move surveyed by British spies, who were attempting to get him extradited through all sorts of devious maneuvers, including planting compromising papers in his house and then denouncing him to the French police.* Once they even tried to kidnap him. Sri Aurobindo would finally be left in peace the day the French police superintendent came to search his room and discovered in his desk drawers the works of Homer. After inquiring whether these writings were "really Greek," the superintendent became so filled with awe and respect for this gentleman-yogi, who read scholarly books and spoke French, that he simply left, never to return. The newcomer could now receive whomsoever he wished and move about as he pleased. Several comrades-in-arms had followed him, waiting for their "leader" to resume the political struggle, but since "the Voice" remained silent, Sri Aurobindo did not move. Besides, he saw that the political process was now under way; the spirit of independence had been awakened in his compatriots, and things

---

* Pondicherry was then a French possession.

would follow their inevitable course until India's total liberation, as he had foreseen. Now he had other things to do.

The Written Works

The highlight of those first years of exile was his reading of the Veda in the original Sanskrit. Until then, Sri Aurobindo had read only English or Indian translations and, along with the Sanskrit scholars, he had seen in the Veda only rather obscure, ritualistic texts . . . *of small value or importance for the history of thought or for a living spiritual experience.*[1] But in the original, he discovered *a constant vein of the richest gold of thought and spiritual experience.*[2] . . . *I found that the mantras of the Veda illuminated with a clear and exact light psychological experiences of my own for which I had found no sufficient explanation either in European psychology or in the teachings of Yoga or of Vedanta.*[3] It can well be imagined how Sri Aurobindo might have become a little perplexed by his own experiences, and how it took him several years to understand exactly what was happening to him. We have described the supramental experience of Chandernagore as if the steps had neatly followed one another, each with its own explanatory note, but, in reality, the explanations came long afterwards. At the time, there were no signposts at all to guide him. Yet here was the most ancient of the four Vedas,* the Rig Veda, unexpectedly suggesting that he was not completely alone or astray on this planet. That the Western and even the Indian scholars had not understood the extraordinary vision of these texts is perhaps not so surprising when we realize that Sanskrit roots lend themselves to a double or even a triple meaning, which in turn can be invested with a double symbolism, esoteric and exoteric. These hymns can be read on two or three different levels of meaning, and even after one finds the right meaning, it is still difficult to fully comprehend the "Fire in

---

* Rig Veda, Sama Veda, Yajur Veda, Atharva Veda.

the water," "the mountain pregnant with the supreme birth," or the quest for the "lost Sun" followed by the discovery of the "Sun in the darkness," unless one has experienced the spiritual Fire in Matter, the explosion of the rock of the Inconscient or the illumination in the cells of the body. The rishis themselves spoke of "secret words, seer-wisdoms that utter their inner meaning to the seer." (IV.3.16) Because of his experiences, Sri Aurobindo knew immediately what was meant, and he set out to translate a large fragment of the Rig Veda, in particular the marvelous *Hymns to the Mystic Fire*. It is astounding to think that the rishis of five or six thousand years ago were alluding not only to their own experiences but also to those of their "ancestors," "the fathers of men," as they called them—how many millennia before?—which had been repeated generation after generation without a single distortion or without omitting a single syllable, because the effectiveness of a mantra depended precisely upon the accuracy of its pronunciation. We are here before the most ancient tradition in the world, intact. That Sri Aurobindo rediscovered the Secret of the beginning of our human cycle (perhaps there were others before?) in an age the Indians call "black," *Kali-yuga*, is not without significance. For if it is true that the Rockbottom is contiguous with a new layer, then we must be approaching "something."*

It would be wrong, however, to identify Sri Aurobindo with the Vedic revelation. As striking as it may seem to us, it was for him only one sign along the way—a confirmation after the fact, as it were. To resurrect the Veda in the twentieth century, as if it

---

* According to Indian tradition, each cycle has four periods: *Satya-yuga*, the age of truth (or golden age), followed by the age with "three-fourths of the truth," *Treta-yuga*, then "half of the truth," *Dwapara-yuga*, and finally the age when all the truth has disappeared, *Kali-yuga*, and when the Password has been lost. The Kali-yuga is followed by a new Satya-yuga, but between the two there is a complete disintegration, *pralaya*, and the universe is "swallowed back up." For Sri Aurobindo, however, the discovery of the Supermind opens up other possibilities.

embodied the total Truth once and for all, would be a futile endeavor since the Truth never repeats itself twice. Sri Aurobindo himself wrote in a humorous vein: *Truly this shocked reverence for the past is a wonderful and fearful thing! After all, the Divine is infinite and the unrolling of the Truth may be an infinite process . . . not a thing in a nutshell cracked and its contents exhausted once and for all by the first seer or sage, while the others must religiously crack the same nutshell all over again.*[4] Sri Aurobindo was not going to work only toward an individual realization, like the rishis, but toward a collective one, and in conditions that were no longer those of the prehistoric shepherds. First, he was to devote a great deal of time to writing, which, for the moment, is probably the most visible sign of his collective action. In 1910, a French writer, Paul Richard, came to Pondicherry, met Sri Aurobindo, and was so impressed by the breadth of his views that he made a second trip to see him in 1914, this time urging him to put his thoughts into written form. A bilingual review was founded, with Richard in charge of the French section. Thus the *Arya,* or *Review of the Great Synthesis,* would be born. But the war broke out, Richard was called back to France, and Sri Aurobindo found himself alone with sixty-four pages of philosophy to produce every month. Nevertheless, he was no philosopher. *And philosophy! Let me tell you in confidence that I never, never, never was a philosopher—although I have written philosophy which is another story altogether. I knew precious little about philosophy before I did the Yoga and came to Pondicherry—I was a poet and a politician, not a philosopher. How I managed to do it and why? First, because Paul Richard proposed to me to cooperate in a philosophical review—and as my theory was that a Yogi ought to be able to turn his hand to anything, I could not very well refuse; and then he had to go to the war and left me in the lurch with sixty-four pages a month of philosophy all to write by my lonely self. Secondly, because I had only to write down in the terms of the intellect all that I had observed and come to know in practising Yoga daily and the philosophy was there automatically. But that is not being a philosopher!*[5] And so it was that Sri Aurobindo became a writer.

He was forty-two. Typically, he himself had decided nothing: "outer" circumstances had launched him upon this path.

In six uninterrupted years, until 1920, Sri Aurobindo would publish nearly all of his written work, close to five thousand pages. But he wrote in an unusual manner—not one book after another, but four and even six books concurrently, on the most varied subjects, such as *The Life Divine,* his fundamental "philosophical" work and spiritual vision of evolution; *The Synthesis of Yoga,* in which he describes the various stages and experiences of the integral yoga, and surveys all the past and present yogic disciplines; the *Essays on the Gita,* which expounds his philosophy of action; *The Secret of the Veda,* with a study of the origins of language; and *The Ideal of Human Unity* and *The Human Cycle,* which approach evolution from its sociological and psychological standpoints and examine the future possibilities of human societies. He had found

The single sign interpreting every sign.[6]

Day after day, quietly, Sri Aurobindo filled his pages. Anyone else would have been exhausted, but he did not "think" about what he was writing. *I have made no endeavour in writing,* he explains to a disciple, *I have simply left the higher Power to work and when it did not work, I made no effort at all. It was in the old intellectual days that I had sometimes tried to force things and not after I started development of poetry and prose by Yoga. Let me remind you also that when I was writing the* Arya *and also whenever I write these letters or replies, I never think. . . . It is out of a silent mind that I write whatever comes ready-shaped from above.*[7] Often, those among his disciples who were writers or poets would ask him to explain the yogic process of literary creation. He would explain it at great length, knowing that creative activities are a powerful means of pushing back the superconscious boundary and precipitating into Matter the luminous possibilities of the future. His letters are quite instructive: *The best relief for the brain,* he writes in one of them, *is when the thinking takes place outside the body and above the head (or in space or at other levels but still outside the body). At any rate it was so in my case; for as soon as that happened there was an immense relief; I have felt body strain since then but never any kind of brain fatigue.*[8] Let us stress that "thinking outside the body" is not at all a supramental phenomenon, but a very simple experience accessible with the onset of mental silence. The true method, according to Sri Aurobindo, is to reach a state devoid of any personal effort, to step aside as completely as one can and simply let the current pass through. *There are two ways of arriving at the Grand Trunk Road. One is to climb and struggle and effortise (like the pilgrim who traverses India prostrating and measuring the way with his body: that is the way of effort). One day you suddenly find yourself on the G.T.R. when you least expect it. The other is to quiet the mind to such a point that a greater Mind can speak through it (I am not here talking of the Supramental).*[9] But then, asked a disciple, if it is not our own mind that thinks, if thoughts come from outside, how is it that there is such a difference between one person's thoughts and another's? *First of all,* replied Sri Aurobindo, *these thought-waves, thought-seeds or thought-forms or whatever they are, are of different values and come from different planes of consciousness. And the same thought substance can take higher or lower vibrations according to the plane of consciousness through which the thoughts come in (e.g. thinking mind, vital mind, physical mind, subconscient mind) or the power of consciousness which catches them and pushes them into one man or another. Moreover there is a stuff of mind in each man and the incoming thought uses that for shaping itself or translating itself (transcribing we usually call it), but the stuff is finer or coarser, stronger or weaker, etc., etc., in one mind than in another. Also there is a mind-energy actual or potential in each which differs and this mind-energy in its recipience of the thought can be luminous or obscure, sattwic (serene), rajasic (impassioned) or tamasic (inert) with consequences which vary in each case.*[10] And Sri Aurobindo added: *The intellect is an absurdly overactive part of the nature; it always thinks that nothing can be well done unless it puts its finger into the pie and therefore it instinctively interferes with the inspiration, blocks half or more than half of it and labours to substitute its own inferior and toilsome productions for the true speech and rhythm that ought to have come. The poet labours in anguish to get the one true word, the authentic rhythm, the real divine substance of what he has to say, while all the time it is waiting complete and ready behind.*[11] But effort helps, the disciple protested again, and by dint of beating one's brains, the inspiration comes. *Exactly! When any real effect is produced, it is not because of the beating and the hammering, but because an inspiration slips down between the raising of the hammer and the falling and gets in under cover of the beastly noise.*[12] After writing so many books for his disciples, Sri Aurobindo finally avowed that the sole purpose of books and philosophies was not really to enlighten the mind, but to silence it so that it can experience things directly and receive direct inspirations. He summed up the role of the mind in the evolutionary process as follows: *Mind is a clumsy interlude between Nature's vast and precise subconscient action and the vaster infallible superconscient action of the Godhead. There is nothing mind can do that cannot be better done in the mind's immobility and thought-free stillness.*[13]

At the end of six years, in 1920, Sri Aurobindo felt he had said enough, for the time being, and the *Arya* drew to a close. The rest of his written work would be comprised almost entirely of letters to his disciples—thousands upon thousands of them, containing all kinds of practical indications about yogic experiences, difficulties, and progress. But most importantly, over a period of thirty years, he would write and rewrite his extraordinary 28,813-line epic poem, *Savitri*, like a fifth Veda—his message, in which he describes the experiences of the higher and lower worlds, his own battles in the Subconscient and Inconscient, the whole occult history of evolution on the earth and in the universe, and his vision of the future:

> *Interpreting the universe by soul signs*
> *He read from within the text of the without.*[14]

The Mother

Sri Aurobindo had not come only to write; he had other things to do. He stopped the *Arya* in 1920, the year the Mother came to join him in Pondicherry. *When I came to Pondicherry*, Sri Aurobindo once told his early disciples, *a programme was dictated to me from within for my sadhana [discipline]. I followed it and progressed for myself but could not do much by way of helping others. Then came the Mother and with her help I found the necessary method.*[15]

It is difficult to speak of the Mother, probably because a personality such as hers cannot be easily captured in words; she is a Force in movement. Everything that happened yesterday, all that may have been said, done, or experienced even on the previous evening is already old for her, and uninteresting. She is always farther ahead, always beyond. She was born to *break the limits*, like Savitri. It would then scarcely be appropriate to imprison her in a curriculum vitae.

Let us say simply that she was born in Paris on February 21, 1878, and that she, too, had the supramental vision. It is not surprising, then, that with such consciousness she knew of Sri Aurobindo's existence long before meeting him physically and coming to join him in Pondicherry. *Between the ages of eleven and thirteen*, she explains, *a series of psychic and spiritual experiences revealed to me not only the existence of God, but man's possibility of finding Him and revealing Him integrally in consciousness and action, and of manifesting Him on earth in a divine life. This revelation, along with the practical discipline for achieving it, were given to me during my body's sleep by several teachers, some of whom I met afterwards on the physical plane. Later on, as the inner and outer development progressed, my spiritual and psychic relationship with one of these beings became increasingly clear and rich. . . . The moment I saw Sri Aurobindo, I knew it was he who had come to do the work on earth and that it was with him I was to work.* The "transformation" was under way. It was the Mother who took charge of the Ashram when Sri Aurobindo retired into complete solitude in 1926, and it is she who would continue the Work after his departure in 1950. *The Mother's consciousness and mine are the same.*[16] It is quite significant that the living synthesis of East and West, which Sri Aurobindo already symbolized, would become perfected by this meeting between East and West, as if the world could only be fulfilled by the coming together of the two poles of existence, Consciousness and Force, Spirit and Earth, He and She forever.

An Outline of Evolution

One day or another, we may all join in the work of transformation that Sri Aurobindo and the Mother have undertaken, because this is our evolutionary future. If we wish to understand what this process really is, its difficulties as well as the chances of failure or success, we must first understand the meaning of our own evolution, so that we can take an active part in it, instead of letting the centuries and millennia do the job after interminable meanderings. Sri Aurobindo is not dealing in theories: his vision of evolution rests essentially upon an experience. If he has attempted to express it in terms that may appear theoretical to us (since we do not yet have the experience), this is not in order to add one more idea to the millions of idea-forces in the world, but to help us seize the key to our own dynamism and accelerate the evolutionary process. For humanity's present condition is scarcely worth lingering on.

The key is *Agni*, the Consciousness-Force, and the whole evolution can be described as Agni's journey in four movements—involution, devolution, involution, evolution—from the eternal Center and within Him. The fourfold movement is in fact He. All is He. *Himself the play, Himself the player, Himself the playground.*[17] He outside time, outside space, the pure Being, the pure Consciousness, the great white Silence where all is in a state of *involution*, self-contained, still formless. Then He who becomes:

Force separates from Consciousness, She from Him, and Agni's journey begins:

> *. . . scattered on sealed depths, her luminous smile*
> *Kindled to fire the silence of the worlds.*[18]

She casts herself forth from Him in an outburst of joy, to play at finding Him again in Time—He and She, two in one. *What then was the commencement of the whole matter? Existence that multiplied itself for sheer delight of being and plunged into numberless trillions of forms so that it might find itself innumerably.*[19] But this beginning is perpetual; it is not situated at any point in Time. When we say "first" the Eternal, "then" the Becoming, we are back in the illusion of our spatio-temporal language, just as when we say "high" or "low." Our language is false, as is our vision of the world. In reality, Being and Becoming, He and She, are two *concurrent* faces of the same eternal FACT. The universe is a perpetual phenomenon, as perpetual as the Silence beyond time: *In the beginning, it is said, was the Eternal, the Infinite, the One. In the middle, it is said, is the finite, the transient, the Many. In the end, it is said, shall be the One, the Infinite, the Eternal. For when was the beginning? At no moment in Time, for the beginning is at every moment; the beginning always was, always is and always shall be. The divine beginning is before Time, in Time and beyond Time for ever. The Eternal, Infinite and One is an endless beginning. And where is the middle? There is no middle; for there is only the junction of the perpetual end and the eternal beginning; it is the sign of a creation which is new at every moment. The creation was for ever, is for ever, shall be for ever. The Eternal, Infinite and One is the magical middle-term of his own existence; it is he that is the beginningless and endless creation. And when is the end? There is no end. At no conceivable moment can there be a cessation. For all end of things is the beginning of new things which are still the same One in an ever developing and ever recurring figure. Nothing can be destroyed, for all is He who is forever. The Eternal, Infinite and One is the unimaginable end that is never closing upon new interminable vistas of his glory.*[20] And Sri Aurobindo added: *The experiment of human life on an earth is not now for the first time enacted. It has been conducted a million times before and the long drama will again a million times be repeated. In all that we do now, our dreams, our discoveries, our swift or difficult attainments, we profit subconsciously by the experience of innumerable precursors and our labour will be fecund in planets unknown to us and in worlds yet uncreated. The plan, the peripetia, the denouement differ continually, yet are always governed by the conventions of an eternal Art. God, Man, Nature are the three perpetual symbols. The idea of eternal recurrence affects with a shudder of alarm the mind entrenched in the minute, the hour, the years, the centuries, all the finite's unreal defences. But the strong soul conscious of its own immortal stuff and the inexhaustible ocean of its ever-flowing energies is seized by it with the thrill of an inconceivable rapture. It hears behind the thought the childlike laughter and ecstasy of the Infinite.*[21]

This ceaseless movement from Being to Becoming is what Sri Aurobindo calls *devolution.* The transition is gradual; the supreme Consciousness does not all at once become Matter. Matter is the final precipitate, the end product of an increasing fragmentation or "materialization" of consciousness, which is worked out slowly, one level at a time. At the "top" of this devolutive course—though it is not a top but a supreme Point that is everywhere at once—stands the supramental Consciousness-Force, which encompasses in a single Glance all the infinite possibilities of the Becoming, as the solar Fire contains all its rays within its center: "They unyoked the horses of the Sun," says the Rig Veda, "the ten hundreds stood together, there was that One, *tad ekam.*" (V.62.1) Then comes the Overmind: the "great cleavage" of consciousness begins; the rays of the Sun branch off; the single Consciousness-Force is henceforth scattered into trillions of forces, each seeking its own absolute realization. Once begun, the Play will not stop until all the possibilities have been exhausted, including those that seem to be the very contradiction of the eternal Player. Force is cast in an ever more passionate movement, as if it wanted to burst forth to its utmost frontiers, to meet itself always farther in order to replace the One by an impossible sum. Then consciousness scatters. It breaks up into smaller and smaller fragments, becoming increasingly heavy and obscure, forming layers or worlds inhabited by their own beings and forces, each with its particular life; all the traditions have described them; we, too, can see them in our sleep, or with our eyes open once our inner vision has become unsealed. From the gods to the symbolic gnomes, consciousness shrinks, crumbles, and falls to dust—overmind, intuitive mind, illumined mind, higher mind, then vital, and subtle physical. It becomes more and more ensnared and mired in its force, scattered into microscopic instincts or survival-oriented tropisms, until its final dispersion in Matter, in which everything becomes fragmented. "In the beginning," says the Veda, "darkness was hidden by darkness, all this was one ocean of inconscience. Universal being was concealed by fragmentation." (X.129.1-5) The devolution is complete; it is the *plunge of Light into its own shadow,*[22] i.e., Matter.

Now we are before two poles. At the top, a supreme Negative (or Positive, depending upon one's personal bias), where Force seems annihilated in a luminous Nothingness, a gulf of peace without a ripple, where everything is self-contained, and there is no need for even the slightest movement in order to be—*it is*. At the other pole, a supreme Positive (or Negative, if we prefer), where Consciousness seems to be engulfed in an obscure Nothingness, an abyss of blind Force forever engrossed in its own dark whirl—an inexorable and ceaseless becoming. This is the first duality from which all others follow: the One and the Innumerable, the Infinite and the Finite, Consciousness and Force, Spirit and Matter, the Formless and a frenzy of forms—He and She. Our whole existence is caught between these two poles, some of us wishing to see only the Transcendent, which is then called the supreme Positive, and dismissing Matter as a kind of temporary falsehood to be endured while awaiting the time of the Great Return; while the rest of us swear by Matter alone, likewise calling it the supreme Positive, and rejecting the Spirit as a definitive and negative falsehood, since according to human logic, plus cannot be also minus, or vice versa. But all this is still an illusion. Consciousness does not contradict Force, nor Matter the Spirit, nor the Infinite the Finite, no more than high contradicts low: *In the world as we see it, for our mental consciousness however high we carry it, we find that to every positive there is a negative. But the negative is not a zero,—indeed whatever appears to us a zero is packed with force, teeming with power of existence. . . . Neither does the existence of the negative make its corresponding positive nonexistent or an unreality; it only makes the positive an incomplete statement of the truth of things and even, we may say, of the positive's own truth. For the positive and the negative exist not only side by side, but in relation to each other and by each other; they complete and would to the all-view, which a limited mind cannot reach, explain one another. Each by itself is not really known; we only begin to know it in its deeper truth when we can read into it the suggestions of its apparent opposite.*[23] In the heights, She is as if asleep within Him; in the depths, He is as if asleep within Her. Force dissolved in Consciousness and Consciousness dissolved in Force, the Infinite contained in the Finite as the tree and all its branches are contained in the seed. This is what Sri Aurobindo calls "involution": *The nescience of Matter is a veiled, an involved or somnambulist consciousness which contains all the latent powers of the Spirit. In every particle, atom, molecule, cell of Matter there lives hidden and works unknown all the omniscience of the Eternal and all the omnipotence of the Infinite.*[24] The involution above is followed by a new involution below, whereby everything is contained latently within the Night, the way everything was contained latently within the Light above. *Agni* is there "like a warm gold dust"; "*Agni* has entered earth and heaven as if they were one," says the Rig Veda (III.7.4). *In a sense, the whole of creation may be said to be a movement between two involutions, Spirit in which all is involved and out of which all evolves downward (or devolves) to the other pole of Matter, Matter in which also all is involved and out of which all evolves upwards to the other pole of Spirit.*[25]

Without this involution no evolution would be possible, for how could something come out of nothing? For an evolution to take place, something must indeed be growing or evolving from within! *Nothing can evolve out of Matter which is not therein already contained.*[26] It is *Agni* that impels and goads in the depths of this awakening stupor, behind the evolutionary explosion of forms. It is Force in quest of Consciousness, She seeking Him, seeking forms more suitable for manifesting Him. It is She emerging from her unconscious Night and groping in her millions of works and millions of species to rediscover the beauty of the one lost Form, and to rediscover innumerably the Joy that was one—*a million-bodied beatitude*[27] instead of a blank ecstasy. If we possess that "ear of ears" the Veda spoke of, perhaps we will hear everywhere the Night crying out to the Light, the walled-in Consciousness crying out to Joy, *the deep spiritual cry in all that is.*[28] This is what impels us deep within; there is a Fire within, a flame in Matter, a flame of Life, a flame in our Mind and in our soul. This is the Fire we must seize: it is the leader of the journey and the key, the secret evolutionary impetus, the soul and flame of the world. If this world were made only of lifeless and inert stone, it would never have become anything but lifeless and inert stone; if the soul were not already in Matter, it could never have emerged in man: *But what after all, behind appearances, is this seeming mystery? We can see that it is the Consciousness which had lost itself returning again to itself, emerging out of its giant self-forgetfulness, slowly, painfully, as a Life that is would-be sentient, half-sentient, dimly sentient, wholly sentient and finally struggles to be more than sentient, to be again divinely self-conscious, free, infinite, immortal.*[29]

Until the day She comes to the human being, Her conscious instrument in whom, by whom and through whom She will be able to recover Him, *Our humanity is the conscious meeting-place of the finite and the infinite and to grow more and more towards the Infinite even in this physical birth is our privilege.*[30] A special phenomenon occurs when *Agni* reaches the human stage of its journey. During the preceding stages of evolution, the evolutionary flame seems to have subsided of its own accord once the new emergence was assured. The explosion of vegetal life seems to have subsided once the animal became firmly established in Life. The teeming of animal life seems similarly to have subsided once humankind became definitively settled in evolution. It does not seem that Nature has created any new animal or plant species since the human species has occupied the crest of evolution. The various species have become stationary; they have attained a degree of perfection, each in its own order, and they remain there. With man, however, the evolutionary urge has not abated, even though he is firmly established in evolution. He is not fulfilled, not satisfied as other species are; he does not know the peace and joy that come with equilibrium. *Man is an abnormal who has not found his own normality,—he may imagine he has, he may appear to be normal in his own kind, but that normality is only a sort of provisional order; therefore, though man is infinitely greater than the plant or animal, he is not perfect in his own nature like the plant and the animal.*[31]

This imperfection should not at all be deplored, Sri Aurobindo says; it is, on the contrary, *a privilege and a promise.*[31] If we were perfect and harmonious within our own kind, without sin or flaw, we would already be a stationary species, like the amphibians or the mollusks. But in us, who reproduce the great cosmic Play, the force has not completely found its consciousness, or our nature its own spirit. Was Plato ever satisfied or Michelangelo ever at peace? "One night I took Beauty upon my knees, and I found her bitter!" exclaimed Rimbaud. This is a sign that the peak of mental intelligence or aesthetic refinement is not the end of the journey, not total plenitude, not the great Equilibrium of She and He together again. The spirit within, the little flame at the center that slowly awakens and grows, has first touched minute fragments, molecules, genes, protoplasms; it has settled psychologically around a separate and fragmentary ego; it does not see very well, groping in the darkness; it, too, is doubly "involved," and it perceives things only through a narrow mental shutter between an abysmal subconscient and a vast superconscient. It is this childish fragmentation—for it really belongs to our human childhood—that is the cause of all our errors and sufferings; all our woes proceed from this narrowness of vision, which is a false vision of ourselves and of the world. For in truth, the world and each cell of our body is *Sat-chit-ananda*, Existence-Consciousness-Bliss; we are light and joy. *Our sense by its incapacity has invented darkness. In truth there is nothing but Light, only it is a power of light either above or below our poor human vision's limited range.*[32] All is joy: "For who could live or breathe if there were not this delight of existence as the ether in which we dwell?" says the Upanishad.* It is our faulty vision that hides from us *the happiness absolute in the heart of things,*[33] it is *our pallid sense,*[34] still immature, that does not yet know how to contain all that great vastness. As Sri Aurobindo points out, man is not the last term of evolution, but *a transitional being.*[35] *We speak of the evolution of Life in Matter, the evolution of Mind in Matter; but evolution is a word which merely states the phenomenon without explaining it. For there seems to be no reason why Life should evolve out of material elements or Mind out of living form, unless we accept . . . that Life is already involved in Matter and Mind in Life because in essence Matter is a form of veiled Life, Life a form of veiled Consciousness. And then there seems to be little objection to a farther step in the series and the admission that mental consciousness may itself be only a form and a veil of higher states which are beyond Mind. In that case, the unconquerable impulse of man towards God, Light, Bliss, Freedom, Immortality presents itself in its right place in the chain as simply the imperative impulse by which Nature is seeking to evolve beyond Mind, and appears to be as natural, true and just as the impulse towards Life which she has planted in forms of Matter or the impulse towards Mind which she has planted in certain forms of life. . . . The animal is a living laboratory in which Nature has, it is said, worked out man. Man himself may well be a thinking and living laboratory in whom and with whose conscious*

---

* *Taittiriya Upanishad* II.7.

cooperation she wills to work out the superman, the god. Or shall we not say, rather, to manifest God? [36] If evolution succeeds in making this difficult transition, the great Equilibrium will be attained; we will enter "the vast home" (*Rig Veda* V.68.5); Force will have recovered all its Consciousness instead of wandering aimlessly, and Consciousness will have recovered all its Force instead of understanding and loving powerlessly.

The rishis, too, knew that the journey was not over. They said that Agni "conceals his two extremities," that Agni is "without head and without feet." (*Rig Veda* IV.1.7,11) We are a tiny flame lost between the superconscious Agni of heaven and the subconscious Agni of the earth, and we suffer, tossing and turning upon our bed of misery, some of us seeking their heaven, others their earth, yet without ever joining the two. Another race is to be born among us, a whole Being, if only we consent to it: "Weave an inviolate work, become the human being, create the divine race. . . . Seers of Truth are you, sharpen the shining spears with which you cut the way to that which is Immortal; knowers of the secret planes, form them, the steps by which the gods attained to immortality." (X.53) Then we will regain our solar totality, our two concealed extremities, our two Mothers in one: "O Flame, O Agni, thou goest to the ocean of Heaven, towards the gods; thou makest to meet together the godheads of the planes, the waters that are in the realm of light above the sun and the waters that abide below." (III.22.3) Then we will know the joy of both worlds and of all the worlds, *Ananda*, of the earth and heaven as if they were one: "O Flame, thou foundest the mortal in a supreme immortality . . . for the seer who has thirst for the dual birth, thou createst divine bliss and human joy." (I.31.7) For joy is the ultimate goal of our evolution. People speak of "love," but is there a word more falsified by our sentimentalities, our political factions, or our churches? Whereas no one can falsify that joy, for it is a child laughing in the sun; it loves, seeking to sweep up everything in its dance. Joy, yes, if we have the courage to want it. *The laurel and not the cross should be the aim of the conquering* human soul[37]—but *men are still in love with grief. . . . Therefore Christ still hangs on the cross in Jerusalem.*[38] The joy of being, of being fully, in all that is, has been, and will be—here, there, and everywhere—*as if honey could taste itself and all its drops together and all its drops could taste each other and each the whole honey-comb.*[39] Then evolution will emerge from the Night to enter the Solar cycle. We will live under the Auspices of the One. The crucified god in us will descend from his cross and man will at last be Himself—normal. For to be normal is to be divine. *There are only two spontaneous harmonic movements, that of the life, incon-scient or largely subconscient, the harmony that we find in the animal creation and in the lower Nature, and that of the spirit. The human condition is a stage of transition, effort and imperfection between the one and the other, between the natural and the ideal or spiritual life.*[40]*

---

* According to the Mother, the serpent of the earthly paradise is a symbol of the evolutionary force that drove man out of a state of animal bliss to regain the state of a divine happiness by eating the fruit of Knowledge and developing his mental capacity until it reached a point of transformation. In Greece, too, winged serpents pull the chariot of Demeter. The serpent is not only a symbol of cosmic evolution but also a symbol of the individual evolutionary force: when the ascending force (*kundalini*) awakens at the base of our spine and emerges from our physical consciousness, where it was asleep, coiled up like a serpent in its hole (*kundalini* means "the coiled one"), when it rises from center to center, the evolved human being emerges from ordinary unconsciousness to enter a cosmic consciousness; then, through the opening above the head, he enters the divine solar consciousness. For Sri Aurobindo and the rishis, and probably for other sources of wisdom that have now vanished, the discovery of this solar consciousness above is only a first evolutionary stage which has to be followed by the discovery of the same solar consciousness below, in Matter. This is the serpent biting its own tail, or what Sri Aurobindo calls the "transformation."

CHAPTER 17

The Transformation

The manifestation of the Spirit in a supramental consciousness and in a new body, a new race, is something as inevitable as was the advent of Homo sapiens after the primates. The only real question now is whether this new evolution will take place with us or without us. This is how Sri Aurobindo expressed the dilemma: *If a spiritual unfolding on earth is the hidden truth of our birth into Matter, if it is fundamentally an evolution of consciousness that has been taking place in Nature, then man as he is cannot be the last term of that evolution: he is too imperfect an expression of the spirit, mind itself a too limited form and instrumentation; mind is only a middle term of consciousness, the mental being can only be a transitional being. If, then, man is incapable of exceeding mentality, he must be surpassed and supermind and superman must manifest and take the lead of the creation. But if his mind is capable of opening to what exceeds it, then there is no reason why man himself should not arrive at supermind and supermanhood or at least lend his mentality, life and body to an evolution of that greater term of the Spirit manifesting in Nature.*[1] We are facing, Sri Aurobindo says, a new *crisis of transformation*[2] as crucial as the crisis that marked the appearance of Life in Matter, or the appearance of Mind in Life. Our own choice is crucial, too, because this time, instead of leaving Nature to do her work of transmutation without much concern for existing contingencies, we can become conscious collaborators in our own evolution, accept the challenge, or, as Sri Aurobindo says, let ourselves be surpassed.

Future Prospects

What will this new race be like? To understand the goal is already a great step on the way, because to understand and to aspire for that Future opens up an invisible door within us through which forces greater than our own can enter, and this means the beginning of our collaboration. Indeed, it is not our own human forces that will effect the transition to the supermind but an increasingly conscious surrender to the Force above.

We have already suggested what the consciousness of the supramental being might be like, but it is worth repeating with Sri Aurobindo that *supermanhood is not man climbed to his own natural zenith, not a superior degree of human greatness, knowledge, power, intelligence, will, character, genius, dynamic force, saintliness, love, purity or perfection. Supermind is something beyond mental man and his limits.*[3] Driven to the extreme, Mind can only harden man, not divinize him or even simply give him joy, for the Mind is an instrument of division, and all its hierarchies are inevitably based upon domination, whether religious, moral, political, economic, or emotional, since by its very constitution it is incapable of embracing the totality of human truths—and even when it is capable of embracing, it is still incapable of implementation. Ultimately, if collective evolution had nothing better to offer than a pleasant mixture of human and social "greatness," Saint Vincent de Paul and Mahatma Gandhi with a dash of Marxism-Leninism and paid vacations thrown in, then we could not help concluding that such a goal would be even more insipid than the millions of "golden birds" or the string quartets at the summit of individual mental evolution. If so many thousands of years of suffering and striving culminated only in this sort of truncated earthly parade, then *Pralaya* or any of the other cosmic disintegrations promised by the ancient traditions might not be so bad after all.

If our mental possibilities, even at their zenith, are not adequate, our vital and physical ones are even less so. It is doubtful whether the Spirit, when it manifests in a supramental consciousness, will be satisfied with a body subject to the physical laws of gravity and decay, and whether it will accept as its sole means of expression the limited range of our mental language, the pen, the etching knife, or the brush. This means that Matter will have to change. Such is the purpose of "Transformation," and it begins with our own immediate matter, the body. *In the spiritual tradition the body has been regarded as an obstacle, incapable of spiritualisation or transmutation and a heavy weight holding the soul to earthly nature and preventing its ascent either to spiritual fulfillment in the Supreme or to the dissolution of its individual being in the Supreme. But while this conception of the role of the body in our destiny is suitable enough for a sadhana [discipline] that sees earth only as a field of the ignorance and earth-life as a preparation for a saving withdrawal . . . it is insufficient for a sadhana which conceives of a divine life upon earth and liberation of earth-nature itself as part of a total purpose of the embodiment of the spirit here. If a total transformation of the being is our aim, a transformation of the body must be an indispensable part of it; without that no full divine life on earth is possible.*[4]

According to Sri Aurobindo, the essential quality of supramentalized Matter is its receptivity: it will be capable of responding to the conscious will and of changing according to the will's dictates, the way clay responds to a potter's fingers. As Matter releases the involved spiritual power it contains and becomes openly conscious, it will be able to respond to corresponding vibrations of the supramental consciousness, just as we now respond to a vibration of anger with anger or to a vibration of love with warmth in our heart. Conscious malleability will be the essential attribute of supramentalized Matter. All other qualities derive from that fundamental characteristic: immortality (or at least a capacity to modify one's form or even change forms altogether), lightness, beauty, luminousness. Such will be the natural attributes of supramental Matter. *The body could become a revealing vessel of a supreme beauty and bliss,—casting the beauty of the light of the spirit suffusing and radiating from it as a lamp reflects and diffuses the luminosity of its in dwelling flame, carrying in itself the beatitude of the spirit, its joy of the seeing mind, its joy of life and spiritual happiness, the joy of Matter released into a spiritual consciousness and thrilled with a constant ecstasy.*[5] The Veda has already expressed this: "Then shall thy humanity become as if the workings of the gods; it is as if the visible heaven of light were founded in thee." (*Rig Veda* V.66.2)

Before these spectacular and visible changes, which will likely take place at the very end of the process, Sri Aurobindo foresees substantial changes in our physiology. We will return to this point when we discuss the practical work of transformation. For the moment, let us only mention several functional changes that Sri Aurobindo observed in his own body: *There would have to be a change in the operative processes of the material organs themselves and, it may well be, in their very constitution and their importance; they could not be allowed to impose their limitations imperatively on the new physical life. . . . The brain would be a channel of communication of the form of the thoughts and a battery of their insistence on the body and the outside world where they could then become effective directly, communicating themselves without physical means from mind to mind, producing with a similar directness effects on the thoughts, actions and lives of others or even upon material things. The heart would equally be a direct communicant and medium of interchange for the feelings and emotions thrown outward upon the world by the forces of the psychic centre. Heart could reply directly to heart, the life-force come to the help of other lives and answer their call in spite of strangeness and distance, many beings without any external communication thrill with the message and meet in the secret light from one divine centre. The will might control the organs that deal with food, safeguard automatically the health, eliminate greed and desire, substitute subtler processes or draw in strength and substance from the universal life-force so that the body could maintain for a long time its*

*own strength and substance without loss or waste, remaining thus with
no need of sustenance by material aliments, and yet continue a
strenuous action with no fatigue or pause for sleep or repose. . . .
Conceivably, one might rediscover and re-establish at the summit of
the evolution of life the phenomenon we see at its base, the power to
draw from all around it the means of sustenance and self-renewal.*[6]
Beyond Mind, the complete man rediscovers consciously what
Matter already is unconsciously—Energy and Peace—since Matter is really but a sleep of the Spirit.

At a further stage of transformation, Sri Aurobindo foresees our
organs being replaced by a dynamic functioning of our centers of
consciousness or *chakras.* This is the real transition from the
animal-man conceived by the lower evolution to the human-man
of the new evolution. It is one of the tasks undertaken by Sri
Aurobindo and the Mother. From the earliest stages of yoga we
have found that each of our activities, from the highest to the most
material, was set in motion and fueled by a current of consciousness-force that seemed to converge at different levels of our being,
within certain centers and with different intensities depending
upon the type of activity; whenever we have tried to manipulate
this current, we have found it to be an extraordinary source of
energy, limited only by our own capacity. Therefore, it is not
inconceivable that our organs, which are only the physical translation or the material concentration of this current behind, may
in the course of evolution be replaced by a direct action of the
centers of consciousness, which would simply radiate their energy
throughout the new body, just as the heart, blood and nerves now
radiate throughout our present body. This is how the Mother once
explained the future body to the ashram children: *Transformation
implies that all this purely physical organization be replaced by
concentrations of force, each with a particular type of vibration;
instead of organs, there will be centers of conscious energy moved by
the conscious will. No more stomach, no more heart, no more blood
circulation, no more lungs; all that is gone and is replaced by a play
of vibrations representing what these organs symbolically are. For*

*organs are merely the material symbols of the centers of energy; they
are not the essential reality: they simply give it a form or a material
support in certain circumstances. The transformed body will then
operate through its* true *centers of energy and no longer through their
symbolic representatives as developed in the animal body. Thus, you
must first know what your heart represents in terms of the cosmic
energy, what your circulation, your brain, and your lungs represent in
terms of the cosmic energy, then you must be able to muster the original
vibrations that these organs symbolize, and progressively concentrate
all those energies in your body and change each organ into a center of
conscious energy that will replace the symbolic functioning by the true
one. For example, behind the symbolic movement of the lungs, there
is a true movement that gives the capacity of lightness, and you escape
the law of gravity.** And likewise *for each organ. There is a true
movement behind every symbolic one. This doesn't mean that there
will no longer be any recognizable form; form will be made up of
qualities rather than solid particles. It will be a practical or pragmatic
form, so to speak—supple, mobile and light at will, in contrast to the
present fixity of the gross material form.* Thus Matter will become a
divine expression; the supramental Will will be able to translate
the whole gamut of its inner life into corresponding changes in its
own substance, much as our faces now change (although so little
and so imperfectly) according to our emotions: the body will be
made of *concentrated energy obeying the will.* Instead of being, in
the powerful words of Epictetus, "a little soul carrying a corpse,"**
we will become a living soul in a living body.

It is not just the body and the mind that will have to change
with the supramental consciousness, but also life's very substance.
If there is one sign that characterizes our mental civilization, it is

---

* This "true movement" behind our breathing is, according to Sri Aurobindo,
the same as the one governing electromagnetic fields, what the ancient
yogis termed *vayu,* the Life-Energy. The well-known breathing exercises
(*pranayama*) are simply one system (among others) of controlling *vayu,*
which eventually enables one to escape gravity.

** Quoted by Sri Aurobindo.

the use of artifices. Nothing happens naturally; we are the prisoners of a thick web of substitutes: airplanes, telephones, televisions, and the plethora of instruments and devices that mask our impotence. We unabashedly forsake all our natural capacities, which dwindle from generation to generation through laziness or ignorance. We forget that our marvelous inventions are only the material extensions of powers that exist within us; if they were not already there, we would never have been able to invent them. We are that *thaumaturge sceptic of miracles*,[7] Sri Aurobindo spoke of. Having delegated to machines the task of seeing for us, hearing for us, and traveling for us, we have now become helpless without them. Our human civilization, created for the joy of life, has become the slave of the means required for enjoying life: sixty percent of our lifetime is spent acquiring means and another thirty percent sleeping. *What is absurd here*, says the Mother, *is all the artificial devices we must use. Any idiot has more power provided he has the means of acquiring the necessary devices. But in a true world, a supramental world, the more conscious and in harmony with the truth of things you are, the more your will has authority over substance; substance responds to the will. There, authority is a true authority. If you want a dress, you must have the power to make it, a true power. If you don't have that power, well, you go naked! There is no artifice to substitute for the lack of power. While here, not once in a million times is authority the expression of something true. Everything is colossally stupid.* This supramental "authority" is not some kind of supermagic, far from it; it is an extremely precise process, as precise and exact as a chemistry experiment, except that instead of dealing with external objects, the supramental being acts upon the true vibration in the core of each thing and combines it with other vibrations in order to achieve a particular result, like a painter mixing colors for a picture or a poet combining sounds for a poem. He is truly a poet, for he creates what he names. The true name of an object is the vibration constituting it; to name an object is to have the power to evoke it or to destroy it.

The spontaneous and natural quality of supramental life—for

ultimately only Truth is natural—will be expressed also in a supramental art, which will be a direct and exact representation of our particular spiritual tonality; an art in which cheating will have become impossible because only our inner light will be able to touch and play upon the same lights involved in Matter and mold from it the corresponding forms. If our vibration is gray, our creation will be similarly gray, and everything we touch will be gray. Our physical, external environment will be the exact image of our inner environment; we will be able to manifest only what we are. Life itself will be a work of art, our outer dominion the changing stage of our inner states. Our language, likewise, will have power only through the true spiritual force within us; it will be a living *mantra*, a visible language like the play of emotions upon a human face. All shams will draw to an end, whether they be political, religious, literary, artistic, or emotional. Once, when a skeptical disciple commented that the Supermind was an impossible invention, first of all, because it had never been seen or realized before, Sri Aurobindo replied with his typical humor: *What a wonderful argument! Since it has not been done, it can't be done! At that rate the whole history of the earth must have stopped long before the protoplasm. When it was a mass of gases, no life had been born, ergo, life could not be born—when only life was there, mind was not born, so mind could not be born. Since mind is there but nothing beyond, as there is no Supermind manifested in anybody, so Supermind can never be born.* Sobhanallah! *Glory, Glory, Glory to the human reason! Luckily the Divine or the Cosmic Spirit or Nature or whatever is there cares a damn for the human reason. He or She or It does what He or She or It has to do, whether it can or can't be done.*[8] Thousands of years ago, the rishis had already spoken of the skeptics' misfortune: "In these there is not the Wonder and the Might." (*Rig Veda* VII.61.5)

The Work (First Phase)

As remarkable as the end result will be, the work of getting there is modest and humble and patient, exactly like the work of a scientist with his vials and test tubes: *a microscopic work*, says the Mother. For it is not a question of performing miracles, but of securing a new physical base by freeing the consciousness-force in each atom and each cell. One might think that this work on the body involves psychophysical methods similar to hatha-yoga, but it is nothing of the kind. Consciousness is and remains the main tool: *The change of consciousness will be the chief factor, the initial movement, the physical modification will be a subordinate factor, a consequence.*[9] With his usual clarity, Sri Aurobindo puts us before the fact: *In the previous stages of the evolution Nature's first care and effort had to be directed towards a change in the physical organisation, for only so could there be a change of consciousness; this was a necessity imposed by the insufficiency of the force of consciousness already in formation to effect a change in the body. But in man a reversal is possible, indeed inevitable; for it is through his consciousness, through its transmutation and no longer through a new bodily organism as a first instrumentation that the evolution can and must be effected. In the inner reality of things a change of consciousness was always a major fact, the evolution has always had a spiritual significance and the physical change was only instrumental; but this relation was concealed by the first abnormal balance of the two factors, the body of the external Inconscience outweighing and obscuring in importance the spiritual element, the conscious being. But once the balance has been righted, it is no longer the change of body that must precede the change of consciousness; the consciousness itself by its mutation will necessitate and operate whatever mutation is needed for the body.*[10]

We can distinguish three phases in this work, corresponding to Sri Aurobindo's and the Mother's own progress and discoveries; three phases that seem to go from bright to dark, from the miraculous to the significant commonplace, and from the individual cell to the earth. The first phase was devoted to testing the powers of consciousness. This is what some disciples have called the "bright period," lasting from 1920 to 1926, after which Sri Aurobindo would retire into complete solitude for twenty-four years, to concentrate exclusively on the Work. Using the new, supramental power they had discovered, Sri Aurobindo and the Mother first made several experiments on their own bodies. "Testing" is one of the key words in Sri Aurobindo's vocabulary: *I have been testing day and night for years upon years more scrupulously than any scientist his theory or his method on the physical plane.*[11] From this huge body of experiences, which pervade Sri Aurobindo's written works and correspondence, we might draw four symbolic events illustrating the power of consciousness and Sri Aurobindo's "testing," bearing in mind that these are only instances among many others, and that neither Sri Aurobindo nor Mother attributed any special importance to them. It is through chance conversations or letters that their existence came to be known. Sri Aurobindo had just arrived in Pondicherry when he undertook a prolonged fast, "to see." Years later, when a disciple asked him whether it was possible to go without food, he was told: *Yes, it is. When I once fasted for about 23 days or more. . . . I very nearly solved the problem. I could walk eight hours a day as usual. I continued my mental work and sadhana as usual and I found that I was not in the least weak at the end of 23 days. But the flesh began to waste away and I did not find a clue to replacing the very material reduced in the body. When I broke the fast, I also did not observe the usual rule of people who observe long fasts,—by beginning with little food. I began with the same quantity I used to take before. . . . I tried fasting once in jail but that was for ten days when I used to sleep also once in three nights. I lost ten pounds in weight but I felt stronger at the end of ten days than I was before I began the fast . . . I was able to raise a pail of water above my head, a thing I could not do ordinarily.*[12] Another experience goes back to the time of the Alipore jail: *I was concentrated. And my mind was questioning: Were such siddhis [powers] possible? when I suddenly found myself raised up. . . . I could not have held my body like that normally even if I had wanted to and I found that the body remained suspended like that without any exertion on my part.*[13] Another time, Sri Aurobindo had a large quantity of opium purchased from the Pondicherry bazaar, enough to overwhelm several people, and absorbed it entirely without suffering any adverse effects, just to test the control of his consciousness. We owe the fourth item to the impatience of a disciple who was complaining that he had not received an answer to his letters soon enough. *You do not realise,* Sri Aurobindo replied, *that I have to spend 12 hours over the ordinary correspondence. I work 3 hours in the afternoon and the whole night up to 6 in the morning over this . . . even the rocky heart of a disciple would be touched.*[14]

Sleep, food, gravity, cause and effect—Sri Aurobindo tested one by one all the so-called laws of nature, to find that they hold only insofar as we believe in their hold; if we change our consciousness, the "groove" also changes. All our laws are only "habits":

Her firm and changeless habits aping Law,[15]

says *Savitri* of Nature. Indeed, there is only one true Law, that of the Spirit, which can modify all the lower habits of Nature: *The Spirit made it and the Spirit can exceed it, but we must first open the doors of our prison-house and learn to live less in Nature than in the Spirit.*[16] Sri Aurobindo has no miraculous recipes, no magic formulas; his entire yoga rests upon a very simple double certainty: the certainty of the Spirit that is within us and the certainty of the Spirit's earthly manifestation. This is the only key, the real agency for doing his work. *In each man there is a God and to make him manifest is the aim of the divine life. That we can all do.*[17] When a disciple argued that it was easy for exceptional beings such as Sri Aurobindo and the Mother to defy natural laws, while poor mortals had only their ordinary resources, Sri Aurobindo protested vehemently: *My sadhana is not a freak or a monstrosity or a miracle done outside the laws of Nature and the conditions of life and consciousness on earth. If I could do these things or if they could happen in my Yoga, it means that they can be done and that therefore these*

*developments and transformations are possible in the terrestrial con-
sciousness. . . . I had no urge towards spirituality in me, I developed
spirituality. I was incapable of understanding metaphysics, I developed into a philosopher. I had no eye for painting—I developed it by
Yoga. I transformed my nature from what it was to what it was not.
I did it by a special manner, not by a miracle, and I did it to show
what could be done and how it could be done. I did not do it out of
any personal necessity of my own or by a miracle without any process.
I say that if it is not so, then my Yoga is useless and my life was a
mistake—a mere absurd freak of Nature without meaning or consequence.*[18] For Sri Aurobindo, the key is to understand that the
Spirit is not the opposite of life but the fulfillment of life, that the
inner realization is the key to an outer realization:

Heaven's touch fulfils but cancels not our earth.[19]

Once humanity understands this simple fact, once it gives up its
age-old habit of cloistering the Spirit in heaven and believing in
death, believing in its laws and its smallness, then we will be saved
and ready for a divine life. This is what Sri Aurobindo came to
show us above all else: there is no need to fly off to heaven to find
the Spirit, we are *free*, we are *stronger* than all the "laws," because
God is within us. All we need to do is believe this, for faith hastens
the world's fairy tale. *That was the thing that saved me all through,
I mean a perfect balance. First of all I believed that nothing was
impossible and at the same time I could question everything.*[20] One
day, as he was again being urged to resume his political struggle,
Sri Aurobindo promptly replied that what was needed was *not a
revolt against the British Government, which anyone could easily
manage . . . [but] a revolt against the whole universal Nature.*[21]

The few disciples—there were about fifteen of them—all remember the very special, highly concentrated atmosphere prevailing during this first phase. They had dazzling experiences almost
at will; divine manifestations were common, and the natural laws
seemed to begin to yield. The veil between the physical world and
the other planes of consciousness was growing thinner, and the

beings we call gods, or the forces of the overmind, were able to manifest, bend the laws, and produce so-called miracles. Had this trend continued, Sri Aurobindo and the Mother would have been well on their way to founding a new religion, and Pondicherry to becoming one of the "holy places" where spiritual fragrances mask the more common odors. But one day, as the Mother was describing one of the latest extraordinary occurrences to Sri Aurobindo, he remarked humorously: *Yes, it is very interesting, you will work miracles that will make us famous the world over; you will be able to turn earthly events topsy-turvy; indeed* (Sri Aurobindo smiled), *it will be a grand success.* Then he added: *But this is an overmental creation, not the highest truth. It is not the success we want; we want to establish the supermind on earth, create a new world. Half an hour later,* narrates the Mother, *everything had stopped. I did not say anything to anyone, not a word, but in half an hour I had torn down everything, severed the connection between the gods and the disciples, demolished everything. For I knew that as long as this was going on, it was so alluring (one saw astounding things all the time) that we would have been tempted to continue. . . . I tore down everything. From then on, we started over on a different footing.*

That was the end of the first phase. Sri Aurobindo and Mother had verified the power of consciousness, and they had found that "miracles with a method," or interventions of higher powers of consciousness, merely sugar the pill without changing the essence of things. These particular "miracles" are useless from the standpoint of transforming the world. *The real thing,* as the Mother would say, is not to change Matter from the outside through fleeting "supernatural" interventions, but to change it from within, lastingly—to establish a new physical order. History is full of "holy places," and they have all failed us. We have lived long enough under the auspices of the gods and religions. *I have no intention of giving my sanction to a new edition of the old fiasco,* wrote Sri Aurobindo, *a partial and transient spiritual opening within with no true and radical change in the law of the external nature.*[22] Levitation, the conquest of sleep, hunger and even illness barely touch the surface of the problem. These are negative efforts directed *against* a prevalent order, which still implies a recognition (in negative terms) of the old laws, while it is the order itself that must change. All such "miracles" are but the reverse side of our impotence. What we need is not a better world, but a *new* world, not a "highly concentrated" atmosphere, but a "lowly" concentrated one, as it were. Everything here below must become holy. Suddenly, on November 24, 1926, Sri Aurobindo announced that he was retiring into complete solitude. Thus would the ashram become founded officially under the Mother's direction. There was no need to tell the disciples that the yoga would henceforth take place "in the subconscient and the inconscient": They all tumbled down from their marvelous experiences . . . soon to confront far harsher realities. Now began the second phase of the work of transformation.

The Fundamental Agni

At the outset of the second phase, a little before his retirement, we find a rather strange conversation that Sri Aurobindo had in 1926 with a French physicist. These few words of Sri Aurobindo's, which must then have seemed rather enigmatic, show the particular orientation of his experiences:

There are two statements of modern science that would stir up deeper ranges in an occultist:

1) Atoms are whirling systems like the solar system.

2) The atoms of all the elements are made out of the same constituents. A different arrangement is the only cause of different properties.

If these statements were considered under their true aspect, they could lead science to new discoveries of which it has no idea at present and in comparison with which the present knowledge is poor.

Let us remember that the year was then 1926.

Sri Aurobindo continued: *According to the experience of ancient*

Yogis . . . Agni is threefold:
  1) ordinary fire, jada Agni
  2) electric fire, vaidyuta Agni
  3) solar fire, saura Agni
  Science has only entered upon the first and second of these fires. The fact that the atom is like the solar system could lead it to the knowledge of the third.[23]

What was Sri Aurobindo driving at? And how is it that he—not to mention the rishis of six thousand years ago—knew before all our scientific laboratories that solar heat, *Saura Agni,* has a different origin from what we usually call fire or electricity, that it is produced by nuclear fusion and that it is the very same energy found in the atom's core? It is a fact—perhaps disconcerting for science, which needs to deal with "concrete realities"—that every physical reality is lined with an inner reality which is both its cause and its foundation; even the most infinitesimal material elements have their inner counterparts, and foremost among them are our own physical organs, which are only the material linings or supports of the centers of consciousness. Everything here is the symbolic translation or shadow thrown by a light or a force that is behind, on another plane. This whole world is but a vast Symbol. Science observes and analyzes phenomena, devises equations for gravitation, weight, atomic fission, etc., but it only touches the effects, never the true cause. The yogi sees the cause before the effect. A scientist can deduce a certain cause from the effects produced, whereas a yogi deduces the effects from the cause; he can even deduce effects that do not yet exist from a cause that already exists (e.g., the accident that will happen tomorrow from the force of the accident that is already there in the background). The scientist manipulates effects, at times bringing about catastrophes; the yogi sees the cause, or, rather, identifies with the Cause, and thereby he can alter the effects, or as Sri Aurobindo puts it, the "habits" we call laws. Ultimately, all our physical effects, which we have codified into laws, are nothing more than a convenient *support* for the manifestation of forces that are behind, exactly as a performance of magic requires certain ritual-istic diagrams, certain ingredients or formulas, so that the forces invoked can manifest themselves. This whole world is a gigantic magical performance, a constant act of magic. But the earthly diagram, all the ingredients we have so earnestly and unchangeably codified, all our infallible formulas, are merely conventions. The earthly ritual can change if, instead of remaining mesmerized by the effects, we go back to the cause behind them—on the side of the Magician. There is a tale about a Hindu Brahmin who, every day at the hour of his worship, had the family cat tied up so that he would not be disturbed in his ritual. Eventually, both the Brahmin and the cat died, and the Brahmin's son, now in charge of the worship ceremony, procured a new cat, which he then conscientiously tied up during the sacrifice! From father to son, the cat had become an indispensable element in the effective performance of the ritual. Our own unassailable laws, too, may contain a few little cats. If we go back to the original force concealed behind the physical support, to the "true movement," as the Mother describes it, then we begin to witness the Great Play, and to realize just how different it is from the rigid notions we have of it. Behind the phenomenon of gravitation, to take one of the rituals, there is what the ancient yogis called *Vayu*, which causes gravitation and the electromagnetic fields (as Sri Aurobindo mentioned also during that conversation of 1926), and this is how a yogi can eventually defy gravity. Behind the solar or nuclear fire there is the fundamental *Agni*, "the child of the waters, the child of the forests, the child of things stable and the child of things that move. Even in the stone he is there," says the Rig Veda. (I.70.2) This is the "warm gold dust" the Mother speaks of, the real cause behind the effect, the original force behind the material, atomic support; "other flames are only branches of thy stock." (I.59) It is because Sri Aurobindo and the rishis saw this spiritual *Agni* in Matter, this "sun in the darkness," that they were able to know of its material, atomic effects, and hence of nuclear fusion, long before our own scientific experiments revealed this phenomenom.

This is also why, since they knew the cause, they dared to speak of transformation.*

Finally, the whole universe is composed of a single substance of divine Consciousness-Force, and *Agni* is the element of force or energy in consciousness: "O Son of Energy," says the Rig Veda. (VIII.84.4) It is Force-Consciousness, a warmth, a flame, at whatever level we feel it. When we concentrate in our mind, we feel the subtle heat of mental energy or mental *Agni*; when we concentrate in our heart or in our emotions, we feel the subtle heat of Life-Energy or vital *Agni*; when we plunge into our soul, we experience the soul's subtle heat or psychic *Agni*. There is only one *Agni* throughout, one current of Consciousness-Force or consciousness-energy or consciousness-heat taking on different intensities at different levels. Then there is the fundamental *Agni*, or material *Agni*, which is the ultimate state of the energy of consciousness, prior to its conversion or densification into Matter. This is how one becomes the other. (Let us here recall the Mother's words: "It is a movement greater than the force or power holding the cells in an individual form.") Modern science has also finally realized that Matter and Energy can be converted into each other ($E = mc^2$ is its great breakthrough), but it has yet to see that Energy is consciousness, that Matter is consciousness, and that by acting upon consciousness one can act upon Energy and Matter. To transform Matter into Energy, modern science knows only of physical processes that produce heat, but by knowing the fundamental *Agni*, which is the foundation of Energy or Consciousness-Force, one can, in principle, act directly upon Matter and achieve

---

* Physical light, the extreme combination of speed and immobility, is a remarkable symbol of the supreme Consciousness. Similarly, the physical sun is another symbol of the supreme Power, as many ancient traditions, which were less childish than we might suppose, have seen. "But the Hindu Yogis who had realized these experiences did not elaborate them and turn them into scientific knowledge," remarked Sri Aurobindo. "Other fields of action and sources of knowledge being open before them, they neglected what for them was the most exterior aspect of the manifestation."

the same transmutation without setting one's body on fire in the process.

The conversation of 1926 then introduces us to two material facts (and their spiritual basis) that are extremely important from the standpoint of transformation: first, that all earthly forms are made up of the same elements, and only different atomic arrangements account for the different features (this is the physical counterpart to the spiritual truth of the world's divine Oneness: "Thou art man and woman, boy and girl, old and worn thou walkest bent over a staff; thou art the blue bird and the green and the scarlet-eyed"*); and second, that the solar fire in Matter is the material counterpart of the fundamental *Agni*, which, as Sri Aurobindo stressed in another part of the same conversation, is *the builder of forms.* To wield *Agni* is to be able to change forms, to transform Matter: "He tastes not that delight (of the twice-born) who is unripe and whose body has not suffered in the heat of the fire," says the Rig Veda; "they alone are able to bear that and enjoy it who have been prepared by the flame." (IX.83.1) It is the warm gold dust that will transmute its material counterpart, the nuclear dust in our body: *The subtle process will be more powerful than the gross, so that a subtle action of Agni will be able to do the action which would now need a physical change such as increased temperature.*[24] Our atoms too are merely a convenient translation of the eternal ritual; nothing is fixed or inevitable. There is no end to the possible combinations, no end to the new human Being.

Second Phase—The Body

The second phase began in 1926 and continued until 1940. It was a phase of individual work on the body and in the subconscient. Up to this point, we have all the clues to achieve the supramental

---

* *Swetaswatara Upanishad* IV.3.4

change of consciousness ourselves, and we know the basic principle of transformation. It is *Agni* "who does the work," says the Rig Veda. (I.1.5) But how, practically, is *Agni* going to change Matter? We cannot yet say; we know only some bits here and there. *If we knew the process,* says the Mother, *it would already be done.* All the other realizations have been meticulously recorded by the Indian traditions; we know all the methods for attaining Nirvana; realizing the cosmic Spirit; finding the soul; conquering gravity, hunger, cold, sleep and illnesses; leaving one's body at will; or prolonging life. Everyone can achieve these feats; the way is well charted, and the stages have been described by the seers or the Hindu *shastras* for thousands of years. It is merely a question of discipline and patience and proper timing. But the transformation is something no one has ever done, an entirely unknown journey, like traveling through a country that does not yet exist. Perhaps it is something equivalent to what happened when the first mental forms began to emerge in the world of Matter and Life. How could the first semi-animal organism that received these mental vibrations understand and describe what was happening to it, and, above all, how could it say what had to be done to control thought? To quote the Mother: *You don't know whether this or that experience is part of the way or not; you don't even know if you are progressing or not, because if you knew you were progressing, it would mean that you knew the way—but there is no way! No one has ever been there! We won't really be able to say what it is until it has been done.* It is *an adventure into the unknown,* as Sri Aurobindo would emphasize. We are truly like the old primates before this new creation. From here on, therefore, we can only indicate some broad lines of development, or of difficulty, without being sure whether or not they really belong to the path. The experience is in process. When it has succeeded once, just once, in a single human being, then the very conditions of the transformation will be different, because the path will have been trodden, charted, and the prime difficulties cleared away. The day Plato conceived *Phaedrus,* he raised up all of humankind to the possibility of Phaedrus. The day a single human being overcomes the difficulties of the transformation, he will raise up all humanity to the possibility of a luminous, immortal, true life.

It is possible, however, to have some idea in advance of the major problems confronting the seeker. When *Agni* burns in our mind, in our moments of inspiration, we know it creates a great tension, an almost physical heat. When it burns in our heart, in our soul-moments, we know that our breast feels like a red-hot hearth, hot enough for the skin to change color and to such a degree that even an inexperienced eye can perceive a kind of glowing radiance around the yogi. When *Agni* burns in our vital, and as we call the force or open to the cosmic world, there is likewise a kind of concentrated pulsation at the level of the navel, almost a tremor of fever throughout the body (since a large amount of force is entering through a tiny channel). But what about the warm gold dust, *this wine of lightning*,[25] in the cells of the body? *It begins to boil everywhere,* says the Mother in her simple language, *like a boiler about to explode.* The rishis, too, spoke of being broken "like a half-baked jar" if one went too quickly. Furthermore, if it were uniquely a matter of creating something entirely new, the problem would be somewhat simpler, but we must do with what we have, *evolve* from our present state to another state, from an old form of organization to a new one. The old heart, the old lungs are still there; at what *moment*, wondered the Mother, is the heart going to be stopped and the Force set in motion? The difficulty is in the change-over. Countless experiences in tiny doses are therefore necessary to accustom the cells so that they do not panic during the transition. Thus, the first problem is to prepare the body, and this requires years and years, perhaps centuries. Sri Aurobindo worked for forty years and the Mother for fifty years at this preparation. The practical, immediate necessity, then, is to endure, to outrun death. *The basic question,* the Mother said, *in this race toward transformation is to know which of the two will arrive first: the person seeking to transform the body in the image of the divine Truth, or the body's old habit of disintegra-*

tion.

For, naturally, the work must be done in one lifetime. From one life to another, it is possible to recover the achievements of the soul, the mind, and even the vital, which in the current life will result in spontaneous blossomings, innate talents, something already developed. One needs only go over the lesson for ten or twenty years to capture the thread of former lives; there is even a rather striking experience in which one sees precisely the cutoff point where the work already accomplished in past lives ends and the new phase begins. Thus one simply picks up the trail where one had left it. But the cellular progress in the body, the progress of the physical consciousness obviously cannot pass into the next life; everything gets scattered on the funeral pyre or dissipates in the earth. So if we want a continuity in human evolution, if we want the supramental being to manifest in our own flesh rather than in some new, unknown organism that would supersede our mental humanity, it is necessary for *one* human being to accomplish the work in *one* lifetime. If it succeeds once, it can be transmitted to others (we will return to this point later). Sri Aurobindo used to say that it would take three centuries—and he had a clear vision—for a full supramental being to emerge, luminous, light, etc., as we have previously tried to describe him. Short of a full supramental being (even Plato was not born in a day), we must then build in our flesh a *transitional* being, a link between the human and the superhuman, that is, a being who not only would have realized the supramental consciousness but whose body would also have acquired enough immortality, as it were, to last through the transition period, and enough power and suppleness to effect its own transmutation, or to engender a supramental being through its own energy, bypassing the usual method of earthly birth. Indeed, the heavy animal and human heredity weighing on our subconscient, and automatically transmitted by physical conception, is one of the major hurdles to the transformation, at least as difficult as the boiling *Agni*, if not more difficult. This is the second problem. Perhaps it is, in fact, the true problem, far greater than the other, more conspicuous problems of the body. Such are the two fundamental problems confronting the seeker: to impart to the cells of the body the consciousness of immortality, which is already there in our soul and even in our mind, and to cleanse the subconscient completely. The progress of *Agni* in the body depends, *it seems*, on these two conditions. Thus, as always, the work is a work of consciousness.

First, the ability to endure. In practice, one finds that immortality is always closely related to truth: what is true is immortal. If we were completely true, we would be completely immortal, from head to toe. Until now, however, hardly anything except our soul has been immortal, because it is the truth of the Spirit within us, passing from one life to the next, growing, evolving, becoming more and more conscious. The mind, too, as it becomes sufficiently integrated around the central Truth of our being, as it thinks the Truth and wants the Truth, is immortal. One can fairly easily remember one's past formations: some truths appear exceedingly familiar, some yearnings for truth inexplicably poignant. The vital also is capable of immortality as it becomes sufficiently integrated with the central psychic Truth: we emerge into another dimension, as familiar as eternity, though this is rather uncommon since our life-force is generally engrossed in all kinds of petty activities instead of building a true life. The more we go down the scale of consciousness, the thicker the falsehood and the more real is death—naturally, because in essence falsehood means decay. The vital is already fairly obscure, but the body is full of falsehood. Old age and illnesses are among its most prominent falsehoods; how could what is True become old, ugly, worn-out, or ill? Truth is so obviously radiant, beautiful, luminous, and eternal. Truth is invincible. Death and old age can only attain us because of our lack of Truth.

Admittedly, Death is wise for a long part of the way, for an immortal Mr. Smith would be a total waste of immortality. All things considered, Death is a faithful guardian of the Truth. It is remarkable how everything has two faces: if we look one way, we must struggle, fight, say *No*; if we look the other way, we can only give thanks and thanks again, and say *Yes* and *Yes* again. And we must be capable of both. Thus, the battle against the "falsehoods of the body"—illness, unconsciousness, old age—can only proceed after the transformation of the higher mental and vital levels has been secured, when the rest of the being lives in Truth and is settled in Truth. It would be a great error to presume that one can undertake the supramental yoga before completing all the other steps; one must reach all the way to the top in order to be able to reach the bottom.

As silence is the basic condition for mental transformation, and peace the basic condition for vital transformation, so immobility is the basis for physical transformation—not an outer immobility but an inner one, in the cellular consciousness. By mental silence and vital peace we have been able to sort out the countless vibrations of the world, the secret stimuli that set us in motion and trigger our feelings or thoughts. Similarly, by an immobility of the physical consciousness, we begin to expose another nest of swarming vibrations and to realize what we are really made of. In cellular terms, we live in a total chaos: a maelstrom of sensations— strong, pleasant, painful, acute, with very high highs or very low lows—and if the maelstrom stops only for a second, a terrible anguish ensues, calling for more and more sensations. We feel alive only when we feel this movement. The basic task, therefore, is to bring all this chaos to a standstill—not an equanimity of the soul but an equanimity of the cells. Only then can the work of truth begin. In this cellular equanimity, our body will become like a transparent pool in which the slightest vibrations become perceptible, hence controllable. All the forces of illness, decay and falsehood, all the subconscious distortions and deformities with their horrible little denizens will begin to wiggle *visibly* in this clearing, and we will then be able to catch them in the act. In fact, the effervescence of *Agni* is due not so much to a basic cellular incapacity as to the resistance of "our" obscurities. This purifying stillness alone can clear the way and help release Agni's overwhelming Movement without causing the body to quake in unison, to panic and run a fever.

Once this cellular immobility has been relatively well established, we will make a first discovery. We will encounter a major obstacle, which is always also a major help in the work of transformation, since on all the planes, every opposition we meet is precisely matched to the force required to take a further step forward; it is both the dead weight and the trigger. We had already isolated, beneath our thinking mind, a "vital mind" that finds wonderful justifications for all our desires and impulses, and then a "physical mind" that repeats the same incidents a thousand times over like a broken record. But there is a deeper layer still, a mental bedrock, as it were, that Sri Aurobindo calls the *cellular mind.* This is actually a mind of the cells or of groups of cells, very similar to the physical mind in its inexhaustible capacity for repeating the same old refrains, but not limited to the brain area or to the mechanical grinding of bits of thought; it is everywhere in the body, like millions of little voices one can easily hear once the other mental layers have been clarified. It ceaselessly churns out not the debris of our conscious activities but of all our sensory impressions; all it takes is for a group of cells to be struck once by an impression (a fear, a shock, or an illness), and they will begin repeating their fear, their contraction, the particular tendency toward disorder, or the memory of their illness. It is a gregarious, absurd mental process that spreads from one cell to the next, quivering and quivering everywhere, endlessly, forever picking up the same wavelengths, the same decaying suggestions, and forever responding to the same stimuli, like a Pavlovian dog to its bell. This is the very fear of life embedded in Matter, which is related to Matter's first conscious efforts to become "alive." Yet unfortunately, the bit of initiative this cellular mind does have is always used to attract every possible disorder—through fear—and then to attract death's final unconsciousness as a relief. Yet this cellular mind, which has quite a formidable power if we begin to reflect upon it, like ants upon an elephant, can put its absurd routine at the service of truth just as well as of falsehood. If it is once turned to a vibration of light, it will repeat that vibration, too, with the stubbornness of a mule, and most remarkably, it will repeat it day and *night,* nonstop.* Whatever we may be doing outwardly (working, talking, or sleeping), it repeats its own vibration over and over again, automatically and independently. Hence, its great value for the transformation: it can become an extraordinary means of fixing the supramental vibration in the body. This is what Sri Aurobindo says about it: *There is too an obscure mind of the body, of the very cells, molecules, corpuscles. Haeckel, the German materialist, spoke somewhere of the will in the atom, and recent science, dealing with the incalculable individual variation in the activity of the electrons, comes near to perceiving that this is not a figure but the shadow thrown by a secret reality. This body mind is a very tangible truth; owing to its obscurity and mechanical clinging to past movements and facile oblivion and rejection of the new, we find in it one of the chief obstacles to permeation by the supermind Force and the transformation of the functioning of the body. On the other hand, once effectively converted, it will be one of the most precious instruments of the stabilisation of the supramental Light and Force in material Nature.*[26]

This work is so minute that it is hard to describe. The only way of working is not to go into deep meditations, which affect only the summits of our being, or to attain an extraordinary concentration or ecstasies, but to remain right in the midst of things, to work at the level of the body, at the very lowest rungs of the ladder, so to speak, every minute of the day and night. This is why Sri Aurobindo insisted on the need for outer work and basic physical exercises, because such activities are the only way to measure oneself against Matter and to drive a little bit of true consciousness into it, or, rather, to allow *Agni* to emerge. This is why, too, he used to walk for many hours every day and then work at night.

---

* Hence the usefulness of a mantra, which can direct a vibration of a certain intensity to any point in the body, or to all points, if the cellular mind picks it up.

Through this external work, and *because of it,* the seeker will see all the false vibrations appear in broad daylight, all the *creases* of the body, as the Mother calls them. Next each false vibration will have to be rectified. But this is still a negative way of putting it, for there is only one Vibration of divine joy in the world and in things—*the* Vibration—because God is Joy. The moment falsehood sets in, that *very* vibration begins to become discolored, hardened, tense, and everything begins grating. Suffering is the most certain sign of falsehood. Pain is the Falsehood of the world. The task of the seeker, then, is not so much to struggle against so-called bad vibrations as to keep the true vibration alive, the divine joy in the body, for this joy has the power to set things right again, to ease the pain, to harmonize and to heal all those tight, wearisome, deceitful little vibrations in which our cells constantly live. It would be tedious, as tedious as the work itself, to describe the countless tiny falsehoods of the body through which old age, disease, and death manage to creep in. *To do each thing in the true way,* as the Mother says, while there are so many false ways of doing the slightest daily gesture. To give an example, this is one direction of the work among many others: we do everything in a state of tension, hurriedly, carelessly, unconsciously; in response to the thousand and one stimuli of outer life, not to mention crises, we behave physically like a patient in a dentist's chair; we are tense and nervous, because we are forever in a rush, afraid, anxious, or eager. This is the legacy of several millions of years of animal nature; our substance has retained the memory of all our struggles for survival, and its immediate response is to tense up. This tension is one of the causes of death, as well as a major obstacle to establishing the true vibration. When we become tense because of a blow, we concentrate all our vital force in one point, as a defense; an enormous current abruptly passes through a tiny opening, which turns red and hurts. If we could learn to expand our physical consciousness and to absorb the blow instead of rejecting it, we would not suffer; all suffering, at any level whatsoever, is a narrowness of consciousness. Similarly, if the warm, gold supramental dust were suddenly to fill our cells and the body reacted with its usual contraction, everything would explode. In other words, our cellular consciousness, like our mental and vital consciousness, must learn to expand and to universalize itself. Cosmic consciousness must be introduced there also. In mental silence, the mental consciousness universalizes itself; in vital peace, the vital consciousness universalizes itself; in the stillness of the body, the physical consciousness universalizes itself. Stillness, receptivity, and cellular expansion seem to be among the basic conditions for the bodily substance to be able to withstand *Agni* and to endure.

Immediately, however, a momentous difficulty arises. Universalization of the physical consciousness? But then, if the body is *one* with all other bodies, it means that all the other bodies are right there inside it, along with all the falsehoods of the world! This is no longer only one person's battle; it becomes the whole world's battle. We are now approaching the real problem. In this new physical transparency the seeker makes yet another, rather brutal discovery: all his yogic achievements and powers are falling to pieces. He had achieved a control of illnesses, of the body's functions, perhaps even of gravity, had even been able to swallow poison with impunity; he was the master of his house, because his consciousness was in control. But the moment he decides to transform the body, all his powers vanish, like water receding into the sand. Diseases assail him as if he were a mere beginner; the bodily organs begin to deteriorate. Everything goes awry. It would seem that the body has to forget its old false, decay-causing operation for it to learn everything in a new way. Then death enters the picture. Between the old mode of functioning of the body and the new one, in which the symbolic organs will be replaced by the true Vibration, the line separating life from death is often very thin indeed; perhaps one must even be able to cross the line and come back for the conquest to be complete and real. This is what Mother called *dying to death*, after having undergone an experience from which she almost did not return. In other words, one has to face everything, and everything resists. We are already aware of the same phenomenon at the higher levels of consciousness. As the seeker set out on his path, everything began going wrong: he who believed his mind to be firmly anchored in the truth was suddenly visited by a host of the most aggressive suggestions and doubts; he who believed himself pure and honest suddenly experienced an array of vital horrors, enough to scare off the worst villains in this world plus a few others from beyond. As Sri Aurobindo has already explained, one cannot solve a problem, on any plane, without confronting all the opposites of one's Goal. Otherwise, there would be no victory, but only repression. Nowhere, not on any plane, is it a matter of cutting off evil from the rest, but of convincing it of its own light. The yogi who with his power had done away with illnesses had not really solved the problem; he had only muzzled the forces of those illnesses. It is perfectly understandable that no transformation is possible as long as these forces are simply muzzled, prowling around in the dark and awaiting their hour. Moreover, since nothing can be subtracted from the universe, they must be converted. But how? Death and diseases are everywhere, in the subconscient of our bodies and in all the bodies in the world. The yogi who had conquered diseases and defied death (though not indefinitely, of course) had conquered only for himself, and that is why he could not fully conquer. How wise is the Law! He had built a protective shell, shut himself up in it like an embryo of light, and let everything beyond it swarm around as usual. But if the shell opens, everything rushes back in! There is only one body! The example of Ramakrishna lashed by the whip that struck the bullock beside him, or of the Mother struggling against a hemorrhage afflicting a disciple several hundred miles away, without her even knowing about it, places us before the real problem. *The body is everywhere!* exclaimed the Mother. The conquest has to be achieved everywhere—for all the bodies and the whole earth. Nothing can be transformed unless everything is transformed. Otherwise one is simply entrenched alone in one's little hole of light. And what purpose does that serve? What good does it do if one man is transformed while the rest of humanity goes on dying? The body of the pioneer of transformation is therefore like a battlefield: this is where the battle of the world is being fought—where everything meets and where everything resists. There is a central *point* in the ultimate depths, a knot of life and death where the world's destiny hangs. Everything is gathered into one single point.

> *I have been digging deep and long*
> *Mid a horror of filth and mire,*
> *A bed for the golden river's song,*
> *A home for the deathless fire. . .*
> *My gaping wounds are a thousand and one. . .* [27]

The pioneer must therefore confront all difficulties, including Death, not in order to destroy them, but to change them. Nothing can be transformed unless it is taken upon oneself: *Thou shalt bear all things that all things may change*, says Savitri.[28] This is why Sri Aurobindo left his body on December 5, 1950, officially because of uremia, he who could heal others in a few seconds. To die on the cross is moving, to be sure, but crucifixions, especially when worshipped, only perpetuate the law of death. *It is not a crucified body that will save the world*, insists the Mother, *but a glorified body.*

No, it is not spectacular work, but decidedly a "microscopic work," and it is through the very mud of the world that one must dig.

Second Phase—The Subconscient

Thus, there is another category of difficulties (though still the same behind a different mask), which is not due to the resistance of individual, corporeal matter but to the subconscious resistance of the entire earth. This is where Sri Aurobindo met Death. And this is, too, where Mother would resume the work. If we want to understand where the whole story—our story—is unfolding and to follow the process of the work, we must go back to the evolutionary process itself. The advent of a new stage in evolution, whether it be Life in Matter or Mind in Life, has always resulted from a twofold pressure: a pressure from within or below, from the involved principle seeking to emerge, and a pressure from "outside" or "above," from the same principle as it already exists within its own plane. The conjunction of these two pressures—for example, that of the mind involved in certain living forms and that of the Mind as it was created in its own plane in the course of a descending evolution or devolution—eventually led to a rupture of the vital limits, and suddenly Mind emerged in Life. Everything is involved, already there in Matter, but the involution cannot be unlocked except through a pressure from above responding to a call from below and breaking the seal, just as the sun breaks the seed's shell. At present, the supermind involved in Matter pushes from within, in the form of spiritual yearnings, human aspirations for Immortality, Truth, or Beauty, etc.; at the same time, it presses from above, from its own eternal plane, in the form of intuitions, revelations, or illuminations. This is what the Scriptures expressed in their own way when they linked the appearance of a "new earth" to that of a "new heaven" ("a new heaven and a new earth wherein dwelleth the Truth"), because without the new heaven or, rather, the new supramental level of consciousness, the emergence of a new earth would not be possible. The new earth will result from the "new heaven" of the supramental consciousness, just as the present earth resulted from the old mental or overmental "heaven" of the gods and religions. So it is for all the evolutionary stages: high and low go together. But the emergence of the new "high" or new level of consciousness, at any stage of evolution, is not a magical phenomenom, which abruptly alters all the preceding levels. Between the appearance of the first amoeba in the world of Life and that of the mammal, we know that it took many millions of years to overcome Matter's inertia and to "vitalize" it. Similarly, from the Neanderthal man to Plato, thousands of years were needed to overcome the resistance of the two previous levels and to "mentalize" Life, to become the complete mental man. Even today, how many human lives are truly governed by the mind rather than by vital passions? The whole task of the pioneers of evolution, at any level, is precisely to join the new height with the former depth; when high meets low, an evolutionary cycle is completed. Likewise, when the pioneer of mental evolution suddenly emerges in the Supramental, his discovery is not a feat of magic that upsets all the former laws. He does not leap to the complete supramental being any more than the Neanderthal man leapt to Plato; he must first "supramentalize" all the previous levels. Certainly, his consciousness is the meeting point of the supreme High and the supreme Low, Spirit and Matter, Positive and Negative, and his own powers are, of course, considerably increased, but they are increased only in proportion to the new resistances he has to encounter. The more evolution progresses, the deeper the layers it seeks to touch: the principle of Life barely colonized the material crust of the world; the mental principle narrowly colonized its immediate past, the mental subconscient and Life's old profligacies; the Supramental principle confronts not only the mental and vital subconscients, but an even more remote past, the physical subconscient and the inconscient. The higher one rises, the farther one is pulled down. Evolution does not move higher and higher, into an ever more heavenly heaven, but deeper and deeper. Each evolutionary cycle closes a little lower, a little nearer to the Center where the supreme High and Low, heaven and earth, will finally meet. The pioneer must therefore clear up the intermediary mental, vital, and material levels so that the two poles can actually meet. When the joining takes place, not only mentally and vitally but also materially, then the Spirit will emerge in Matter within a complete supramental being and a supramental body.

> *. . . earth shall be the Spirit's manifest home.*[29]

This clearing-up of the intermediary levels is the whole story of Sri Aurobindo and the Mother. The difficulties of accustoming the body to the supramental *Agni* may, ultimately, have a reason and a purpose. It may not be so much a material difficulty as a strategic one, as it were. Indeed, during that second phase, Sri Aurobindo and the Mother would realize that transformation is not just an individual problem but one involving the earth and that no individual transformation is possible (or at least complete) without some degree of collective transformation. Once collective evolution reaches a satisfactory stage of progress, the present material difficulties of transformation, which seem insurmountable, will likely vanish at once. There is never any impossibility, just the question of whether the right time has come. All obstacles, whatever their nature, always ultimately prove themselves to be helpful auxiliaries of a Truth whose meaning and purpose we do not yet know. To our outer, superficial vision, the transformation seems to be exclusively a physical problem, because we always put the cart before the horse, but all difficulties are actually *inner* and psychological; the visible and dramatic difficulties of the body's growing accustomed to the boiling *Agni* may be, as we shall see, less a practical or material problem than one involving the whole terrestrial consciousness. But we are speaking in riddles; the problem Sri Aurobindo and the Mother were soon to confront will be better understood with this simple remark Sri Aurobindo once made to a disciple: *I had been dredging, dredging, dredging the mire of the subconscious. . . . It [the supramental light] was coming down before November [1934], but afterwards all the mud arose and it stopped.*[30] Once again, Sri Aurobindo verified, not individually this time but collectively, that pulling down too strong a light causes all the darkness below to groan and to feel violated. It should be noted that each time Sri Aurobindo and the Mother had some experience indicating a new progress in the transformation, the disciples, without their even knowing anything about it, experienced in their consciousness a period of increased difficulties or even revolts and illnesses, as if everything were grating. Now we begin to understand how things work. If a pigmy were abruptly subjected to the simple mental light of an educated man, it would probably cause in the poor fellow subterranean revolutions that would traumatize him forever and drive him insane. There is still too much jungle underneath. This present world is still full of jungles: such is the problem in a nutshell. Our mental colonization is a very thin crust over a barely dried Stone Age.

The Vedic rishis, speaking of the subconscious forces and subconscious beings, called them "those-who-cover," "those-who-devour," or the "sun-thieves." There could be no better description for them; they are indeed merciless thieves. No sooner do we make some progress, draw a new light or a more intense vibration, than we suddenly become covered over or pulled downward beneath a suffocating bell-jar where everything disintegrates in a dreadful mugginess; the harmonious vibration of the day before, so clear, so luminous, so supple, suddenly become blanketed by a thick, sticky layer, as if finding a bit of light meant wading through miles of seaweed; everything we see, touch, or do becomes as if spoiled, decayed by that invasion from below. Nothing makes sense anymore. And yet, outwardly, the conditions are the same, and apparently nothing has changed. *There is a sort of locked struggle,* wrote Sri Aurobindo, *in which neither side can make a very appreciable advance (somewhat like the trench warfare in Europe), the spiritual force insisting against the resistance of the physical world, that resistance disputing every inch and making more or less effective counter-attacks. . . . And if there were not the strength and Ananda within, it would be harassing and disgusting work.*[31] The battle seems endless. One "digs and digs," said the Vedic rishis, and the more one digs, the more the bottom seems to recede downward: "I have been digging, digging . . . many autumns have I been toiling night and day, the dawns aging me. Age is diminishing the glory of our bodies." Thus, thousands of years ago, lamented Lopamudra, the wife of the rishi Agastya, who was also seeking transformation: "Even the men of old who were wise of the Truth and they spoke with the gods . . . yea, they reached not an end." But Agastya was not easily discouraged; his reply is magnificently characteristic of the conquerors these rishis indeed were: "Not in vain is the labour which the gods protect. Let us have the taste of even all the contesting forces, let us conquer indeed even here, let us run this battle-race of a hundred leadings." (I.179) To be sure, it is a hydra. Night after night, in his sleep or with his eyes wide open, the seeker uncovers very strange worlds. One after another, he unearths all the birthplaces of human perversion, human wars, human concentration camps, where everything we live here is being prepared; he catches in their dens all the sordid forces that move the petty and cruel men.

> *A lone discoverer in these menacing realms*
> *Guarded like termite cities from the sun.*[32]

The more Light he possesses, the more darkness he uncovers. Night after night he tracks down the surreptitious rot that undermines Life; for how can anything change as long as that gangrene is there? Since by now the seeker's mind and vital are too well established in the truth, too pure to be affected by those subterranean forces, it is his body that becomes stricken—for the body is Falsehood's last hiding-place. Then the seeker perceives in minute details through what complicity illnesses and death can penetrate the body—each defeat in those realms means a defeat here—and he understands tangibly, concretely, the enormous vanity of those who pretend to cure the world through external means and new institutions; no sooner is evil cured here or exterminated there than it instantly revives elsewhere, in some other place or some other form. Evil is not outside, but inside and below, and as long as that particular Disease has not been cured, the world can never be cured. As Sri Aurobindo put it: *The old gods . . . know how to transmigrate.*[33]

All the way underneath, beyond the disorders and the fear—the great presiding Fear underneath—the seeker meets a stupendous Weariness, something that refuses and says *NO* to all this pain of living and this violation by the light. He senses that going farther down, to the end of this *NO,* would mean merging into a great release of stone, just as the ecstasy above meant merging into a great release of Light. Yet death is not the opposite of Life! It is the other side of, or the door to, the luminous Superconscient; at the very end of that *NO* there is a *YES* and *YES*, which keeps driving us into one body after another, for the unique purpose of joy. Death is only the regret of that *YES*. The great Weariness at the bottom is only a shadow-form of that Bliss. Death is not the opposite of Life! It is the dark release of a body that has not yet found the luminous release of an eternal joy. When the body finds that particular ecstasy, that vastness of light and rapture within its own flesh, as above, it will no longer need to die.

Where is the "I" in all this? Where is "my" difficulty, "my" death, "my" transformation? The seeker has broken through the thin crust of the personal subconscient only to find himself in the world's totality. It is the whole world that resists: *It is not we who wage the war; it is everything that wages wars against us!* We think we are separate, each in our own little sack of skin, with an "inside" and an "outside," an individual and a collective, like the tiny borders around our countries—but, in reality, everything perfectly interconnects! There is not a single perversion, not a single disease in the world that is not also rooted in ourselves, not a death in which we are not an accomplice. We are all equally guilty and in the same boat; no one is saved unless everyone is saved! It is not the difficulty of *one* body, says the Mother, but the difficulty of *the* Body. Sri Aurobindo and the Mother thus discovered *materially*, experientially, the oneness of the world's substance: we cannot touch a point without touching all points, take a step ahead or upward without the rest of the world also taking a step ahead or upward. We spoke earlier of a "strategic" difficulty; it may well be that the divine strategy is to prevent any single point from progressing all by itself without all the other points. This is why the Vedic rishis failed six thousand years ago. There cannot be any complete and lasting individual transformation without a minimum of world transformation.

The second phase of the work of transformation thus drew to a close. After working for fourteen years, from 1926 to 1940, in an individual, concentrated manner, with a handful of carefully chosen disciples, Sri Aurobindo and the Mother had come up against a wall. The moment the supramental light approached the earth to join with the same light involved in Matter, torrents of mud would rise up from the collective subconscient and drown everything. *To help humanity out,* Sri Aurobindo remarked, *it was not enough for an individual, however great, to achieve an ultimate solution individually, [because] even when the Light is ready to descend it cannot come to stay till the lower plane is also ready to bear the pressure of the Descent.*[34] It is very significant that the culmination of the second phase of the work of transformation should coincide with the outbreak of the Second World War. When the pressure of the Light descends into one human body, the body of the world, too, begins to glow. What do we really know of the good of the world, or of its evil?

Confronted with that collective resistance, Sri Aurobindo and the Mother hesitated momentarily, wondering whether they should not cut themselves off from the rest of the world, forge ahead alone with just a few disciples, effect the transformation, then return to the collective work by communicating to the rest of the earth the transformation accomplished (or partially accomplished) in themselves. (This same idea has impelled many spiritual, occult, or chivalrous groups in the past to select a secret place far away from the rest of the world, sheltered from the contamination of collective vibrations, to do their work.) But they soon realized that this was an illusion and that afterward the gap or the *atmospheric gulf,*[35] as Sri Aurobindo would put it, between the new accomplishment and the old world would be too great to be bridged. Furthermore, what is the point of an individual success if it is not communicable to the rest of the world? If a supramental being suddenly appeared on earth, no one would even see him! Our eyes must first be unsealed to another way of life. *If you advance on the path that is open in front of you,* said the Mother, *without patiently waiting for the rest of creation, that is, if you achieve alone something very close to the Truth as compared to the present state of the world—what will happen? The whole is thrown off balance; not only the harmony but the equilibrium of the whole will be upset, because a certain part of the creation will not be able to follow. And instead of a full realization of the Divine, you will have a small, local, infinitesimal realization, and nothing of the goal will be achieved. Moreover,* emphasized the Mother, *if you want to do the work in a solitary way, you absolutely cannot do it in a total way, because every physical being, however complete he may be, even if he is of an altogether superior nature, even if he was made for an altogether special Work, is only partial and limited. He embodies only* one truth, one *law in the world—it may be a very complex law, but it is still only one law—and the full transformation cannot be realized through him alone, through one body. . . . Alone, you can attain your own perfection, become infinite and perfect in your consciousness. Inner realization knows no limits. But outer realization, on the contrary, is necessarily limited, and a minimum number of physical persons are necessary in order to achieve a general action.*

In 1940, after fourteen years of individual concentration, Sri Aurobindo and the Mother opened the doors of their ashram. The third phase of the transformation began, a phase that has expanded today to a world scale.

Third Phase—The Ashram

Author's Note: The following subchapter should be entirely revised, as the conditions in the Ashram have drastically changed since the Mother's departure in 1973. The "Sri Aurobindo Ashram" has become an "institution," as opposed to the living experiment it was meant to be. Therefore, the following description now has merely (and regretfully) an historical value. For more details concerning the Mother's own work in the body refer to *Mother's Agenda* (her own recorded account to Satprem from 1951 to 1973).

In India an "ashram" is traditionally a spiritual or religious community whose members are gathered around a Master and who have renounced the world to devote themselves to meditation, concentration, and yogic practices in order to attain "liberation." As we might imagine, though, Sri Aurobindo's Ashram had little to do with this particular definition, except for the fact that the disciples were indeed gathered around Sri Aurobindo and the Mother. It was not an exotic kind of monastery, and still less a place for refuge and peace; it was more like a forge: *This Ashram has been created . . . not for the renunciation of the world but as a centre and a field of practice for the evolution of another kind and form of life.*[36] Even before his arrest in Bengal, at a time when he was not even remotely dreaming of founding an ashram, Sri Aurobindo had said: *The spiritual life finds its most potent expression in the man who lives the ordinary life of men in the strength of the Yoga. . . . It is by such a union of the inner life and the outer that mankind will eventually be lifted up and become mighty and divine.*[37] Hence, Sri Aurobindo wanted his Ashram to be fully involved in everyday life, right in the midst of the world-at-large, since that is where the transformation had to take place, and not upon some Himalayan peak. Except for the main building, where the Mother lived and where Sri Aurobindo's monument is located, the 1,200-odd disciples of all nationalities and all social classes (men, women and four to five hundred children) were scattered throughout the city of Pondicherry in more than three hundred different houses. There were no protective walls in the Ashram, except for one's own inner light; the bustle of the bazaar was just next door.

Any Westerner journeying there with the idea of finding peace or learning "yoga" was certainly disappointed. First of all, no one would try to teach him anything (rather, "unlearning" was what was required); there were no classes and no "teaching," except for Sri Aurobindo's written works and the Mother's *Questions and Answers,* which were at everyone's disposal (as well as all other teachings, in fact, both traditional and nontraditional). There were no rules, either. A disciple had to discover everything for

himself, within himself, in the midst of a very active life. He was
left to himself. How could mental rules possibly be drawn up for
a work embracing all the levels of evolution—mental, vital, and
psychic, all the human types and all the traditions and cultures
(some disciples had been raised as Christians, others as Taoists,
Moslems, Buddhists, atheists, etc.)? Each one had to find his own
truth, which is never the same as the next man's truth. Some people
in the Ashram believed in the virtues of asceticism—in spite of all
Sri Aurobindo had said about it—and they lived as ascetics; others
favored judo or football; others liked books and studies, while still
others did not; some were involved in business, or manufactured
stainless steel, perfumes, and even tons of sugar in a modern sugar
mill. There was something to satisfy every taste. Those who liked
painting painted; those who liked music had every possible instrument, Indian or Western, at their disposal; those who liked
teaching became teachers at the International Centre of Education, which covered the whole academic spectrum, from kinder-
garten to the college level. There were also a printing press;
scientific laboratories; gardens; rice fields; workshops for cars,
tractors and trucks; an X-ray department and an operating room.
Every conceivable human activity was represented. The Ashram
was a microcosm. One could be a baker, too, or wash dishes, or
try one's hand at carpentry, if one believed in the virtues of simple
work. But there was no hierarchy among these activities; none was
remunerated, nor was any considered superior to any other. All
the practical necessities of life were provided for by the Mother—
to each person according to his or her needs. The only essential
task was to discover the truth of one's being, for which the external
work was merely a pretext or a means. It was remarkable, in fact,
to observe people changing activities as their consciousness awakened; soon, all the values attached to the former profession would
fall away, and because money no longer had any meaning, one
who had considered himself a doctor, say, found that he was really
more comfortable as an artisan, while a man with no particular
education might discover that he had a talent for poetry or

painting, or might become engrossed in the study of Sanskrit or Ayurvedic medicine. There was a complete recasting of all external values according to the one inner criterion. When a disciple once asked the Mother about the best way of collaborating in the supramental transformation, he was given this answer: *It is always the same thing: by realizing one's own being, in whatever form, by whatever means—it doesn't matter—but that is the only way. Each person carries a truth within himself; he must become one with that truth, live that truth. When he does that, the path he follows to unite with and realize that truth is also the path that brings him closest to the Transformation. In other words, the two—personal realization and transformation—are inseparably connected. Perhaps this multiplicity of approaches will even yield the Secret and open the door, who knows?*

There was no communal life either, only the inner connection. Some disciples kept the habit, from the days when the Mother used to talk to the Ashram children, of assembling twice a week for a collective meditation. But it was especially for sports that the disciples would get together. (There was a common dining room, too, although many chose to eat at home with their families, or alone.) There were all kinds of sports, from the traditional hatha yoga to tennis to boxing, and almost every disciple devoted an hour or two each day to sports. Although the sea was nearby, there was also an Olympic-sized swimming pool, as well as basketball and volleyball courts, running tracks, a gymnasium, a boxing ring, a dojo for judo, etc. Every possible sport was practiced there, with participants from the ages of five to eighty. There was also a theater and a cinema. Yet sports were not an article of faith; nothing was an article of faith, except, of course, for the faith in man's divine possibilities and in a truer life upon the earth. *All of you here, my children, live in exceptional freedom,* the Mother would say to the youngest . . . *No social constraints, no moral constraints, no intellectual constraints, no rules; nothing but a Light which is here.* But it was a very demanding Light, and this was where the terrestrial work began.

How can anything be "terrestrial" with 1,200 disciples, or even a hundred thousand? The Ashram was actually only a concentrated point for the work. The real Ashram is in fact *everywhere* in the world, wherever human beings yearn for a truer life, whether they know of Sri Aurobindo or not, because their inner orientation and their inner need automatically place them in the same evolutionary crucible. Transformation is not one individual's prerogative; on the contrary, it requires many individuals, as diverse as possible. The Ashram was only a *symbolic* point of the work, as a laboratory is the symbolic testing-ground for a vaccine that will benefit millions of people. Sri Aurobindo himself often called his Ashram *the laboratory.* This might be better appreciated if we understand that each individual represents a certain aggregate of vibrations and is in contact with a certain zone of the subconscient. These worlds, apparently full of diversity, are in fact each made up of a few typical vibrations; the multiplicity of forms (of deformations, rather), of beings, places, or events within a given zone merely mask an identical vibration. The moment we become somewhat conscious and begin to descend into the subconscient (without becoming overwhelmed) in order to work, we are surprised, or sometimes even amused, to find that some persons we know, who are outwardly very different from one another when we meet them on the mental or vital planes, are almost the same and interchangeable in the subconscient! Thus, people separated by different religions, different backgrounds, different social classes, or even different ethics, can belong to a perfectly identical *type* and be entirely alike in the subconscient, *as if you could see one through the other,* says the Mother. Since our vision is limited, we see only two or three people, one through the other, but if we had total vision, we would see thousands and thousands more behind them, arrayed in well-defined categories. Some people are never seen together in the subconscient, although they may be quite close in outer life, and vice versa. Now we understand how the work can assume a world scale: *Each person,* says the Mother, *is an instrument for controlling the set of vibrations that represent his own particular field of work.* Each of us, through his qualities *and his defects,* is in touch with a special region of the terrestrial consciousness that represents his part in the overall transformation. So we now understand why the transformation cannot take place through a single individual, for no matter how great he is, how complex his inner organization, how extensive his mental, vital, and subconscious colonization, he represents only *one* set of vibrations. At most, he can transform the type of vibration he represents, and, if that, because in the final analysis everything is interconnected. We understand, too, why the transformation cannot be realized by saints. It is not from saintliness that one makes a vaccine, but from that very share of human illness one has the courage to acknowledge and to take upon oneself. In any case, the illness undeniably exits, only one person closes his eyes to it and escapes into ecstasy, while the other person rolls up his sleeves and gets to work with his test tubes. When an older disciple once bitterly complained about the odd human mixture in the Ashram and all those "impossible" individuals who were in it, Sri Aurobindo replied: *It is necessary or rather inevitable that in an Ashram which is a "laboratory" . . . for a spiritual and supramental yoga, humanity should be variously represented. For the problem of transformation has to deal with all sorts of elements favourable and unfavourable. The element favourable carries in him a mixture of these two things. If only sattwic [virtuous] and cultured men come for yoga, men without very much of the vital difficulty in them, then, because the difficulty of the vital element in terrestrial nature has not been faced and overcome, it might well be that the endeavour would fail.*[38] In a moment of remorse, another disciple wrote to Sri Aurobindo, "What disciples we are! . . . You should have chosen or called some better stuff—perhaps somebody like Z." Sri Aurobindo replied: *As to the disciples, I agree!—Yes, but would the better stuff, supposing it to exist, be typical of humanity? To deal with a few exceptional types would hardly solve the problem. And would they consent to follow my path—that is another question. And if they were put to the test, would not the common humanity suddenly reveal itself—that is still another* question.[39] *I do not want hundreds of thousands of disciples. It will be enough if I can get a hundred complete men, empty of petty egoism, who will be instruments of God.*[40]

Practically, the work is done through each of our psychological difficulties, which are symbols of the same difficulties in the world; if a particular vibration is touched in one individual, then the same vibration is touched in the entire world. *Each one of you,* said the Mother, *represents one of the difficulties to be overcome for the transformation to be complete—and that makes a lot of difficulties! It's even more than a difficulty; I think I told you before that each one represents an impossibility to be resolved; when all these impossibilities are resolved, the Work will be over.* As previously mentioned, each person has a shadow that keeps pursuing him and that seems to contradict the very aim of his existence. This is the particular vibration he must transform, his field of work, his impossible knot. At once the challenge of his life and its potential triumph, it is his share in the progress of the collective evolution upon the earth. But something curious happens in this particular laboratory: in ordinary life, or in an individual yoga, the shadow is more or less dormant, more or less bothersome, and usually dissolves by itself or, rather, sinks below, into oblivion; but the moment we are involved in a terrestrial yoga, we find that it does not dissolve at all, but resurges again and again, relentlessly, as if the battle had never really been won—indeed, as if we were waging a contest against that particular vibratory knot for the entire earth. It appears as if the seeker has become a special battlefield for a fierce and symbolic war against the same knot of darkness in all the rest of humanity. *You no longer do yoga for yourself alone; you do it for everybody, unintentionally, automatically,* says the Mother. The seeker verifies *in vivo* the principle of the world's substantial oneness: trying to straighten a vibration in oneself triggers reactions from myriads of vibrations all over the world. This is what Sri Aurobindo calls a "yoga for the earth-consciousness." [41] *Accepting life, he [the seeker of the integral yoga] has to bear not only his own burden, but a great part of the world's burden too along with it, as a continuation of his own sufficiently heavy load. Therefore his Yoga has much more the nature of a battle than others'; but this is not only an individual battle, it is a collective war waged over a considerable country. He has not only to conquer in himself the forces of egoistic falsehood and disorder, but to conquer them as representatives of the same adverse and inexhaustible forces in the world. Their representative character gives them a much more obstinate capacity of resistance, an almost endless right to recurrence. Often he finds that even after he has won persistently his own personal battle, he has still to win it over and over again in a seemingly interminable war, because his inner existence has already been so much enlarged that not only it contains his own being with its well-defined needs and experiences, but is in solidarity with the being of others, because in himself he contains the universe.*[42]

Will the end of the work ever be reached? We might conclude that the subconscient is an endless sewer—the rishis themselves called it "the bottomless pit"—and that if we have to wait for it to be totally cleansed before we can achieve a supramental transformation, we might have to wait for a very long time, indeed. But this is only an appearance. The birth of a new individual does not bring with it a new load of subconscious or unconscious material; that individual merely draws from the common source, repeating the same vibrations which circle endlessly through the earth's atmosphere. Man cannot create new darkness any more than he can create new light. He is only an instrument—whether conscious or unconscious—of the one or of the other (though most often of both). No new vibrations can be brought into the world except those of the superconscious Future, which gradually become the present ones and dissolve or transmute the vibrations from our evolutionary past. Today's Subconscient and Inconscient are obviously less subconscious and unconscious than they were two thousand years ago, and we have all paid to bring about this result. This descent of the Future into the present is the key to the transmutation of the world. Yoga is the process of accelerating the Future, and the pioneer of evolution is the instrument who brings down more and more powerful vibrations. The task of the seeker, therefore, is not so much a negative endeavor of scouring the Subconscient as it is a positive one of calling the light and bringing down the vibrations of the Future to accelerate the cleansing or purification process. This is what Sri Aurobindo calls "descent," which is the main characteristic of his yoga, as has been said earlier. *If there is a descent in other Yogas, yet it is only an incident on the way or resulting from the ascent—the ascent is the real thing. Here the ascent is the first step, but it is a means for the descent. It is the descent of the new consciousness attained by the ascent that is the stamp and seal of the sadhana . . . here the object is the divine fulfilment of life.*[43] When Sri Aurobindo speaks of "descent," he does not mean a sharp and quick movement upward followed by a sharp and quick movement downward. He does not mean coming down for a brief stint of hard labor to sweep up the dust; he means that the bottom must actually cease to be the bottom. To take an example, a very prosaic one—and as one soon learns, the transformation process is prosaic enough—we may be shopping at the grocery store amid a rather opaque and gray humanity, or we may be visiting at night rather noxious regions of the subconscient, yet do both things with the same intensity of consciousness, light, and peace as when we are sitting alone in our room, eyes closed, in deep meditation. This is what is meant by "descending." No longer is there any difference between the high and the low; both have become equally luminous and peaceful. Too, this is how the transformation works on a world scale, for the oneness of substance in the world works both ways. We cannot touch a shadow without touching all the corresponding shadows in the world; but the opposite is equally true: we cannot touch a light without affecting all the surrounding shadows. All vibrations are contagious, including the good ones. Every victory is a victory for all. *It is all the same Being!* exclaimed the Mother. There is but one consciousness, one substance, one force, and one body in the world. This is why Sri Aurobindo could say of the Mother and of himself: *If the Supermind comes down into our physical, it would* mean that it has come down into Matter and so there is no reason why it should not manifest in the sadhaks [disciples].[44]

The higher the seeker reaches, the wider his access to the regions below—the Past he can come into contact with is exactly in proportion to the Future he has discovered—and the greater his capacity for collective transformation. Until now, the only power brought down was a mental power, or overmental at best, which was incapable of touching the bottommost layers, but now that a supramental or spiritual power has descended into the earth-consciousness through Sri Aurobindo's and the Mother's realization, we can conceivably expect this supreme Future to touch the supreme Depths and hasten the cleansing, that is, ultimately hasten the evolution of all humanity. Yoga is a process of accelerated evolution, and the progression is geometric: *The first obscure material movement of the evolutionary Force is marked by an aeonic graduality; the movement of Life progress proceeds slowly but still with a quicker step, it is concentrated into the figure of millenniums; mind can still further compress the tardy leisureliness of Time and make long paces of the centuries; but when the conscious spirit intervenes, a supremely concentrated pace of evolutionary swiftness becomes possible.*[45] We have now reached that very point. The convulsions of the present world are undoubtedly a sign that the descending Pressure is increasing and that we are approaching a true solution. *It may well be that, once started, the [supramental] endeavour may not advance rapidly even to its first decisive stage; it may be that it will take long centuries of effort to come into some kind of permanent birth. But that is not altogether inevitable, for the principle of such changes in Nature seems to be a long obscure preparation followed by a swift gathering up and precipitation of the elements into the new birth, a rapid conversion, a transformation that in its luminous moment figures like a miracle. Even when the first decisive change is reached, it is certain that all humanity will not be able to rise to that level. There cannot fail to be a division into those who are able to live on the spiritual level and those who are only able to live in the light that descends from it into the mental level. And below these too there* *might still be a great mass influenced from above but not yet ready for the light. But even that would be a transformation and a beginning far beyond anything yet attained. This hierarchy would not mean as in our present vital living an egoistic domination of the undeveloped by the more developed, but a guidance of the younger by the elder brothers of the race and a constant working to lift them up to a greater spiritual level and wider horizons. And for the leaders too this ascent to the first spiritual levels would not be the end of the divine march, a culmination that left nothing more to be achieved on earth. For there would be still yet higher levels within the supramental realm,* as the old Vedic poets knew when they spoke of the spiritual life as a constant ascent,—*[46]

"The priests of the word climb thee like a ladder, O hundred-powered. As one ascends from peak to peak, there is made clear the much that has still to be done."**

We have in fact spent all these centuries preparing the Base: a base of security and well-being through our science, a base of charity through our religions and morals, a base of beauty and harmony through our arts, and a mental base of rigorous exactitude, but these are all bases for *something else*. Absorbed as we are in our effort for perfection, we see only one angle of the great Work—the angle of earthly immortality, like the rishis; the angle of eternal Permanence, like the Buddha; the angle of charity, of well-being, all kinds of angles—but we are not going to continue playing forever like children with building blocks! None of these is an end, but only a negative condition of the Play. Nothing has really yet begun! Perhaps we are expected, first, to become conscious of the Play in order for it to begin. We have exhausted all kinds of adventures since Jules Verne, and they have all gradually closed in on us. What war, what revolution is still worth giving

---

*   Sri Aurobindo recognized three degrees or planes of consciousness within the Supermind. It does not seem necessary to expound upon them here.
** *Rig Veda* I.10.1.

one's blood for? Our Everests have all been deflowered, and the high seas are patrolled night and day; everything is monitored, precalculated, even the stratosphere. Could this be intended to lead us to the only possibility left in this increasingly asphyxiating world? We had assumed we were only shortsighted little moles on a big planet, so we proceeded to rectify the great Eye within, and our wings, by substituting a steel machinery that is now crushing us mercilessly—perhaps to compel us to believe as much in ourselves as we do in our machines, and to understand that we can realize far more than they. "They go round and round, battered and stumbling, like blind men led by one who is blind," said the Upanishad long ago.* Perhaps the time has come to look beyond all our small constructions and to begin the Play? Instead of playing with shovels, bulldozers, gospels, and neutrons, let us clear the consciousness and cast *that* seed to the winds of time, that life may truly begin.

> *O Force-compelled, Fate-driven earth-born race,*
> *O petty adventurers in an infinite world*
> *And prisoners of a dwarf humanity,*
> *How long will you tread the circling tracks of mind*
> *Around your little self and petty things?*
> *But not for a changeless littleness were you meant,*
> *Not for vain repetition were you built. . .*
> *Almighty powers are shut in Nature's cells.*
> *A greater destiny awaits you in your front. . .*
> *The life you lead conceals the light you are.*[47]

Glancing beyond the old wall, we see that everything is already there, only waiting for us to want it:

> *I saw them cross the twilight of an age,*
> *The sun-eyed children of a marvellous dawn. . .*
> *The massive barrier-breakers of the world. . .*
> *The architects of immortality. . .*
> *Bodies made beautiful by the Spirit's light,*

---

* *Mundaka Upanishad* I.2.8.

Carrying the magic word, the mystic fire,
Carrying the Dionysian cup of joy. . .[48]

The Iron Age Is Ended[49]

The prerequisites of the Age of Truth may seem harsh—the perilous descent into the Inconscient, the battle against Darkness, Death at every bend in the road. But have we not risked our lives for lesser undertakings? *Man's greatness is not in what he is, but in what he makes possible,*[50] said Sri Aurobindo. The Victory must be won *once*, in one body. When one human being has won that Victory, it will be a victory for all humankind and in all the worlds. For this little earth, so insignificant in appearance, is the symbolic ground of a battle involving all the cosmic hierarchies, just as a conscious human being is the symbolic ground of a battle being waged for all humankind. If we conquer here, we conquer everywhere. We are the deliverers of the dead—the deliverers of life. By becoming conscious, each of us becomes a builder of heaven and a redeemer of the earth. That is why this life on earth takes on such an exceptional significance among all our other forms of life, and also why the guardians of Falsehood persist on preaching to us the hereafter. *We must not waste a minute to do our work here,* says the Mother, *because it is here that we can really do it. Do not expect anything from death; life is your salvation. It is in life that the transformation must be achieved; it is on the earth that one progresses, on the earth that one realizes. It is in the body that the Victory is won.* Then the law of evolution will no longer be a law of opposites exhorting us through endless dualisms in order to uproot us from our human childhood. It will be a law of light and unending progress, a new evolution in the joy of Truth. The Victory must be won only once. One glorious body. One body must break the iron law for all bodies. And all human beings must collaborate in that one Victory. The strategic difficulty of the transformation is fully before us. If earth calls and the Supreme answers, the hour can be even now.*

---

* From *The Hour of God,* a posthumous collection of Sri Aurobindo's writings.

The End
Which Ever Begins Again[*]

The realization of the Vedic rishis has become a collective one. The Supermind has entered the earth-consciousness, descending right into the physical subconscient, at the last frontiers of Matter. There remains only one final bridge to cross for the connection to be established. *A new world is born,* said the Mother. *At present, we are in the midst of a transitional period in which the two are intermingled: the old world hangs on, still very powerful, still controlling the ordinary consciousness, but the new one is slipping in, so modest and unobtrusive that, externally, it doesn't change too much, for the moment. . . . But it is working, growing, and one day it will be strong enough to assert itself visibly.* Indeed, not all difficulties come from the subconscient.

One difficulty in particular is of a very "conscious" nature, hindering the new world like a massive bronze door. It is not our materialism, as we so often imagine—for scientists, if they are sincere, may be the first to emerge in the Truth—but the enormous spiritual carapace under which we have buried the Spirit. The real mischief of the devil is not to sow falsehood and hatred

---

[*] From *Savitri.*

in the world, such as Attila or the Nazis have done—he is far too clever for that—but to lay hands on a grain of truth and then to twist it ever so slightly. Nothing is more intractable than a perverted truth, because the falsehood is made that much stronger by the power of truth it contains. We have been told repeatedly that "salvation is in heaven," and it is true. There is no salvation for man so long as his nose remains completely buried in matter; his salvation is in the superconscious heaven. It was probably necessary to preach heaven to us in order to pull us out of our initial evolutionary sclerosis, but this was just a first stage of evolution, which we then turned into an ultimate and rigid end. Now, however, this same end has turned against us. We have denied the Divinity in Matter, to confine it instead in our holy places, but now Matter is taking its revenge. We called Matter crude, and crude it is. As long as we tolerate this Imbalance, there is no hope for the earth. We will only continue to swing from one extreme to another, both equally false—from material enjoyment to spiritual austerity—without ever finding any true fulfillment. *The ancient intellectual cultures of Europe ended in disruptive doubt and sceptical impotence, the pieties of Asia in stagnation and decline.*[1]* We need both the vigor of Matter and the fresh waters of the Spirit, while our materialisms are stupefying us and our beliefs are merely the reverse of our disbeliefs. *The Atheist is God playing at hide-and-seek with Himself; but is the Theist any other? Well, perhaps; for he has seen the shadow of God and clutched at it.*[2]

If we wish to remedy this Imbalance—for everything that lacks balance in our bodies, our societies, or our cosmic cycles eventually perishes—we must become lucid. We have lost the Password; such is the bottom line of our era. We have replaced true power with devices, and true wisdom with dogmas. This is the reign of the gnomes, on every plane. And it will become more and more a reign of gnomes, unless we relinquish these mortifying half-truths, from above or below, and immerse ourselves in the true Source, within,

---

* This was written in 1914. Perhaps things have improved since then, but this is far from being evident.

to recover the practical secret of the Spirit in Matter. "That which is immortal in mortals . . . is a god and established inwardly as an energy working out in our divine powers." (*Rig Veda* IV.2.1) Because they knew this Secret, neither the rishis nor the sages of the ancient Mysteries ever created the monumental schism that presently undermines our lives: "our Father in heaven, our Mother the earth"; and they did not ever attempt to settle the problem by relegating an earthly human fulfillment to a celestial hereafter: "Let us conquer even here, let us run this battle-race of a hundred leadings." Having reached the summits of consciousness, they did not vanish in a pale ecstasy: "I am a son of Earth, the soil is my mother. . . . " (*Atharva Veda* XII.1) Having traveled to the frontiers of the Infinite, they did not find that the small things here were small: "O Godhead, guard for us the Infinite and lavish the finite." (*Rig Veda* IV.2.11) "May we speak the beauty of thee, O Earth, that is in thy villages and forests and assemblies and wars and battles." (*Atharva Veda* XII.44.56) They battled, and they were invincible, for they knew that God is within us: "O Son of the body . . . full of happiness and light, victorious, to whom no hurt can come." (III.4.2,9.1) A conquering truth of upright men, for whom death is both a falsehood and a defeat. A truth of a divine joy upon the earth. Certainly their truth was premature for the hordes of Europe, who still needed to hear about heaven before earth, but now the time may have come at last to unveil the Mysteries—whether they be Vedic, Orphic, Alchemical, or Catharist—and to recover the whole truth of the two poles within a *third* position, which is neither that of the materialists nor that of the spiritualists. *The ascent of man into heaven is not the key, but rather his ascent here into the spirit and the descent also of the spirit into his normal humanity and the transformation of this earthly nature. For that and not some post mortem salvation is the real new birth for which humanity waits as the crowning movement of its long, obscure and painful course.*[3]

Sri Aurobindo brings us a message of hope. Ultimately, our present reign of gnomes is the sign of a new emergence. Our darkness and declines always signal the advent of a greater light, which had to descend to break the prevailing limits. There are only two ways of breaking the limits: through an excess of light or an excess of darkness, but while one draws our darkness up into the light and dissolves it, the other precipitates the light into our darkness and transmutes it. One way liberates a few individuals, while the other liberates the whole earth. Ten thousand years ago, a few giants among men had wrestled out the Secret of the world, but this was the privilege of a few initiates, while now we must all become initiates. Ten thousand years ago reigned the Golden Age, while today everything seems to have been swallowed up in darkness. In truth, though, night has not descended upon the world, as the preachers of doom would have us believe; it is only that the light has been buried in the world. The Secret had to be forgotten, humanity had to descend the dark curve of the age of reason and religions, so that all could recover the Secret and the Light everywhere, beneath all the darkness, all the misery, and the pettiness, instead of in a high brazier in some Vedic or Persian sanctuary. We are at the beginning of Time. Evolution does not follow an increasingly sublime and vanishing trajectory, but a spiral: *It is not a tortuous path leading you back, relatively battered, to the starting-point; on the contrary, it seeks to bring to the whole creation the joy of being, the beauty of being, the greatness of being, and the perpetual development, perpetually progressive, of this joy, this beauty, and this greatness. Then everything makes sense.* An eternal spiral that does not end in an ultimate point—for the Ultimate is everywhere in the world, in every being, every body, every atom— but a gradual ascent reaching higher and higher in order to descend lower and lower, to embrace ever more, and to reveal ever more. We are at the beginning of the "Vast," which will become ever vaster. The pioneers of evolution have already recognized other levels within the Supermind, opening up new trajectories in an eternal Becoming. Each conquered height brings about a new change, a complete reversal of consciousness, a new heaven, a new earth—for the physical world itself will soon mutate before our incredulous eyes. This is surely not the first change in history; how many were there before us? How many more *with* us, if only we consent to become conscious? *Successive reversals of consciousness, which will bring an always renewed richness of creation, will take place from one stage to the next.* Each time, the Magus in us turns his kaleidoscope, and everything becomes astonishing—vaster, truer, and more beautiful. We just have to open our eyes, for the joy of the world is at our door, if only we wish it.

> *Earth's pains were the ransom of its prisoned delight. . . .*
> *For joy and not for sorrow earth was made.*[4]

Such is the Secret. It is here, everywhere, within the very heart of the world. The "well of honey beneath the rock," the "childlike laughter of the Infinite" that we are, the luminous Future that pushes back our past. Evolution is far from being over. It is not an absurd merry-go-round, not a fall, nor a vanity fair. It is

> *. . . the adventure of consciousness and joy.*[5]

Pondicherry
April 14, 1963

REFERENCES

Most quotations refer to the complete edition of Sri Aurobindo's works in 30 volumes (The Centenary Edition). Figures in bold indicate the volume number. Other quotations are taken from the following editions and books.

Sri Aurobindo: *Essays on the Gita* (1959)
Sri Aurobindo: *On Yoga II, Tome 2* (1958)
Sri Aurobindo: *Life, Literature and Yoga* (1952)
Sri Aurobindo: *The Riddle of this World* (1951)
Sri Aurobindo: *Letters,* 3rd series (1949)
Sri Aurobindo: *Poems Past and Present* (1952)
Sri Aurobindo: *The Human Cycle* (1949)
Sri Aurobindo: *On the Veda* (1956)
Sri Aurobindo: *The Life Divine* (1960)
Sri Aurobindo: *The Ideal of the Karmayogin* (1950)

A. B. Purani: *Evening Talks with Sri Aurobindo* (1959)
A. B. Purani: *Life of Sri Aurobindo* (1958)
D. K. Roy: *Sri Aurobindo Came to Me* (1952)
G. Monod-Herzen: *Shri Aurobindo* (1954)
Nirodbaran: *Correspondence with Sri Aurobindo* (1959)

Most of the Mother's quotations are taken from *Mother's Agenda.*

Introduction
1. Thoughts and Glimpses, **16**:378
2. The Hour of God, **17**:148
3. The Human Cycle, **15**:36

Chapter 1
1. On Himself, **26**:1
2. *ibid*, **26**:7
3. Life of Sri Aurobindo, 8
4. The Human Cycle, **15**:166
5. Thoughts and Aphorisms, **17**:138
6. On Yoga II, Tome 2, 871
7. Life of Sri Aurobindo, 43

Chapter 2
1. New Lamps for Old,**1**:44
2. Thoughts and Aphorisms, **17**:138
3. The Synthesis of Yoga, **20**:51
4. *ibid*, **20**:439
5. The Problem of Rebirth, **16**:241
6. Savitri, **29**:664

Chapter 3
1. Thoughts and Aphorisms, **17**:88
2. Shri Aurobindo, 342
3. New Lamps for Old,**1**:8
4. Evening Talks, 199
5. Life of Sri Aurobindo, 102
6. On Himself, **26**:12
7. Speeches, 2:7

Chapter 4
1. Life, Literature and Yoga, 86
2. The Synthesis of Yoga, **20**:302
3. *ibid*, **20**:65
4. On Himself, **26**:85
5. Sri Aurobindo Came to Me, 219
6. The Synthesis of Yoga, **20**:86
7. On Yoga II, Tome 2, 41
8. Letters on Yoga, **22**:166
9. On Yoga II, Tome 2, 302
10. *ibid*, 277

11. The Hour of God, **17**:11
12. On Himself, **26**:83
13. Letters on Yoga, **23**:637

Chapter 5
1. Letters on Yoga, **22**:234
2. The Synthesis of Yoga, **20**:370
3. *ibid*, **20**:203
4. Letters on Yoga, **22**:358
5. The Synthesis of Yoga, **20**:170
6. Correspondence with Sri
    Aurobindo, Vol. II, 119
7. Savitri, **28**:93
8. On Yoga II, Tome 2, 197
9. Correspondence with Sri
    Aurobindo, Vol. II, 83
10. Sri Aurobindo Came to Me, 206

Chapter 6
1. The Life Divine, **18**:48
2. The Synthesis of Yoga, **20**:321
3. Letters on Yoga, **22**:314
4. On Yoga II, Tome 2, 451
5. ibid, 489
6. The Life Divine, **19**:989
7. Letter on Yoga, **23**:654
8. The Synthesis of Yoga, **20**:322
9. Correspondence with Sri
    Aurobindo, Vol. II, 112
10. The Synthesis of Yoga, **20**:53
11. The Riddle of this World, 79
12. Thoughts and Aphorisms, **17**:146
13. The Synthesis of Yoga, **20**:71
14. Letters on Yoga, **22**:125
15. The Synthesis of Yoga, **20**:217
16. Correspondence with Sri
    Aurobindo, Vol. II, 86
17. On Himself, **26**:355
18. On Yoga II, Tome 2, 671
19. Letters on Yoga, **22**:84
20. On Yoga II, Tome 2, 184

Chapter 7
1. Essays on the Gita, 193
2. Thoughts and Aphorisms, **17**:138
3. Savitri, **28**:74
4. Thoughts and Aphorisms, **17**:124
5. The Synthesis of Yoga, **20**:353
6. TheProblem of Rebirth, **16**:111
7. *ibid*, **16**:110
8. The Synthesis of Yoga, **20**:294

Chapter 8
1. The Life Divine, **18**:63
2. The Synthesis of Yoga, **21**:833
3. Letters on Yoga, **22**:314
4. The Synthesis of Yoga, **20**:328

Chapter 9
1. The Life Divine, **18**:193
2. Mother India (Journal)
3. Savitri, **28**:120
4. On Yoga II, Tome 2, 110
5. Savitri, **28**:30
6. Thoughts and Aphorisms, **17**:137

Chapter 10
1. Savitri, **28**:64
2. *ibid;*, **28**:169
3. The Human Cycle, 301
4. On Himself, **26**:98
5. *ibid*, **26**:22
6. Essays on the Gita, 55
7. Ideal of Human Unity, **15**:320
8. Letters on Yoga, **22**:153
9. Savitri, **28**:256
10. On Himself, **26**:375
11. *ibid*, **26**:279
12. *ibid*, **26**:79
13. Savitri, **28**:82
14. On Himself, **26**:101
15. *ibid*, 154
16. Letters on Yoga, **22**:273
17. *ibid*, 71

18. The Human Cycle, **15**:177
19. On Himself, **26**:102
20. Life of Sri Aurobindo, 109
21. On Himself, **26**:49
22. Speeches, **1**:664

Chapter 11
1. Speeches, **2**:3
2. *ibid*, **2**:7
3. The Synthesis of Yoga, **29**:109
5. *ibid*, **2**:5
4. Speeches, **2**:4
6. The Synthesis of Yoga, **20**:285
7. Essays on the Gita, 59,516
8. The Life Divine, **19**:805
9. Savitri, **28**:66
10. The Synthesis of Yoga, **20**:313
11. Savitri, **28**:260
12. *ibid*, **29**:625
13. Collected Poems and Plays, **5**:311
14. The Life Divine, 677
15. The Problem of Rebirth, **16**:272
16. The Life Divine, **19**:1023
17. Savitri, **28**:24
18. The Synthesis of Yoga, **20**:348
19. The Superman, **16**:289
20. Letters on Yoga, **22**:316
21. Evening Talks, 180
22. The Synthesis of Yoga, **20**:48
23. Savitri, **28**:325

Chapter 12
1. The Hour of God, **17**:62
2. The Synthesis of Yoga, **20**:320
3. Savitri, **29**:454
4. The Synthesis of Yoga, **20**:162
5. Savitri, **29**:686
6. The Synthesis of Yoga, **20**:110
7. The Life Divine, **19**:761
8. Essays on the Gita, 646
9. The Synthesis of Yoga, **20**:185
10. *ibid*, **20**:14

11. On Yoga II, Tome 2, 739
12. Thoughts and Aphorisms, 17:79
13. Savitri, 28:143
14. The Synthesis of Yoga, 29:315
15. Savitri, 28:239
16. On Yoga II, Tome 2, 246
17. The Synthesis of Yoga, 20:281
18. Letters on Yoga, 23:743
19. The Synthesis of Yoga, 20:281
20. Correspondence, Vol. II, 119
21. Letters on Yoga, 22:235
22. On Yoga II, Tome 2, 197
23. Savitri, 29:525
24. ibid, 28:279
25. The Human Cycle, 209
26. The Hour of God, 17:15
27. Letters, 3rd Series, 124
28. ibid, 124
29. Sri Aurobindo Came to Me, 127
30. Savitri, 28:315
31. The life Divine, 1127
32. Letters on Yoga, 22:264
33. The Synthesis of Yoga, 21:772
34. On Yoga II, Tome 2, 263
35. Poems Past and Present, 1
36. The Human Cycle, 15:5
37. The Future Poetry, 9:233
38. ibid, 9:9
39. Letters, 3rd Series, 97
40. Savitri, 28:120
41. Speeches, 2:6

Chapter 13
1. Evening Talks, 120
2. The Human Cycle, 133
3. ibid, 131, 136
4. The life Divine, 19:722
5. On Yoga II, Tome 2, 263
6. Letters, 3rd Series, 128
7. The Life Divine, 19:954
8. The Synthesis of Yoga, 20:82
9. the Life Divine, 19:1159

Chapter 14
1. Life of Sri Aurobindo, 132
2. ibid, 122
3. Savitri, 28:227
4. ibid, 29:446
5. On Yoga II, Tome 2, 686
6. ibid, 689
7. Savitri, 28:172
8. The Synthesis of Yoga, 20:123
9. Savitri, 517
10. On Yoga II, Tome 2, 733
11. Savitri, 28:192
12. Thoughts and Aphorisms, 17:15
13. The Life Divine, 18:12
14. The Synthesis of Yoga, 20:123
15. The Human Cycle, 133
16. Savitri, 29:613
17. ibid, 29:625
18. Mother India, March 1962,
19. Savitri, 29:317
20. On Himself, 26:153
21. Savitri, 28:7
22. Poems Past and Present, 5,99
23. Savitri, 28:91
24. Last Poems, 5:150
25. Savitri, 28:42
26. ibid, 29:541
27. ibid, 28:169
28. ibid, 29:370
29. Letters on Yoga, 22:388
30. On Yoga II, Tome 2, 34
31. On Himself, 26:425
32. Savitri, 29:684

Chapter 15
1. Savitri, 29:566
2. The Sythesis of Yoga, 21:808
3. ibid, 20:234
4. Thoughts and Aphorisms, 17:133
5. Letters on Yoga, 22:451
6. The Life Divine, 19:983
7. The Synthesis of Yoga, 20:316

8. *ibid*, 21:835
9. *ibid*, 20:464
10. Savitri, 29:660
11. The Synthesis of Yoga, 20:393
12. *ibid*, 20:408
13. Savitri, 29:657
14. *ibid*, 29:614
15. *ibid*, 28:196
16. The Synthesis of Yoga, 20:164
17. Savitri, 20:63
18. Life, Literature and Yoga, 11
19. Evening Talks, 91
20. Savitri, 29:600
21. The Life Divine, 19:642,766
22. Savitri, 29:709
23. Letters, 3rd Series, 103
24. The Synthesis of Yoga, 20:95
25. Thoughts and Aphorisms, 17:92
26. The Hour of God, 17:12
27. Savitri, 28:183
28. On Himself, 26:378
29. The Ideal of the Karmayogin, 2:17
30. On Himself, 26:58
31. Letters on Yoga, 22:69
32. *ibid*, 22:139

Chapter 16
1. On the Veda, 42
2. *ibid*, 47
3. *ibid*, 46
4. Letters on Yoga, 22:93
5. On Himself, 26:374
6. Savitri, 28:97
7. Sri Aurobindo Came to Me, 247
8. On Himself, 26:361
9. Correspondence, Vol. II, 154
10. *ibid*, 155
11. Letters, 3rd Series, 5
12. Correspondence, Vol. II, 150
13. The Hour of God, 17:11
14. Savitri, 28:76
15. Anilbaran's Journal (unpublished)

16. On Himself, 26:455
17. The Life Divine, 18:103
18. Savitri, 28:4
19. Thoughts and Glimpses, 16:384
20. The Hour of God, 17:148
21. *ibid*, 17:149
22. The Life Divine, 18:162
23. *ibid*, 18:378
24. The Hour of God, 17:15
25. The Life Divine, 18:129
26. *ibid*, 18:87
27. The Synthesis of Yoga, 20:151
28. Savitri, 28:90
29. The Life Divine, 18:243
30. The Problem of Rebirth, 16:241
31. The Human Cycle, 290
32. The Hour of God, 17:48
33. The Synthesis of Yoga, 20:216
34. Savitri, 28:235
35. The Hour of God, 17:7
36. The Life Divine, 18:3-4
37. Thoughts and Glimpses, 32
38. Thoughts and Aphorisms, 17:82
39. Thoughts and Glimpses, 16:384
40. The Synthesis of Yoga, 21:798

Chapter 17
1. The Life Divine, 109
2. The Human Cycle, 292
3. The Hour of God, 17:7
4. The Supramental Manifestation, 15:24
5. *ibid*, 16:8
6. *ibid*, 16:29,37
7. Savitri, 28:338
8. Correspondence, Vol. 1, 56
9. The Life Divine, 19:842
10. *ibid*, 19:843
11. On Himself, 26:469
12. Life of Sri Aurobindo, 142
13. *ibid*, 121

14. On Himself, 26:186
    Correspondence, Vol. II, 152
15. Savitri, **28**:20
16. Thoughts and Aphorisms, **17**:93
17. Life of Sri Aurobindo, 167
18. Correspondence, Vol. I, 53,71
19. Savitri, **29**:719
20. Evening Talks, 198
21. *ibid,* 45
22. On Yoga II, Tome 2, 406
23. *France-Asie* (Journal) April 1953
24. On Yoga II, Tome 2, 340
25. Savitri, **29**:383
26. Letters on Yoga, **22**:340
27. Poems Past and Present, 6
28. Savitri, **29**:700
29. *ibid,* **29**:707
30. Sri Aurobindo Came to Me, 73
31. On Himself, **26**:425
32. Savitri, **28**:216
33. The Ideal of Human Unity, **15**:80
34. Sri Aurobindo Came to Me, 251
35. The Synthesis of Yoga, **20**:348

36. Letters on Yoga, **23**:847
37. The Ideal of the Karmayogin, 10
38. Letters on Yoga, **22**:856
39. Correspondence, Vol. I, 101
40. Life of Sri Aurobindo, 167
41. On Himself, **26**:109
42. The Synthesis of Yoga, **20**:71
43. On Himself, **26**:109
44. *ibid,* **26**:450
45. The Life Divine, **19**:932,
46. The Human Cycle, 332
47. Savitri, **29**:370
48. *ibid,* **28**:343
49. Collected Poems and Plays, I, **5**:61
50. The Hour of God, **17**:9

Conclusion
1. The Human Cycle, 278
2. Thoughts and Aphorisms, **17**:82
3. The Human Cycle, 329
4. Savitri, **28**:43 **29**:629
5. *ibid,* **28**:2

WORKS OF SRI AUROBINDO

Most of the following titles can be found in the complete edition
of Sri Aurobindo's works in 30 volumes (the Centenary Edition).

1 – Indian Tradition

The Foundations of Indian Culture, 'Arya' Dec. 1918-Jan. 1921 (New York)	1st ed. 1953
On the Veda, 'Arya' Aug. 1914-Jan. 1920	1st ed. 1956
Hymns to the Mystic Fire	1st ed. 1946
Isha Upanishad (translation & commentaries), 'Arya' Aug. 1914-May 1915	1st ed. 1921
Eight Upanishads (translation & introduction)	1st ed. 1953
Essays on the Gita, 'Arya' Aug. 1916-July 1920	1st ed. 1922
The Renaissance in India, 'Arya' Aug. 1918-Nov. 1918	1st ed. 1920
The Significance of Indian Art, 'Arya' 1918-1921	1st ed. 1947

2 – Philosophy-Sociology

The Life Divine, 'Arya' Aug. 1914-Jan. 1919	1st ed. 1939
Ideals and Progress, 'Arya' 1915-1916	1st ed. 1920
The Superman, 'Arya' March 1915-Aug. 1915	1st ed. 1920
Thoughts and Glimpses, 'Arya' 1915-1917	1st ed. 1920
Thoughts and Aphorisms	1st ed. 1958
The Hour of God	1st ed. 1959
Evolution, 'Arya' 1915-1918	1st ed. 1920
Heraclitus, 'Arya' Dec. 1916-June 1917	1st ed. 1941

The Supramental Manifestation upon Earth, 'Bulletin' 1949-1950	1st ed. 1952
The Problem of Rebirth, 'Arya' Nov. 1915-Jan. 1921	1st ed. 1952
The Human Cycle, 'Arya' Aug. 1916-July 1918	1st ed. 1949
The Ideal of Human Unity, 'Arya' Sept. 1915-July 1918	1st ed. 1919 Revised 1950
On the War, 1940-1943	1st ed. 1944
War and Self Determination, 1916-1920	1st ed. 1920
Man-Salve or Free? 'Karmayogin' 1909-1910	1st ed. 1922

3 – Yoga

Elements of Yoga, 1933-1936	1st ed. 1953
Lights on Yoga,	1st ed. 1935
More Lights on Yoga	1st ed. 1948
Sri Aurobindo on Himself and on the Mother	1st ed. 1953
The Mother	1st ed. 1928
The Yoga and its Objects	1st ed. 1921
The Synthesis of Yoga, 'Arya' Aug. 914-Jan. 1921	1st ed. 1948
Letters, 2volumes (On Yoga I & II)	1st ed. 1958
The Riddle of this World	1st ed. 1933
Bases of Yoga	1st ed. 1936
Correspondence with Nirodbaran, vol. I	1st ed. 1954
Correspondence with Nirodbaran, vol. II	1st ed. 1959
Letters (translated from Bengali)	1st ed. 1961

4 – Literature-Poetry-Drama

Views and Reviews, 'Arya' 1914-1920	1st ed. 1941
Letters, third series	1st ed. 1949
Life-Literature-Yoga	1st ed. 1952
Conversations of the Dead, 1909-1910	1st ed. 1951
The Phantom Hour (a short story), 1910-1912	1st ed. 1951
Kalidasa, 2 volumes, 1893-1905 (Baroda)	1st ed. 1929
Vyasa and Valmiki, 1893-1905 (Baroda)	1st ed. 1956

The Future Poetry, 'Arya' Dec. 1917-July 1920	1st ed. 1953
Collected Poems and Plays, 2 volumes	1st ed. 1942
Poems Past and Present	1st ed. 1946
Poems from Bengali, 1893-1905 (translation)	1st ed. 1956
Savitri	1st ed. 1950
Last Poems, 1937-1944	1st ed. 1952
More Poems	1st ed. 1957
Vikramorvasie, 1903-1904 (Baroda)	1st ed. 1911
Songs of Vidyapati, 1893-1905 (Baroda)	1st ed. 1956
Rodogune, 1893-1905 (Baroda)	1st ed. 1958
Ilion	1st ed. 1957
Vasavadutta 1915-1916	1st ed. 1957
Urvasie, 1893-1896	1st ed. 1896
Ahana and Other Poems, 1895-1915	1st ed. 1915
Love and Death, 1899	1st ed. 1921
The Viziers of Bassora, 1893-1905 (Baroda)	1st ed. 1959
Eric, 1912 or 1913	1st ed. 1960
The Chariot of Jagannath, 1918 (translated from Bengali)	1st ed. 1972

5 – Political Period

The Ideal of the Karmayogin, '*Karmayogin' 1909-10*	1st ed. 1918
A System of National Education, 'Karmayogin'1910	1st ed. 1921
The National Value of Art, 'Karmayogin' 1909	1st ed. 1922
The Speeches, 1908-1909	1st ed. 1922
The Doctrine of Passive Resistance, 1907	1st ed. 1948
Bankim-Tilak-Dayananda, 1907-1916-1918	1st ed. 1940
The Brain of India, 'Karmayogin' 1909	1st ed. 1921
Tales of Prison Life (translated from Bengali)	1st ed. 1974